SACRED SORROWS

This *New Consciousness Reader* is part of a new series of original and classic writing by renowned experts on leading-edge concepts in personal development, psychology, spiritual growth, and healing. Other books in this series include:

Founding Series Editor: CONNIE ZWEIG, PH.D.

Sacred Sorrows

EMBRACING AND TRANSFORMING DEPRESSION

Edited by John E. Nelson, M.D.
and Andrea Nelson, Psy.D.

A Jeremy P. Tarcher/Putnam Book
Published by G. P. Putnam's Sons
New York

Most Tarcher/Putnam books are available at special quantity discounts for bulk purchases for sales promotions, premiums, fundraising, and educational needs. Special books or book excerpts also can be created to fit specific needs.

For details, write or telephone Special Markets, The Putnam Publishing Group, 200 Madison Avenue, New York, NY 10016; (212) 951-8891.

For permissions and copyrights, please see page 235

A Jeremy P. Tarcher/Putnam Book
Published by G. P. Putnam's Sons
Publishers Since 1838
200 Madison Avenue
New York, NY 10016

http://www.putnam.com/putnam

Library of Congress Cataloging-in-Publication Data

Sacred sorrows: embracing and transforming depression /
    edited by John E. Nelson and Andrea Nelson.
        p.   cm.
    ISBN 0-87477-822-0
    1. Depression, Mental.   2. Depression, Mental—Religious aspects.
    3. Depression, Mental—Alternative treatment.   I. Nelson, John E.
    II. Nelson, Andrea.
    RC537.S29   1996   95-24790 CIP
    616.85′27—dc20

Design by Jaime Robles
Cover design by Susan Shankin

Printed in the United States of America

10   9   8   7   6   5   4   3   2

This book is printed on acid-free paper.∞

I love the dark hours of my being
In which my senses drop into the deep.
I have found in them, as in old letters,
my private life that is already lived through,
and become wide and powerful now, like legends.
Then I know that there is room in me
for a second huge and timeless life.

—RAINER MARIA RILKE

A NOTE ON GENDER

Recognizing that our shared language *creates* as well as reflects our culture's unspoken attitudes, we acknowledge that the exclusive use of the masculine *he*, *his, or him* for the impersonal pronoun perpetuates an archaic view of sexual inequality. Yet, in practice, the common alternatives prove to be even more unsatisfactory in that they place upon the reader a burden of confusing syntax that detracts from the flow of ideas.

Therefore, in the service of clarity, we have requested all male authors to employ the masculine form of the impersonal pronoun, and all female authors to use the feminine form.

—Editors

Contents

Acknowledgments

The editors wish to express their gratitude to the extraordinary people who contributed to the research and writing of this anthology over the past three years. Special thanks to Mark Waldman, whose timely editorial assistance, organizational skills, and contagious enthusiasm during the final stages of the project enriched this work immeasurably. Connie Zweig, whose work appears herein, lent her sensitive insights and foresights throughout the conception and planning stage. Jeremy Tarcher's wisdom, patience, and encouragement sustained the effort from its inception. Thoughtful contributions were made by Brian Conlan, Charles Grob, Jonna Lannert, and David Lukoff. Our companions of The Circle ennobled this work in more subtle ways. We acknowledge our debt to our many patients who, by sharing their sacred sorrows, became teachers of our hearts.

Prologue: Depression in Body, Mind, and Spirit

Few maladies touch so many aspects of the self as depression. Informed discussions of this ancient and pervasive human affliction must range freely from the faint rattlings of molecules in the brain, through the fleeting thoughts and emotions that comprise mind, to the unfathomable mysteries of Spirit—the subtle essence of consciousness itself. We, the editors, were therefore inspired to compile this anthology to draw together a diverse group of writers who can help depressed people and therapists alike expand their grasp of this complex disorder that undermines body, mind, heart, and spirit.

More than one hundred million people throughout the world suffer from depression. Each year, more people seek relief from this disabling condition than any medical disease, including the common cold. The economic toll is staggering: in 1990, the cost of depression exceeded $43 billion in the United States alone, including medical treatment, lost work-time, and depression-related suicide.[1]

Until modern times, people who became depressed were said to be afflicted with a malaise of the soul, caused by offending a wrathful deity or behaving in ways that conflicted with the stern dogmas of medieval religion. Melancholia and other derangements of consciousness were thought to originate in a privileged sphere, an exclusive domain of supernatural events that stood above the mechanical workings of the body or the fruits of life's experience.

Following the Enlightenment, newly empowered secular thinkers founded the science of psychology, which in turn generated psychoanalysis and its credo that persistent unhappiness derives from faulty childhood learning that conflicts with primal instincts emerging from the unconscious mind. Followers of Sigmund Freud's revolutionary method casually relegated spirituality to the dustbin of rank superstition. In deference to nascent discoveries in neuroscience, they gave lip service to the idea that mind and brain comprised a unity, only begrudgingly allowing a little biology to creep into their mind-dominated theories.

Recent decades have brought about a second paradigm shift that de-emphasizes both mind and spirit in favor of biologic determinants of mood and even personality. Armed with rigorously controlled studies using high-technology brain-imaging devices, the biologists' arguments take on a compelling tone that we ignore only at risk of finding ourselves out of touch with modern times. In tune with this generally mechanistic view of human nature, many modern psychological theorists turned to behavior modification as their dominant treatment method, assigning low priority to deep insight and personal growth.

We believe there is great peril in stringently materialistic approaches that reduce consciousness to an impotent minion of matter, that view the unfathomable depths of human passion, creativity, curiosity, reason, intuition, will, compassion, and spiritual insight as mere secretions of the brain, akin to the way the kidney secretes urine. This narrow paradigm overlooks the most essential aspect of humanity: its consciousness, its indomitable spirit, so hard to define but impossible to overlook. Modern biological research challenges spiritually-friendly psychologies to devise theories that do not contradict the facts about biological effects on the mind but complement and balance them.

Today, our conception of depression is primed for another radical restructuring, one that retains enduring insights from mental and spiritual theories of past eras while casting off their excesses. To understand why some people become depressed and others don't, we now must consider genetic predisposition, birth experience, childhood traumas, personality, nutrition, life-style, substance abuse, capacity for insight, and spiritual receptivity. A new, more integrative paradigm is beginning to emerge, one that accepts both brain chemistry and consciousness as essential features of human existence, adding an eclectic spiritual perspective that draws on ancient, modern, and cross-cultural traditions to forge a contemporary technology of the sacred.

Our anthology advances this more comprehensive paradigm for understanding depression by incorporating insights from personal experience, biological science, psychological theory, and sophisticated spiritual traditions that point the way to transcending suffering inherent in human existence. The first step, we believe, is to embrace sadness, emptiness, and despair as powerful teachers of life's most profound lessons, not simply as diseases or symptoms to be eliminated by any means necessary. Our goal is to return a sense of sacredness to all human experience, especially those sorrows that most try our souls. For this reason, we have named our book *Sacred Sorrows*.

The articles in this book range from musings about the effects of Prozac, subjective accounts of deep spiritual alienation and renewal, techniques for altering mood by changing thinking, to methods for renewing the spirit by cultivating higher insight. Authors include psychiatrists, psychologists, social workers, novelists, philosophers, and teachers, each providing the reader with a unique perspective about a major source of suffering that afflicts men and women, rich and poor, adults and children alike.

We have divided our book into three sections. Part One emphasizes the first-hand experience of depression through stories of people who have personally felt its devastating effects on their lives, careers, and families. These poignant narratives provide depressed people with a feeling that they are not alone in their suffering, while enabling therapists to deepen their empathic connection with their depressed patients.

Part Two combines a spectrum of theories about why people become depressed with practical therapeutic strategies for reducing its damaging effects as its lessons are incorporated. Essays in this section are an eclectic mix, including antidepressant medications, physical exercise, bodywork, psychotherapy, Jungian approaches, and raising planetary awareness. The general goal of these approaches is to prepare a depressed individual to resume his or her path of personal growth. Part Three continues the progression by means of perceptive theories and practical techniques for embracing the lessons inherent in all human suffering in order to remove impediments to spiritual growth and transformation.

As we searched for the original works and previously published articles that comprise this anthology, we took pains to avoid stuffy academic discourses in favor of clearly written essays accessible to both laypersons and therapists alike. We also avoided pop-psychology and self-help essays that offer simplistic solutions to complex feelings and emotions. A few sophisticated original articles have been included because they represent important theoretical contributions to understanding depression. Because these are rather advanced, they challenge the reader to spend a bit of extra effort to grasp their complexities. We feel that we have succeeded in compiling a unique and diverse collection of essays on a subject about which there is much known and much yet to learn.

PART ONE

Living with Depression

1. The Many Faces of Depression

HOW DEPRESSION AFFECTS THE HUMAN PSYCHE

BY JOHN E. NELSON, M.D.

This article describes the myriad ways that depression disrupts people's lives. Following a review of how people experience the classic symptoms of major depression, the author describes three common variations of the depressive syndrome. How depression engenders vicious cycles that insidiously undermine a person's physical, mental, social, and spiritual well-being concludes this introductory essay to Sacred Sorrows.

During my psychiatric training at a major California State Hospital, some of my teachers often referred to depression as "the common cold of psychiatry." The implication was that it is a universal but relatively mild and self-limited ailment that is easy to treat and bears a good prognosis.

Now, some twenty-five years later, the difficult lessons that I have learned from observing the misery caused by this disease indicate that my teachers must never have been depressed, or that they simply weren't attentive to the bleak reality of their patients' suffering. In its more severe forms, depression can devitalize a person's soul to the point that he is unable to work, to love, or to find meaning in life. Recurrent depressive episodes can lead to pernicious alterations of personality, sapping an individual's self-confidence, abridging independence, impoverishing his ties to the world and people who care for him. Depression can turn fatal; between 10 and 30 percent of depressives and manic-depressives eventually kill themselves, surpassing even schizophrenia and chronic alcoholism in lethality.

Even when not fatal, depression leads to career underachievement, marriage and relationship failures, and shortfalls in parenting. When a family member becomes depressed, everyone close to him suffers too. Depressed children endure more than their share of social and academic torments. Depressed parents may be unreasonably harsh and irritable with their children, or they may withdraw, becoming emotionally and physically unavailable. In turn, these pernicious outgrowths engender guilt feelings that spin the depressed parent downward to the next level in his vicious cycle.

Depression insidiously undermines the physical body, disrupting glandular function, enfeebling the immune system, rendering the sufferer vulnerable to a host of diseases, and reducing life expectancy of people who are battling serious illness, such as cancer.[1] Some depressed people may simply lack the self-concern or physical energy to seek help when confronted with a life-threatening physical illness.

Although the issue is controversial, it is likely that chronic, low-level depression underlies many addictive and compulsive behaviors, including drunkenness, stimulant craving, overeating, and self-starvation. The quick, giddy high from a shot of alcohol or a jolt of cocaine temporarily numbs awareness of the self-loathing and alienation that depression bequeaths its victims. This understandable but hazardous urge to "self-medicate" also plays into the vicious cycle of depression, for alcohol and many stimulants deplete the brain of hormones essential for maintaining one's energy level and emotional stability.

Although there are several effective strategies to treat depression, we must first be sure that we are not dealing with some other physical disease that mimics it. Hormonal disorders, infectious agents, certain kinds of tumors, and side effects of commonly prescribed medicines can echo the discordant rumblings of authentic depression. Some of these are covered in detail in a later chapter of this book. Prudent practitioners insist on a complete physical examination and appropriate laboratory studies before beginning specific treatment for severe depression.

DO DIAGNOSES HELP OR HARM?

Although many people use the term "depression" to describe fleeting moments of discouragement—perhaps from losing a lover or failing to achieve an important goal—modern mental health professionals are more careful in defining the term. For centuries, physicians have observed that like other diseases, symptoms of depression fall into patterns that are fairly constant from one individual to another. In recent years, these have been cataloged in the diagnostic bible of modern psychiatry, *DSM-IV.*[2]

Despite the widespread acceptance of *DSM-IV,* some idealistic therapists argue that making a diagnosis is unnecessary at best, degrading to a suffering individual at worst. They argue that putting unflattering labels on people ignores their individuality and dehumanizes them, subtly preparing them for assembly-line treatments that characterize modern medical systems. Others contend that a diagnosis is bad for the *healer,* blinding him to aspects of the patient's total selfhood that fall outside the expected range of symptoms. Some of psychiatry's most vocal antagonists even hold that a diagnosis *creates* the mental disorder that it names, programming a vulnerable person to conform to the expectations of a powerful medical authority.

Nevertheless, the disciplined process of organizing one's observations into clusters of symptoms has passed the test of time, and we would sacrifice much of proven value should we abandon it hastily. Experienced therapists know that many depressed people feel relief when they learn that the source of their solitary distress has a name, and is therefore understood as part of the human condition. For a person who feels that he is uniquely alone in his suffering, or interprets his symptoms as evidence of moral turpitude, a timely diagnosis can reassure him that he is not being punished for some obscure shortcoming and that help is on the way. If used with *artfulness* by a healer who takes time to establish trust and rapport, a thoughtful diagnosis can be the first step in establishing the therapeutic alliance necessary for recovery to begin.

The medical archives—a vast body of literature dating back thousands of years—is a major healing resource of humanity. But this information remains inaccessible to those who refuse to categorize their observations. A careful diagnosis can be a tool of communication, guiding a healer toward the experience of others who once grappled with similar problems. The challenge to an enlightened healer is to individualize this knowledge to meet the unique needs of his patient. This takes time and skill.

RECOGNIZING DEPRESSION

A conscientious healer looks for certain signs and symptoms that alert him to the presence of depression in his patient. Although these vary according to the health, temperament, and personality of the person who is experiencing the shift of mood, it is helpful first to recognize the cardinal features of major depression, the most widespread form of the disorder. Once these are familiar, it will be easier to understand the variations. What follows is a brief description of how the most common symptoms feel to those who experience them.

• *Persistent low mood.* Most people normally note their mood shifting as often as several times a day. These swings are usually triggered by disturbing life events, natural daily fluctuations of hormone levels, or even what the individual ate at his last meal. But such lability of mood is not necessarily a symptom of major depression. To qualify for that unfortunate diagnosis, a person must experience an enveloping drop in mood from a previously normal state, sustained for at least two weeks, although certain times of day may be worse than others, especially mornings. In contrast to the pervasive mental paralysis of the seriously depressed, when a nondepressed person experiences an emotional slump from not achieving a goal, it usually motivates him for some form of constructive activity that restores his feeling of well-being.

• *Low energy.*   A depressed person feels that he is "running on empty," or that nothing seems worth the effort. Although he complains of not sleeping, he may spend most of the day in bed, or when he does get up, he turns into the proverbial couch-potato, aimlessly channel-surfing while despising himself for living such an indolent life. Athletic individuals may give up daily exercise as they become depressed, which usually leads to a progressively worsening mood.

• *Loss of interest in one's usual activities.*   As depression tightens its grip on a person's psyche, his hobbies become cloying chores, his job grows tedious, his spouse and children mutate into annoying parasites. Brooding alone in a semi-darkened room seems infinitely more rewarding than going to a weekend movie. He feels languorous and apathetic, losing his zest for activities that he once found fascinating.

• *Difficulty concentrating and setting goals.*   "My mind won't stay put," one depressed patient told me. "Whenever I try to read or even watch a dumb sitcom on TV, my thoughts lurch about like a blind bull, mostly finding ways to beat myself up for being such a useless lout. My life is seven minutes long; five in the past and two in the future. I procrastinate planning dinner, then I end up junking out on cookies and Coke." Such a loss of focus can be the most disabling of depressive symptoms, rendering a person unable to work effectively or plan for the future, which seems desolate, devoid of any possibility for redemption.

• *Slowed thought and speech.*   Experienced therapists recognize this symptom when they experience strong impulses to finish sentences for their patients. It can be quite an exercise of forbearance for a therapist with a sense of time-urgency to sit with a dispirited person who answers questions sluggishly with a weak voice and no spontaneous elaboration. This symptom is technically known as *psychomotor retardation,* and it can often lead to a mistaken impression of feeble-mindedness in a person whose depression masks normal intelligence.

• *Insomnia.*   "My bedroom ceiling is the most familiar scene in my life. I've memorized every crack and crevice," a depressed patient once told me. "Sometimes I fall asleep okay, but then I wake up at four in the morning stuck on the idea that I've failed in life and let down everyone who cares for me. That's when I feel closest to suicide. Not sleeping leaves me exhausted and grumpy all day long." Another depressed patient grimly quipped that he now spells morning with a "u." Biologically oriented psychiatrists consider such early awakening to be a classic sign of *endogenous,* or physically based, depression.

• *Inability to experience pleasure or reward.* "The blue sky and the birds singing just don't turn me on the way they used to," a depressed patient lamented. "I pick at my meals. Making love with my wife is just something I do to please her. I've even stopped reading the comics because they don't seem funny any more. My daughter's report card was all A's, but it didn't matter because I kept thinking that we're all going to die some day no matter what we do. This isn't me; I'm really a passionate and caring person." Such inability to savor life's gratifications is technically called *anhedonia.* Socially, a leaden seriousness and crimped sense of humor naturally follow from losing one's inner sense of reward.

• *Loss of appetite and sexual interest.* One depressed patient told of her husband taking her to an expensive French restaurant to celebrate her birthday, then getting into a nasty argument when she told him that the gourmet meal tasted like soggy cardboard. Dramatic and unexplained weight loss often leads a depressed person to consult an internist rather than a psychologist or psychiatrist. Indifference or aversion to sexual activity follows the general devitalizing pattern of depression and can disrupt an otherwise gratifying relationship.

• *Tendency to cry over relatively minor matters.* "I've always enjoyed a good cry at a sad movie, but the other day I started bawling when I broke an old dish. When I heard that a friend got a promotion, I wanted to cry for all the people who don't get what they want. What's the matter with me? I used to be a happy-go-lucky person." Lachrymose responses to trivial rebuffs or disappointments are part of some people's sensitive character structures, but in depression they are always exaggerated compared to a past state of relative imperturbability.

• *Self-loathing.* "Born loser." "Dregs of the earth." "Worthless parasite." "Defective specimen." "Superfluous rubbish—never have been good for anything and never will be. My family would be better off if I were dead." Such caustic self-abasements reflect the inner world of a depressed person plagued by a haunting sense of personal failure beyond atonement. As self-esteem wanes, a depressed person tends to underestimate himself, his capabilities, and the concern that others hold for him on every level.

• *Inappropriate guilt feelings.* Depression confers a compulsion for self-blaming that may lead a victim to conclude that his parent had a heart attack because he forgot to call that week, or that he is somehow responsible for a sports team losing a game because he was rooting for it. In severe depressions, such guilt feelings can acquire a delusional cast that is impervious to reason, leading a person to conclude that he has been singled out for punishment by an angry deity.

• **Withdrawal.** If a natural extrovert grows standoffish when depressed, an introvert can turn into a stalwart recluse. He may say that it is just too much trouble to be with people or engage in social activities. Those of a more mordant disposition shield themselves behind a wall of acidic misanthropy: "The world is full of rip-off artists, egomaniacs, and jackasses anyway. Any reasonable person prefers to be alone."

• **Spiritual alienation.** As depression depletes an individual's physical, mental, and social vitality, it also disengages him from his innermost intuition of life's meaning and his personal role in the unfolding of the universe. He feels isolated within his limited sphere of consciousness, alienated from whatever deity, higher power, or universal force that grounds his particular belief system. If he previously held a religious faith, he now woodenly goes through the motions of worship lacking passion or inner conviction.

The result is often a cynical outlook, for if human existence is pointless and without credible destiny, then there is scant reason to go on with a life that feels drained of pleasure anyway. A depressed person may express this disunity in various ways, from the personal: "God has abandoned me," or "I'm an accursed sinner," to the cosmic: "The universe is indifferent to my petty concerns," "The world would be better off if human beings never existed."

• **Feelings of hopelessness and helplessness.** "With this black cloud that follows me wherever I go, nothing I do ever turns out right," a previously optimistic depressed patient exclaimed. Accompanying his impotent gloominess was a feeling that nothing anyone else can do will help him to feel better either. Experienced therapists call this *negativity,* a reflexive rejection of all remedial suggestions or offers to help.

• **Restless irritability (dysphoria).** Although some people suffering from major depression become nearly immobile, others find themselves fitfully unable to relax or remain quiet. They feel a pressing urge to pace about, to fidget, to *do* something; they know not what, for nothing they attempt truly satisfies. Accompanying this is an explosive temper detonated by trifling provocations that most people readily shrug off. As one depressed person put it, "I used to enjoy the little mischievous tricks my kids would pull. Now I just yell at them all day. I hate myself for the grouchy old witch I've become." Such behavior tends to alienate friends and family alike, mobilizing yet another of the vicious cycles that energize the vortex of desolation swirling within a depressed psyche.

• **Inability to plan for the future.** "What future?" a depressed patient once exclaimed as I asked him what he envisioned for himself. "There's nothing ahead of me but darkness, a void. I don't have the energy for exercises in futility. If I get really lucky, I'll just die and not have to think about it at all." Empathic therapists appreciate this abbreviated foresight and try not to force their patients beyond a here-and-now orientation until they begin to recover.

• *Increased desire for intoxicants.* Depression underlies many, if not most, addictions to alcohol, cocaine, and opiates, which start off as misguided efforts at self-medication with the goal of emotional regulation. "The only time I feel alive is when I'm high," is a common lament. The problem is that the physical effects of alcohol and many street intoxicants increase depression, and the psychological effect of addiction is to lower self-esteem and inhibit behavior that can relieve depression.

• *Mild distortions of reality.* Although by definition a person with major depression does not express full-scale delusions—fixed and demonstrably false beliefs that are impervious to logic or persuasion—he may express vague feelings that he is being punished for minor foibles or that he is somehow responsible for everyday setbacks experienced by friends or family members.

• *Suicidal urges.* Except for those over age sixty-five, suicide ranks as one of the ten leading causes of death in all age groups, and a majority of people who choose this means of release have classic symptoms of depression. Despite the lifelong emotional scars a suicide imparts to surviving children, spouses, parents, and friends, a depressed person becomes convinced that his significant others will be secretly pleased and relieved to be rid of him.

Although not every depressed person will manifest all of the above symptoms, they are likely to have most, and perhaps some others that are idiosyncratic to individual personalities. In the next section, we will take a closer look at other depressive syndromes and the way they affect a person's experience of himself and the world.

DEPRESSIVE PERSONALITY (DYSTHYMIA)

Although psychiatry's diagnostic manual requires that milder forms of depression be present for only two years to make the diagnosis of dysthymia, or "depressive personality," most people with this kind of depression say that they have felt depressed all of their lives. Although the magnitude of their symptoms do not match that of people with major depression, dysthymic people often lack the vitality and "chutzpah" that lead to successful lives in modern society.

Dysthymic people tend to be brooding, introverted, obsessional, self-sacrificing, guilt-ridden, self-effacing, lethargic, socially maladroit, late sleepers, unable to enjoy leisure, overdedicated to work, tolerant of other people who treat them badly, and overconcerned with detail, missing the big picture. They often have little vigor, but they may learn to use their available energy with precision in order to accomplish great things in a focused area, although they derive little pleasure from their accomplishments.

At this point a question arises as to whether dysthymia is merely a personality style or an authentic illness? When a group of women with chronic minor depression was studied, a distinctive pattern of behavior emerged.[3]

Compared to control subjects, dysthymic women were socially awkward and tended to avoid social interactions, exhibiting decreased eye contact and odd gestures. They were more likely to fear that others would not approve of them. They were slow to engage in novel behaviors and avoided taking risks to get what they desired. They had significantly fewer friends and living offspring. Their incomes were lower, and they lived in smaller homes. These women tended to persevere in hopeless tasks long past the point that most people would quit, leading one researcher to speculate that the last three people in any long line probably have dysthymic disorder. They were also likely to remain locked in ungratifying, co-dependent, or abusive relationships—"women who love too much." It seems that these chronically depressed women's temperamental characteristics—rigidity and social discomfort—lead to a constricted life with few social rewards.

There is evidence to believe that in early childhood, most of these women who later suffer from chronic minor depression were also shy, cautious, and socially inhibited. While these character traits may have been adaptive in earlier historical epochs that valued steadfastness, loyalty, and unassertiveness, they seem hopelessly out of place in modern society, which rewards us for being energetic, flexible, risk-taking, and charismatic. Individual assertiveness is now more likely to get you what you need to remain happy. People whom society does not reward, who do not find appreciation, love, career success, or a sense of competency, tend to become depressed and stay that way. The magnitude of depression experienced by dysthymics may not rival that of biologically driven major depression, but it nevertheless can be as personally disabling as chronic diabetes or emphysema.

DEPRESSION AND THE BORDERLINE PERSONALITY

Unflattering though it may be, "borderline" is the official term for people who spend their lives precariously straddling the border between psychosis and neurosis. Borderlines are the walking wounded in the universal struggle to find a secure place in life for the self. Psychiatrists append this term to "difficult" patients who are consistently unable to consolidate a stable sense of personal selfhood that can stand unsupported without the constant presence of powerful others, to whom they become dependently attached.

Borderlines desperately cling to relationships by passively complying to the will of the other, or by manipulation, including gratuitous threats of suicide. To lose the relationship is perceived as death, for as one patient told me, "When I'm alone, I fall apart, I cease to exist as an individual." Consequently their moods tend to be extremely unstable and contingent upon external sources of admiration and approval. A borderline may feel hopelessly bereft at the end of a love affair, then meet a new attentive partner and feel immediately euphoric, ready to merge their precarious selfhood with this perceived font of unconditional love. Such a person may note short-lived episodes of hopeless depression alternating with fleeting exultation several times a day. Although a borderline rapidly elevates new friends, lovers, or therapists into hero or savior roles, at their first failure to gratify his dependency, he just as rapidly devalues these overvalued figures into enemies or persecutors.

The singularly nasty kind of depression that haunts the emotional life of borderlines has been called *hysteroid dysphoria* by one investigator to indicate the overdramatized presentation of their restless inner disquiet.[4] Others have named this syndrome *atypical depression* to reflect these people's tendency to increase eating and sleeping when depressed, in contrast to people with major depression. Perhaps the essential feature of depression in borderlines is a deep-seated sensitivity to rejection that, coupled with an insatiable craving for compliments and attention, leads to seduction as a full-time imperative.

Other features that help to identify the borderline syndrome include a persistent fear that those on whom the individual feels dependent will abandon him. His efforts to cling to a relationship often become so exaggerated that the underlying fear becomes self-fulfilling. Feelings of inner "emptiness" characterize his subjective state. He projects these unpleasant feelings outward as bitterness or sarcasm directed at a "screwed-up world." He is notorious for his impulsivity, including running away, drunken binges, unreasoned use of drugs, sexual excesses, and explosive tantrums.

Multiple marriages, career changes, and other upheavals mark the life histories of borderline people who act upon their fantasy that a utopian world lies just over the horizon. This causes them to be consistent underachievers, despite intellectual or creative abilities suggestive of potential for higher functioning. Self-destructive acts such as drug-overdosing and superficial wrist-slashing are their way of exacting rescuing responses from others. Although most suicide gestures in borderlines are studiously sublethal, the suicide rate among severe borderlines still approaches 10 percent.

Most experienced therapists agree that the majority of their borderline patients have been sexually molested or otherwise severely traumatized at some
point prior to adolescence, inhibiting their ability to distinguish their own
thoughts and feelings from those of others. Because of their shallow sense of
selfhood and crisis-oriented life-style, borderlines are adept at uncovering deep
feelings of inadequacy and helplessness in their psychotherapists, who tend to
refer these patients to novice therapists unprepared to unravel the knot of
contradictory feelings that emerge in therapy. The outcome is often tragic,
although even this most difficult form of depression can yield to an *artful*
combination of modern medications coupled with specific forms of supportive,
empathic psychotherapy. Beverly Conlan's sensitive article later in this anthology
describes the unique conditions for therapy with borderlines.

MANIC-DEPRESSIVE (BIPOLAR) DISORDER

Some people experience major depression only once in a lifetime; for others it is
a series of storm clouds that sporadically turn their world to gray; for still others
depressive episodes are intermixed with an extreme opposite state of consciousness called *mania*. In mania, consciousness grows more *dense* in the sense that
more experience is crowded into a given time frame. Perception, feeling, thinking, intuition, and sometimes creative inspiration become equally inflated.

As a manic state takes hold, a person initially feels pleasantly alert, vibrantly
alive, at the brink of new insights. Although several sleepless nights pass, he feels
no sense of fatigue, only a gradual opening of exceptional clarity. Sleep is
superfluous, a needless waste of time, of which there is never enough. Sights and
sounds are brilliant, vivid; indeed, all the senses come alive, swollen with wonder.
There is a sensation of ascending above the strictures of ordinary thought, of
being privy to a wealth of insight beyond the reach of others, of unfettered
freedom to feel and act as never before. Things that before had been mysterious
now reveal their secrets. The early manic is empowered with a newfound vision
of the essence of things, not merely how the world functions but the subtle
reasons behind it.

It is nearly impossible to convince someone in such an extraordinary frame of
mind that he is in imminent peril of becoming psychotic. The sane world has
little to match his raptures, and he has never felt more rational in his life. Because
there is no way to keep such important truths to himself, an ebullient extrover-
sion infects the early manic phase, no matter how introverted the core personality. His high-velocity stream of ideas whirls into a torrent of words. He
jumps into every situation that catches his fancy, and there are many, for he

seldom persists in any undertaking past the point when the next intriguing novelty intrudes. With sexual drive quickened, he indiscriminately seeks a rush of partners, but he remains insatiable.

Time rushes for the manic; there is never enough of it. There are no limits to what he can accomplish by pure will alone if others would just get out of his way. And there are no consequences, no dues to pay tomorrow. Personal responsibility or guilt are impediments reserved for the unilluminated. There is a glorious scattering of money for the sheer fun of spending. Credit cards are his means to meet the unquenchable challenge of finding new and interesting ways to dispense it.

At first the manic forfeits little social or vocational competence. Indeed, his infectious confidence and enthusiasm enable him to seduce others into relinquishing their conservative scruples. He seems to be speeding down a dead-end street, but sometimes his arousal stabilizes before disaster occurs, a state known as *hypomania*. Many hypomanics are creative and successful people, leaders in business, science, and the arts. They have the knack of flaunting authority and convention, while halting one step short of crossing the line into psychosis. One physician who studied manic people wrote that such luminaries as Abraham Lincoln, Teddy Roosevelt, Ernest Hemingway, Winston Churchill, and George Patton were beset by episodes of hypomania during times of their most significant accomplishments.[5]

The one percent of humanity who develop full-blown manic episodes are less fortunate. Countless careers, marriages, and families have been destroyed by this hypercharged consciousness spiraling out of control. As arousal escalates beyond a certain threshold, the balance of various mind/brain systems is set askew, and a vicious circle takes hold. Disrupting sleep patterns, such as may happen during east-west travel or at times of stress, can trigger a mild manic episode that itself prevents sleep, in turn escalating the state of arousal until conventional perception and cognition is derailed. As the manic's ego inflates to the point that it can no longer hold the unconscious at bay, telepathic or precognitive information may intrude into his awareness, and he may experience feelings of mystical rapture.

Despite the fascinating aspects of hyperacute experience, an explosively volatile state of consciousness lurks behind the manic's rapidly faltering ego. Visual and auditory hallucinations insidiously blend with objects of the material world. Delusions—the ego's last-gasp effort to make sense of the uncanny—soon follow. These tend to be tinged with a cosmic or mythic quality, imparting a messianic sense of mission to save the world, or even the universe. In the thrall of this sweeping vision, the manic has few inhibitions that paralyze his implacable will to action. Paranoia—a final common pathway for many psychotic states—leads to exaggerated defensive reactions against anyone unwise enough to stand in his way. Many a manic gets roughed up by uncomprehending police after flouting trivial social conventions.

Like Icarus whose fragile wings of wax lifted him too near the ultimate source of power, manics await a hard fall to earth. A manic consumes his vital inner resources at a rate too swift to be contained. A precipitous descent from sunny heights into the dark caves of depression soon follows.

Having sipped the nectar of higher insight, a person who falls from a manic state faces a most profound devitalization, the worst of the many faces of depression. On the average, a manic episode lasts about three months, and the following depression about nine months—an eternity of psychic stagnation that can end in suicide. The spent ashes of manic exaltation now blacken each experience, providing taunting reminders of a momentary flirtation with the deep mysteries of consciousness itself. There remains only a soft whisper of something left undone, an important truth just barely missed, now seemingly forever beyond reach. Where there was once an abundance of purpose to life, now there is a void, a sealing off of a rapidly contracting self from the life-giving energies of union with spirit.

Yet this too eventually passes. One morning the depressed individual awakens to a pleasing shaft of morning light through a window, or takes spontaneous joy in the song of a bird. His ordinary state of consciousness is gradually restored, and with it his premanic personality. He finds no noticeable reason for this fortuitous shift, just as the manic state emerged without perceptible cause. Unlike that of schizophrenics in remission, the core personalities of manic-depressives differ little from those of the population at large. Many are free from everyday neuroses and are sorely distressed by the disruptive interludes in their otherwise goal-directed lives. Even more worrisome is the prospect of another unpredictable manic-depressive cycle in the future.[6]

THE VICIOUS CYCLE OF DEPRESSION

It's depressing to be depressed; depression feeds on itself, creating a deep rut from which escape may seem impossible. If an individual cannot concentrate on his work, forfeits his sexual drive, is surly and morbidly unpleasant to be with, this inflames the worst image he may harbor of himself, sapping his self-esteem and inflating nascent feelings of hopelessness and helplessness. The myriad vicious cycles that ensnare a depressed person gain momentum as his mood deteriorates, often leaving him a lonely and embittered caricature of his former self, the memory of which mocks him from afar.

These vicious circles are not all of psychological origin. There is mounting evidence to believe each episode of depression *physically* predisposes an individual to the next, rewiring the structure and chemistry of his brain, undermining his resistance to stress, rejection, or loss. This phenomenon—known as "kindling"—has long been known to exist for epilepsy, in which each seizure lowers one's threshold for the next. More recently, kindling has been shown to exist for panic attacks and manic episodes. When applied to depression, kindling creates an internal frailty that can magnify a relatively minor disappointment into a devastating blow to the sense of well-being that derails one's ability to cope effectively.

Just as one defective part of a car can overload other parts and cause their premature breakdown, so does a depressed psyche severely tax one's physical and mental stamina. Repeated episodes of depression insidiously undermine an individual's personality, permanently sapping his self-confidence, initiative, and ability to plan for far-reaching goals. For these reasons, we can no longer reasonably entertain the notion that depression is a "common cold" that is hardly worth the bother to treat. We must develop skills to recognize depression early in life, and be alert to early signs of each episode thereafter. Modern treatment methods, many of which will be described in later chapters of this book, can be quite effective in averting these vicious circles, so they must be aggressively offered to depressed people before the psyche is indelibly scarred.

2. *Darkness Visible*

AN AUTHOR'S PERSONAL STRUGGLE WITH DEPRESSION

BY WILLIAM STYRON

In this poignant excerpt from his widely acclaimed book, Darkness Visible, *Pulitzer Prize–winning novelist William Styron gives a moving account of the destructive interplay between alcohol and depression, and his wrenching struggle to overcome both. Styron confronts the depths of his being as he searches for a path of renewal and affirmation of life.*

The storm which swept me into a hospital in December began as a cloud no bigger than a wine goblet the previous June. And the cloud—the manifest crisis—involved alcohol, a substance I had been abusing for forty years. Like a great many American writers, whose sometimes lethal addiction to alcohol has become so legendary as to provide in itself a stream of studies and books, I used alcohol as the magical conduit to fantasy and euphoria, and to the enhancement of the imagination. There is no need to either rue or apologize for my use of this soothing, often sublime agent, which had contributed greatly to my writing; although I never set down a line while under its influence, I did use it—often in conjunction with music—as a means to let my mind conceive visions that the unaltered, sober brain has no access to. Alcohol was an invaluable senior partner of my intellect, besides being a friend whose ministrations I sought daily— sought also, I now see, as a means to calm the anxiety and incipient dread that I had hidden away for so long somewhere in the dungeons of my spirit.

The trouble was, at the beginning of this particular summer, that I was betrayed. It struck me quite suddenly, almost overnight: I could no longer drink. It was as if my body had risen up in protest, along with my mind, and had conspired to reject this daily mood bath which it had so long welcomed and, who knows? perhaps even come to need. Many drinkers have experienced this intolerance as they have grown older. I suspect that the crisis was at least partly metabolic—the liver rebelling, as if to say, "No more, no more"—but at any rate I discovered that alcohol in minuscule amounts, even a mouthful of wine, caused me nausea, a desperate and unpleasant wooziness, a sinking sensation and ultimately a distinct revulsion. The comforting friend had abandoned me not gradually and reluctantly, as a true friend might do, but like a shot—and I was left high and certainly dry, and unhelmed.

Neither by will nor by choice had I became an abstainer; the situation was puzzling to me, but it was also traumatic, and I date the onset of my depressive mood from the beginning of this deprivation. Logically, one would be overjoyed that the body had so summarily dismissed a substance that was undermining its health; it was as if my system had generated a form of Antabuse, which should have allowed me to happily go my way, satisfied that a trick of nature had shut me off from a harmful dependence. But, instead, I began to experience a vaguely troubling malaise, a sense of something having gone cockeyed in the domestic universe I'd dwelt in so long, so comfortably. While depression is by no means unknown when people stop drinking, it is usually on a scale that is not menacing. But it should be kept in mind how idiosyncratic the faces of depression can be.

It was not really alarming at first, since the change was subtle, but I did notice that my surroundings took on a different tone at certain times: the shadows of nightfall seemed more somber, my mornings were less buoyant, walks in the woods became less zestful, and there was a moment during my working hours in the late afternoon when a kind of panic and anxiety overtook me, just for a few minutes, accompanied by a visceral queasiness—such a seizure was at least slightly alarming, after all. As I set down these recollections, I realize that it should have been plain to me that I was already in the grip of the beginning of a mood disorder, but I was ignorant of such a condition at that time.

When I reflected on this curious alteration of my consciousness—and I was baffled enough from time to time to do so—I assumed that it all had to do somehow with my enforced withdrawal from alcohol. And, of course, to a certain extent this was true. But it is my conviction now that alcohol played a perverse trick on me when we said farewell to each other: although, as everyone should know, it is a major depressant, it had never truly depressed me during my drinking career, acting instead as a shield against anxiety. Suddenly vanished, the great ally which for so long had kept my demons at bay was no longer there to prevent those demons from beginning to swarm through the subconscious, and I was emotionally naked, vulnerable as I had never been before. Doubtless depression had hovered near me for years, waiting to swoop down. Now I was in the first stage—premonitory, like a flicker of sheet lightning barely perceived—of depression's black tempest.

I was on Martha's Vineyard, where I've spent a good part of each year since the 1960s, during that exceptionally beautiful summer. But I had begun to respond indifferently to the island's pleasures. I felt a kind of numbness, an enervation, but more particularly an odd fragility—as if my body had actually become frail, hypersensitive, and somehow disjointed and clumsy, lacking normal coordination. And soon I was in the throes of a pervasive hypochondria. Nothing felt quite right with my corporeal self; there were twitches and pains, sometimes intermittent, often seemingly constant, that seemed to presage all sorts of dire infirmities.

One of the unforgettable features of this stage of my disorder was the way in which my old farmhouse, my beloved home for thirty years, took on for me at that point when my spirits regularly sank to their nadir an almost palpable quality of ominousness. The fading evening light—akin to that famous "slant of light" of Emily Dickinson's, which spoke to her of death, of chill extinction—had none of its familiar autumnal loveliness, but ensnared me in a suffocating gloom. I wondered how this friendly place, teeming with such memories of (again in her words) "Lads and Girls," of "laughter and ability and Sighing, And Frocks and Curls," could almost perceptibly seem so hostile and forbidding. Physically, I was not alone. As always Rose was present and listened with unflagging patience to my complaints. But I felt an immense and aching solitude. I could no longer concentrate during those afternoon hours, which for years had been my working time, and the act of writing itself, becoming more and more difficult and exhausting, stalled, then finally ceased.

There were also dreadful, pouncing seizures of anxiety. One bright day on a walk through the woods with my dog I heard a flock of Canada geese honking high above trees ablaze with foliage; ordinarily a sight and sound that would have exhilarated me, the flight of birds caused me to stop, riveted with fear, and I stood stranded there, helpless, shivering, aware for the first time that I had been stricken by no mere pangs of withdrawal but by a serious illness whose name and actuality I was able finally to acknowledge. Going home, I couldn't rid my mind of the line of Baudelaire's, dredged up from the distant past, that for several days had been skittering around at the edge of my consciousness: "I have felt the wind of the wing of madness."

That fall, as the disorder gradually took full possession of my system, I began to conceive that my mind itself was like one of those outmoded small-town telephone exchanges, being gradually inundated by flood-waters: one by one, the normal circuits began to drown, causing some of the functions of the body and nearly all of those of instinct and intellect to slowly disconnect.

There is a well-known checklist of some of these functions and their failures.

Mine conked out fairly close to schedule, many of them following the pattern of depressive seizures. I particularly remember the lamentable near disappearance of my voice. It underwent a strange transformation, becoming at times quite faint, wheezy, and spasmodic—a friend observed later that it was the voice of a ninety-year-old. The libido also made an early exit, as it does in most major illnesses—it is the superfluous need of a body in beleaguered emergency. Many people lose all appetite; mine was relatively normal, but I found myself eating only for subsistence: food, like everything else within the scope of sensation, was utterly without savor. Most distressing of all the instinctual disruptions was that of sleep, along with a complete absence of dreams.

Exhaustion combined with sleeplessness is a rare torture. My few hours of sleep were usually terminated at three or four in the morning, when I stared up into yawning darkness, wondering and writhing at the devastation taking place in my mind, and awaiting the dawn, which usually permitted me a feverish, dreamless nap. I'm fairly certain that it was during one of these insomniac trances that there came over me the knowledge—a weird and shocking revelation, like that of some long-beshrouded metaphysical truth—that this condition would cost me my life if it continued on such a course. This must have been just before my trip to Paris. Death, as I have said, was now a daily presence, blowing over me in cold gusts. I had not conceived precisely how my end would come. In short, I was still keeping the idea of suicide at bay. But plainly the possibility was around the corner, and I would soon meet it face to face.

What I had begun to discover is that, mysteriously and in ways that are totally remote from normal experience, the gray drizzle of horror induced by depression takes on the quality of physical pain. But it is not an immediately identifiable pain, like that of a broken limb. It may be more accurate to say that despair, owing to some evil trick played upon the sick brain by the inhabiting psyche, comes to resemble the diabolical discomfort of being imprisoned in a fiercely overheated room. And because no breeze stirs this caldron, because there is no escape from this smothering confinement, it is entirely natural that the victim begins to think ceaselessly of oblivion.

Loss in all of its manifestations is the touchstone of depression—in the progress of the disease and, most likely, in its origin. At a later date I would gradually be persuaded that devastating loss in childhood figured as a probable genesis of my own disorder; meanwhile, as I monitored my retrograde condition, I felt loss at every hand. The loss of self-esteem is a celebrated symptom, and my own sense of self had all but disappeared, along with any self-reliance. This loss can quickly degenerate into dependence, and from dependence into infantile dread. One dreads the loss of all things, all people close and dear. There is an acute fear of abandonment. Being alone in the house, even for a moment, caused me exquisite panic and trepidation.

Of the images recollected from that time the most bizarre and discomfiting remains the one of me, age four and a half, tagging through a market after my long-suffering wife; not for an instant could I let out of my sight the endlessly patient soul who had become nanny, mommy, comforter, priestess, and, most important, confidante—a counselor of rocklike centrality to my existence. I would hazard the opinion that many disastrous sequels to depression might be averted if the victims received support such as she gave me. But meanwhile my losses mounted and proliferated. There is no doubt that as one nears the penultimate depths of depression—which is to say just before the stage when one begins to act out one's suicide instead of being a mere contemplator of it— the acute sense of loss is connected with a knowledge of life slipping away at accelerated speed. One develops fierce attachments. Ludicrous things—my reading glasses, a handkerchief, a certain writing instrument—became the objects of my demented possessiveness. Each momentary misplacement filled me with a frenzied dismay, each item being the tactile reminder of a world soon to be obliterated.

I reached that phase of the disorder where all sense of hope had vanished, along with the idea of a futurity; my brain, in thrall to its outlaw hormones, had become less an organ of thought than an instrument registering, minute by minute, varying degrees of its own suffering. The mornings themselves were becoming bad now as I wandered about lethargic, following my synthetic sleep, but afternoons were still the worst, beginning at about three o'clock, when I'd feel the horror, like some poisonous fogbank, roll in upon my mind, forcing me into bed. There I would lie for as long as six hours, stuporous and virtually paralyzed, gazing at the ceiling and waiting for that moment of evening when, mysteriously, the crucifixion would ease up just enough to allow me to force down some food and then, like an automaton, seek an hour or two of sleep again. Why wasn't I in a hospital?

A phenomenon that a number of people have noted while in deep depression is the sense of being accompanied by a second self—a wraithlike observer who, not sharing the dementia of his double, is able to watch with dispassionate curiosity as his companion struggles against the oncoming disaster, or decides to embrace it. There is a theatrical quality about all this, and during the next several days, as I went about stolidly preparing for extinction, I couldn't shake off a sense of melodrama—a melodrama in which I, the victim-to-be of self-murder, was both the solitary actor and lone member of the audience. I had not as yet chosen the mode of my departure, but I knew that the step would come next, and soon, as inescapable as nightfall.

I watched myself in mingled terror and fascination as I began to make the necessary preparation: going to see my lawyer in the nearby town—there rewriting my will—and spending part of a couple of afternoons in a muddled attempt to bestow upon posterity a letter of farewell. It turned out that putting together a suicide note, which I felt obsessed with a necessity to compose, was the most difficult task of writing that I had ever tackled. There were too many people to acknowledge, to thank, to bequeath final bouquets. And finally I couldn't manage the sheer dirgelike solemnity of it; there was something I found almost comically offensive in the pomposity of such a comment as "For some time now I have sensed in my work a growing psychosis that is doubtless a reflection of the psychotic strain tainting my life" (this is one of the few lines I recall verbatim), as well as something degrading in the prospect of a testament, which I wished to infuse with at least some dignity and eloquence, reduced to an exhausted stutter of inadequate apologies and self-serving explanations. I should have used as an example the mordant statement of the Italian writer Cesare Pavese, who in parting wrote simply: *No more words. An act. I'll never write again.*

But even a few words came to seem to me too long-winded, and I tore up all my efforts, resolving to go out in silence. Late one bitterly cold night, when I knew that I could not possibly get myself through the following day, I sat in the living room of the house bundled up against the chill; something had happened to the furnace. My wife had gone to bed, and I had forced myself to watch the tape of a movie in which a young actress, who had been in a play of mine, was cast in a small part. At one point in the film, which was set in late-nineteenth-century Boston, the characters moved down the hallway of a music conservatory, beyond the walls of which, from unseen musicians, came a contralto voice, a sudden soaring passage from the Brahms *Alto Rhapsody.*

This sound, which like all music—indeed, like all pleasure—I had been numbly unresponsive to for months, pierced my heart like a dagger, and in a flood of swift recollection I thought of all the joys the house had known: the children who had rushed through its rooms, the festivals, the love and work, the honestly earned slumber, the voices and the nimble commotion, the perennial tribe of cats and dogs and birds, "laughter and ability and Sighing, And Frocks and Curls." All this I realized was more than I could ever abandon, even as what I had set out so deliberately to do was more than I could inflict on those memories, and upon those, so close to me, with whom the memories were bound. And just as powerfully I realized I could not commit this desecration on myself. I drew upon some last gleam of sanity to perceive the terrifying dimensions of the mortal predicament I had fallen into. I woke up my wife and soon telephone calls were made. The next day I was admitted to the hospital.

The hospital was my salvation, and it is something of a paradox that in this austere place with its locked and wired doors and desolate green hallways—ambulances screeching night and day ten floors below—I found the repose, the assuagement of the tempest in my brain, that I was unable to find in my quiet farmhouse.

This is partly the result of sequestration, of safety, of being removed to a world in which the urge to pick up a knife and plunge it into one's own breast disappears in the newfound knowledge, quickly apparent even to the depressive's fuzzy brain, that the knife with which he is attempting to cut his dreadful Swiss steak is bendable plastic. But the hospital also offers the mild, oddly gratifying trauma of sudden stabilization—a transfer out of the too familiar surroundings of home, where all is anxiety and discord, into an orderly and benign detention where one's only duty is to try to get well. For me the real healers were seclusion and time.

To most of those who have experienced it, the horror of depression is so overwhelming as to be quite beyond expression, hence the frustrated sense of inadequacy found in the work of even the greatest artists. But in science and art the search will doubtless go on for a clear representation of its meaning, which sometimes, for those who have known it, is a simulacrum of all the evil of our world: of our everyday discord and chaos, our irrationality, warfare and crime, torture and violence, our impulse toward death and our flight from it held in the intolerable equipoise of history. If our lives had no other configuration but this, we should want, and perhaps deserve, to perish; if depression had no termination, then suicide would, indeed, be the only remedy. But one need not sound the false or inspirational note to stress the truth that depression is not the soul's annihilation; men and women who have recovered from the disease—and they are countless—bear witness to what is probably its only saving grace: it is conquerable.

For those who have dwelt in depression's dark wood, and known its inexplicable agony, their return from the abyss is not unlike the ascent of the poet, trudging upward and upward out of hell's black depths and at last emerging into what he saw as "the shining world." There, whoever has been restored to health has almost always been restored to the capacity for serenity and joy, and this may be indemnity enough for having endured the despair beyond despair.

> *E quindi uscimmo a riveder le stelle.*
> *And so we came forth, and once again beheld the stars.*

3. Beauty and the Beast

EXPLORING THE LINK BETWEEN CREATIVITY AND
DEPRESSION

COMPILED BY KATHY CRONKITE

Kathy Cronkite has compiled an unique collection of first-person accounts by well-known people who were willing to share their personal struggles with depression and its antithesis, mania. In this chapter from On the Edge of Darkness, *several of her subjects speak insightfully of the creative tension that lies between melancholy and art.*

Whether I am trying to write, to express myself musically, or to act, the downward spiral into depression inspires and inhibits creativity at different points along the way. As the melancholy begins, there is a heightened, though self-absorbed, kind of passion that allows the upwelling of those romantically bleak feelings that inspired Emily Dickinson or Gerard Manley Hopkins. Here is where I write poetry, where I can identify with the sadness or anger in a theatrical part, where I walk through the night, singing in full voice old hymns or folk blues. Here I feel most in touch with the deepest corners of my soul, and when I have a creative outlet, the junction of poetry and pain feels if not good at least satisfying.

But as the spiral continues down, I feel so inept, so incapable, so hopeless that there is no point in attempting to create. Anything I fashioned would be dross. Soon any effort at all becomes pointless, activity slows, then stops, and numbness sets in.

Why does it seem almost a given that creativity and madness go hand in hand? Why are we less surprised by the suicidal death of a poet than that of a doctor? From Van Gogh to Jean Seberg, some of humankind's most gifted artists have lost their battles with their inner demons. As tragic as these losses are, still we ask ourselves: Is it their madness that imbues their creativity with genius? If they were well, would their art still move us as profoundly?

Do we as a society have a stake in keeping our artists ill? As we move closer to prenatal gene manipulation, will parents have to choose between a well child and a *potentially brilliant artist? Dr. John Kelsoe poses the question: "If you eliminated bipolar genes from the population, who knows what other beneficial effects you might be losing, even beyond creativity?"*

JOHN KELSOE, M.D.

There is certainly a link between the two—not to say that most people who are creative have an affective disorder, but it certainly occurs at a higher rate, among poets most notably. I think that is partly because when people with bipolar disorder go through the stage of mania called hypomania where they are activated and energized, their brains are going faster than usual. They are not ill to the degree where they are impaired yet, but they probably think better, faster, more creatively than the rest of us. And they are frequently very successful in our society. It is only when they go on beyond that into full mania that they are impaired. Many of these very creative writers and musicians have been creative as a result of or during their depressive episodes as well.

LESLIE GARIS

I have one son with dyslexia, another son with dyslexia, attention deficit disorder, and hyperactivity. All three of my children are incredibly artistic, and they're tremendously gifted, especially the one who is in a way the most afflicted. I have come to see with my family and with my children that the affliction comes with an artistic territory, but it's no gift. For their higher functioning, the price they have paid is a very complicated personality that short-circuits.

BETTY SUE FLOWERS, PH.D.

I think great artists produce in spite of depression, not because of it. The artists I know are more willing than most people to feel the feelings they have. So the depression is more pronounced. Not that they value depression per se, but they value intense feeling.

If you're a materialist, you can look back on a lot of the descriptions of the ecstatic vision of saints, like St. Theresa, and say, "Oh, well, yes, she was undergoing a schizophrenic attack," or "[El Greco] must have had a strange condition that made him paint elongated figures." That doesn't lessen his art, nor does it lessen the artists' visions if they were chemically induced, either through an imbalance or through something ingested.

I know many artists who suffer from clinical depression. What they create is not in itself a product of depression, even though it may reflect their struggle with depression as content. The difference between a mere expression of depression and a work of art that is *informed* by depression is that the first comes out of depression and stays in depression, as opposed to a work of art that takes me to the depths of darkness, to a dimension that is part of the human condition.

Have you ever seen the Rothko Chapel in Houston? To me that's a very moving, spiritual place. [Mark] Rothko was a severely depressed person. You could go into the chapel and if you didn't really *see* those paintings you might say, "Yuck, what is this? Just brown dark paintings—how depressing. . . . " But if you're in there and *look*, you see the light *and* the darkness. You see behind and through those paintings. You see the tremendous power and sheer depth. It's a moving experience that lifts you out of yourself. You end up being transformed rather than depressed. To me, the Rothko Chapel is a place of hope—or perhaps of faith in hope.

MARY JONES

There's the romantic notion of all these wonderful nineteenth-century geeks who wrote romantic poetry and had interesting lives like Byron and Shelley and Baudelaire, and screwed up everything around them. And I keep thinking that it is possible to be sane and also do great creative art. Surely, it's possible.*

I think that in many ways the Romantic tradition is a great trick that's played on people, the idea that to be creative, to be a poet, to be a great writer, to be an artist, to be interesting, you had to be outrageous, to live on the edge, to push things as far as possible. Actually it's a bunch of crap.

I suspect we'd all be far more creative if we went to bed every night at ten o'clock and got up at eight and ate granola. . . . But it's so boring.

JULES FEIFFER

I think artists are more sensitive toward their work, not necessarily toward anything else in life. Some of the most insensitive people I know are artists.

I don't know that it's a given that artists are more susceptible to this illness. I

---

* Dr. Flowers also mentioned this myth. "During the Renaissance, depression itself used to be a romanticized state—melancholia, it was called. Hamlet is the archetypal case of the depressed young man. During the early nineteenth century, in Goethe's *Sorrows of Young Werther,* the depressed young man commits suicide for love.

"The Renaissance suddenly saw human beings as alone. The world was demythologized for the first time, so the natural reaction was depression over the death of God. Then when someone articulates that, that expresses the age."

think what they are more susceptible to, just because of the nature of free-lance work, is the ups and downs of acceptance and rejection. If you're working in an office job, it's likely that you can have a period of years without being tested all the time. While a writer or a painter or a playwright is tested every time out. The notion that this is not a statement on your worth as a human being, as opposed to your last work, doesn't carry very far. In the end you think "This is a statement on me. They don't like me." And in fact that's true, because if your art is representative of who and what you are, it is a statement on your worth.

JOHN KENNETH GALBRAITH

I have a very strong feeling just from talking with other people about this, that there's a strong relationship between somebody who writes or is in some literary public role and depression.

There's a certain introspective tendency. You look at your work and say to yourself, "Well, Galbraith, ah, this isn't so good, this is pretty bad." And if you're working with your hands or repairing buildings or something of that sort, you're not subject to bad reviews.

You hold yourself to a higher standard than most people. Hemingway had some of the same problems. You're depressed when you feel that the intellectual structure you have built somehow isn't up to form. Hemingway took an escape that I've never pursued by getting drunk. It's why so many literary people have resorted to alcohol.

HARRY WILMER, M.D.

There is almost a cliché in Jungian psychology that you welcome the depression as a necessary journey into the unconscious. Most people I know who are creative go through some pretty tough times, and I think some of the best things are done when people are in this mire, and they're trying to find some way out. [But] if a gifted writer, playwright, or artist comes to see me and they're terribly depressed, I don't say, "Oh, that's nice, welcome it." I may feel compelled to work with their depression or give them medication until they can be stabilized, and then deal with the creative side.

I don't intrude in the creative process. When I find a creative person dreaming of a guide, I don't immediately say, "Oh, that's me," I say, "That's you, even if it's projected on me." It's important for the psychiatrist dealing with creative people who are depressed to help them see that their guide is in them, their inner analyst, their wise old man, their wise old woman. When any patient tells me a dream, I take that as a supreme creative act.

JUDITH BELUSHI PISANO

There are a lot of comedians who believe that if they don't have that tortured side they won't know what's funny. I think that it's true that there are a lot of people who are reacting to being unhappy or to negative things in their life by being funny. But I don't think one has to exist to have the other. Now, in my life, I have a new husband, and I have a baby. We have a nice life, it's very comfortable, it's peaceful. So the question is, do you lose your instinct to continue creating if you become too comfortable? I don't think so. I think you create because it's in you. It's almost Zen, opening yourself up for humor, to be funny. You put yourself there.

I've known some comedians who can't turn it off, and it's not something I would call a good quality about them. I think they're blocking something. They're afraid if they turn it off, it won't come back. Likewise, I imagine, depression for some people could get to be so familiar that they're afraid to let go of it, too.

John was not always "on" by any means. He was just funny in general. Just his look and the way he could move or react. He was a funny person, but he wasn't verbally on and making jokes all the time. It was more his mind, the way he saw things, and the ability to use it in political satire or whatever it might be. I don't think that has anything to do with whether you're happy or unhappy or on drugs or not, or depressed or not.

A lot of John's comedy started as a young kid at home; his mother was a funny lady. At the same time, they had a complicated relationship, and there was pain in it, too, so it was multisided. Maybe that's what makes someone more specifically a user of comedy to block things versus someone who's just a funny person.

Once when John was at the height of a binge, he said to me he didn't think he could be funny without drugs. Later, when he was at a period when he had not been doing drugs for some time, he knew that wasn't true. He might have had fears that life was getting a little too comfortable, and wondered if life gets too cushy, are you going to lose your drive and just want to work in the garden all day? And the bottom line is that actually, that's not so bad.

The depressed writer, or actor, or painter asks, "Without the highs of mania or the lows of depression, would I still live a life of creative intensity?" The question also might be, "Without the distraction of mania, would I be free to make the most of my gifts? Without the shackles of depression, would my work soar?"

Writing, painting, acting, singing may help you feel a little better, for a little while, by siphoning off some of the painfully urgent emotions of mania and depression. If the internal pressure can be channeled artistically, at the very least, those around you may be spared some of the emotional fallout from your anger or your pain. The result doesn't have to be "good" by any objective criteria; all it needs to be is a release. If it is also well wrought, ask yourself, "Is that because of or in spite of my illness?" and remember that it is the artist who created the work, not the depression.

My fear is that we will glorify depression as a means to an artistic end, that we will say, "It's not illness, it's art." I believe it is an illusion that art must be much larger or more passionate than life. One of the finest poems I have read in the last few months alluded to the death of a friend, but described riding home on a bicycle and clothes hanging on the line—ordinary experiences, poignantly, sanely rendered through the spare words of an artist. I have written some poems out of pain that I am very proud of, but the ones I remember are those written out of love.

4. *Meeting the Shadow at Mid-life*

THE CHANGING OF THE GODS

BY CONNIE ZWEIG, PH.D.

This sensitive essay casts mid-life depression in both archetypal and personal terms, a headlong plunge into the deep unconscious where the self confronts its disowned shadow in order to emerge empowered for the role of wise elder. Weaving timeless mythic tales with penetrating insights derived from her study of Jungian psychology, the author shows how a timely descent into the underworld of depression can become a journey of renewal.

The dread and resistance which every natural human being experiences when it comes to delving too deeply into himself is, at bottom, the fear of the journey to Hades.

C.G. JUNG
Psychology and Alchemy[1]

When I turned forty, the solid ground beneath my feet cracked open. I dropped through a fissure, down, down, and disappeared into a great blackness. I lived for a long while at the bottom of a dark hole looking up.

Nothing had prepared me for such an eclipse. No betrayal, no wound had shown me the way. I had not felt depressed since adolescence, when I first discovered Sartre and Camus. I had not felt depressed when some of my friends dog-paddled and sank beneath the surface from addictions or failed marriages. I had not felt depressed when world events turned grim and human cruelty looked out at me with hollow eyes.

Instead, I had felt some strange immunity, as if I were vaccinated against descent; as if I walked on buoyant ground filled with helium perhaps, or hope.

And I saw this as a sign of grace, a sign that the gods winked at me and smiled.

Then I turned forty. And, like an unforeseen natural disaster, the earth yawned open, a long hand rose up from the depths of the underworld, grabbed me by the foot—and stopped my dancing.

The music of the underworld plays in a minor key. It hums constantly like a droning lament.

The inhabitants of the underworld, shrouded in black, speak in whispers, as if they could awaken the dead.

The sky in the underworld is not a blue envelope: it is a dusky tunnel that swallows every particle of light. The colors of the underworld pale and fade to gray, not an oceanic blue-gray, not a shiny silver-gray, just gray, flat and unending. Tastes—sweet, salty, bitter—turn to ash on the tongue. Life in the underworld is a still life, drawn without motion in two dimensions.

For a while, I faded into the background, monotone and colorless, part of the still life. Then, like Theseus holding onto Ariadne's golden thread, I began to follow the plumb-line through my dreams. Slowly, I opened my eyes to the darkness; slowly, I opened my heart to the pregnant possibilities that gestated there. Slowly, like a blind poet, I groped my way toward images and words.

I sought an acquaintance with the journeyers who had descended before me: Persephone, Orpheus, Dionysus, Inanna, Odysseus. Their strange-sounding names grew familiar. I recited them like a long litany . . . and slowly I began to feel that I was not alone, but rather that a family of souls encircled me. And then I began to feel that I was not off the path, but rather had stumbled upon another path, a hidden, more treacherous road that led not to enlightenment but, perhaps, to *endarkenment.*

The Greeks had a name for this downward path: *Katabasis,* or Descent. Our ancient forebears understood that we needed not only to fly above with the birds, lightly and full of grace, but also to crawl beneath with the snakes, slowly, silently, on our bellies.

I had not chosen this lower path; it had chosen me. On seeing this, I told myself that I did not have depression; rather, Depression had me. And so, at last, I was able to take the backseat and go along for the ride. Then the real journey began.

This paper explores an archetypal approach to the great descent, known today as depression. This symbolic approach does not preclude a psychodynamic perspective, or a biological one. In fact, I believe that the ideal approach to treating depression includes all three—body, mind, and spirit.

But I wish to address a specific kind of depression here, the kind that often appears, as my own did, at mid-life. And I suspect that this garden variety does not typically stem from early childhood trauma or from neurochemical imbalance.

Instead, mid-life depression is an archetypal event, a meeting with the daimonic. It's a symbolic turning toward the second half of life—an irreversible turning. And just this quality—its irreversibility—carries a depressive weight. For an individual to carry this weight alone, the task may be arduous, even unbearable.

But if a traveler can detect footprints on the path, she might learn the stories of those who've gone before and in this way lighten the weight. She may uncover the pattern that connects her to the past and to the future. For the underworld is the ancestral realm and the mythical realm; it is the land of the dead and the land of the dream.

Archetypal psychologist James Hillman describes it this way: "Underworld is psyche. When we use the word 'underworld,' we are referring to a wholly psychic perspective, where one's entire mode of being has been desubstantialized, killed of natural life . . . the underworld perspective radically alters our experience of life. It no longer matters on its own terms but only in terms of the psyche. To know the psyche at its depths . . . one must go to the underworld."[2]

For some travelers, a katabasis leads to total despair. Carl Jung, who saw descent to the shadow as a stage in the individuation process, warned: "Apparently one has to be 'led' downwards, because it is not easy for people to descend from their heights and remain below. In the first place a loss of social prestige is feared, and in the second a loss of moral self-esteem when they have to admit their own darkness . . . 'Below' means the bed-rock of reality, which despite all self-deceptions is there right enough."[3]

This Hell-realm is bankrupt of feeling, empty of meaning. Some journeyers will refuse to walk through the door to Hell by feverishly doing more of the same: more work for more hours; more alcohol, more jogging; more sex, more gambling; even more books about the promise of immortality. For them, mid-life looks like an uphill marathon race, anything so as not to stop—and hear the call to descend.

THE CALL

If the loss is shattering enough, the disillusionment deep enough, one hears the call. Some may refuse to respond. But others will turn toward it and listen. What does this call ask of us? Mythologist Joseph Campbell describes it this way:

"It happens that if anyone—in whatever society—undertakes for himself the perilous journey into darkness by descending, either intentionally or unintentionally, into the crooked lanes of his own spiritual labyrinth, he soon finds himself in a landscape of symbolical figures (any one of which may swallow him), which is no less marvelous than the wild Siberian world of the *pudak* and sacred mountains."[4]

Campbell likens the mythological descent to the second stage of the classical spiritual way of mystics, which involves "purification of the self," in which the journeyer's senses are "cleansed and humbled," her attention is "concentrated on transcendental things." He also proposes that in psychological terms the descent involves "dissolving, transcending, or transmuting the infantile images of our personal past." Thus the descent to the underworld is both a psychological awakening and a spiritual initiation.

Campbell suggests that this movement inward and downward, toward the deep darkness, is like entering a holy place, which requires metamorphosis. The journeyer cannot bring the persona, which is adapted to the outside world, into the underworld. She sheds it as a snake sheds its old skin. And this act of symbolic death brings new life, the birth of a new self.

The theme of the inner traveler's ego death and spiritual rebirth, which takes place at the bottom of the abyss, or in the world womb, is repeated over and over in mythology. Like the Greek maiden Persephone who is raped by Hades, lord of the underworld, but makes a seasonal return to the realm above, bringing springtime with her; or the Egyptian Osiris who was slain, dismembered, and scattered over the sea, only to return from the dead; or Christ who was hung on the cross and left to die, only to be resurrected, each man or woman who makes the harrowing descent and suffers the required sacrifices engages in a life-renewing act.

A TIMELESS STORY OF DESCENT

In my favorite myth of descent, Inanna, Queen of Heaven in the ancient land of Sumer (near the Tigris and Euphrates rivers in what is now Iraq), "opens her ear to the Great Below."[5] She wishes to descend to witness the funeral rites of the husband of her sister Ereshkigal, Queen of the Underworld. To do so, she must pass through seven gates and at each one sacrifice a precious attribute: her roles as queen and priestess; her royal power; her sexual power. These are symbolized by an adornment—her crown, necklace, breast beads, breastplate, gold ring, measuring rod, and finally her royal robe.

In her nakedness, Inanna is as helpless as an infant. And in this state she meets her sister, the dark goddess, who, like the Hindu goddess Kali, symbolizes death and rebirth, the destructive-transformative energies. Jungian analyst Sylvia Perera suggests that modern women face Ereshkigal in the depths of depression, "an abyssmal agony of helplessness and futility." They may feel stuck in timeless stasis, unable to budge. They may feel evil or ugly in these introverted, undifferentiated states. Or they may sink into the preverbal chaos of psychosis.[6]

At this moment in the story, Ereshkigal fastens the eye of death on her sister Inanna, turning the Goddess of Heaven into a corpse, a piece of rotting meat, which is hung from a hook on the wall.

What alchemy takes place at the bottom of the abyss when a queen becomes a corpse? Inanna's mythological meeting with her shadow sister, her loathsome alter ego, inspires terror and submission. She confronts the death-dealing, rageful indifference of the one who sits on a throne within each of us in the most hidden recesses of our psyches. As a result, she becomes hopeless, formless, lifeless.

Campbell suggests that Inanna and Ereshkigal together represent the one goddess in her two aspects: light and dark. Her task, he says, is to assimilate her opposite either by psychically swallowing it or by being swallowed. This requires putting aside pride, virtue, beauty, and life itself, and submitting to the intolerable.

Perera echoes this idea when she says that to connect the upper-world feminine with the underworld shadow, a woman (and perhaps a man) must suffer the death of the ego-ideal, that part of the psyche that permits us to perform in the conventional world, even to perform well. The maintenance of this ideal is connected to the repression of other parts of our wholeness, our undeveloped or inferior abilities.

So, in meeting her shadow, a woman swallows up or is swallowed up by her opposite. Perera says, "To the extent that she was high, she must go low; from extraverted, active to inert, passive meat; from differentiated and ideal to undifferentiated and primordial."

The lowest point of the labyrinth, where the confrontation with evil takes place, proves to be the place of reversal. Poet Kathleen Raine describes Dante's famous descent and return in this way:

"The journey had been, hitherto, always a descent into darker and worse places, the claustrophobia closing in until Hell's ruler is encountered and identified as the Shadow . . . Now that the ruler of the hells has been seen and identified, Virgil half leads, half carries the horrified Dante through a narrow passage under Satan's throne, below the hairy thighs of the half-animal, half-human figure of the Devil. What takes place is a kind of rebirth through a round opening; and, like the new-born, Dante can now for the first time see the sky and the stars. And there is literally—and how dramatically—a change of point of view: Satan on his towering throne is now seen reversed beneath the traveler's feet; his power is gone. He is no longer the ruler and the center of the psyche. What has taken place Jung has described as the reintegration of the personality when we find the Self—the 'other' within us—and not, as we had supposed, the ego, to be the ruler and center of the soul."[7]

THE CHANGING OF THE GODS

Like the changing of the guards at Buckingham Palace, the changing of the gods in the palace of the psyche is a symbolic shift in power. But the latter is distinct from the former in several ways: it may not happen on schedule, at regular intervals. And it may not be ritually marked.

An unknown archetype may move to center stage swiftly and radically alter an individual's self-presentation. In the language of mythologist Ginette Paris,[8] one archetype is ascending while another is descending. At these times we might say of a woman who is temporarily taken over by an unfamiliar pattern, "She is not herself."

Or when Hades surfaces suddenly in mid-life depression and turns the world topsy-turvy, Eros, our connection to life and love, is pushed aside and Thanatos draws us out of life, making us feel "down," cold, and withdrawn.

Or when an Athena woman, typically independent and intellectual, is seduced by a skilled lover into her Aphrodite nature, she may be able to move into it for moments of lovemaking. But she may resist a deeper, long-lasting change.

Or when Hestia, who keeps order inside a closed house, is pushed outdoors by the winds of change, such as a financial crisis; or when Hera faces the death of a spouse and her identity as wife is at stake, these women face transitions of serious proportions. They are like mini-deaths, catapulting them into a liminal space, a bardo-like realm between lifetimes, which may last moments or years.

For some people the movement between the archetypes is fluid and ever-changing. They can cross over, letting go of old baggage and beginning anew. But for others, the crossing is difficult, painful, overwhelming.

Perhaps some mid-life depression results when we cannot face the death of the old—and we are stuck, motionless, in between, unable to reach the other side where new life begins. In depression we lose our flexibility and feel paralyzed; time stops, the moment seems to drag on forever. Winter, cold and relentless, does not give way to Spring.

As I wrote this last line I realized that it's the metaphor for the most famous underworld story, the rape of Persephone by Hades. When the maiden is kidnapped by the lord of death, her mother, Demeter, wails in grief and stops the grain from growing. When Persephone returns to the upper world for part of the year, she brings the Spring; when she descends to the underworld to live with Hades, she brings the Winter.

These moments of underworld Winter, however difficult, can open out into great depth. They offer time for incubation, for the imagination to deepen by imagining yet greater depths. For the underworld is always with us, simultaneous and continuous with the upper world, offering us the depths in any moment.

Certainly, my mid-life depression, with its great sacrifices and great awaken-ings, has helped me to live in those moments more fully. It has shown me that I was living with only one eye open—the eye of light. Now, whenever possible, I open the eye of darkness, and my vision embraces a deeper, wider, more paradoxical range of life.

5. Despair, Hope, and Survival

NOTES FROM A NAZI CONCENTRATION CAMP

BY BRUNO BETTELHEIM

*Few situations can match the depressing effects of being held prisoner in a Nazi
death camp. One survivor, Bruno Bettelheim, later became a prominent psychiatric
theoretician and author. In this brief excerpt from* Surviving and Other Essays, *he
shares his hard-won insights that link abandonment, despair, and ultimate hope.*

From what I had learned about survival in the camps from observing others and
myself: even the worst mistreatment by the SS failed to extinguish the will to
live—that is, as long as one could muster the wish to go on and maintain one's
self-respect. Then tortures could even strengthen one's resolution not to permit
the mortal enemy to break one's desire to survive, and to remain true to oneself
as much as conditions permitted. Then the actions of the SS tended to make one
livid with rage, and this gave one the feeling of being very much alive. It made
one all the more determined to go on living, so as to be able someday to defeat
the enemy.

Through their actions and the terrible conditions of life that they imposed,
the SS attempted to rob the prisoners of the ability to respect themselves and care
for their lives. If one thus lost all hope for the future, then one's mental state
automatically precluded any possibility of believing that one could defeat the SS's
purpose by surviving. Then one was deprived of the psychological relief which
imagining future revenge and well-being offered, and one could no longer
defend oneself against falling prey to deepest depression. When to this became
added the feeling that one was abandoned by those in the outside world, then, in
utter desperation, one only wished it would all be over.

Wanting to go on living even in so terrible a situation, keeping one's respect
for oneself, and with it for some others, maintaining hope for one's future, and
holding on to the belief—or at least the hope—that one was not abandoned

were all closely related elements; so were disgust with oneself and one's life, despair about one's future, and the conviction that one had been forsaken. If one could maintain one's self-respect and will to live despite the utter exhaustion, physical mistreatment, and extreme degradations one had to endure, then one could continue to hope that one had not been forsaken by the rest of the world, even if there was but little support for such belief. Then any scrap of evidence was sufficient to be experienced as suggesting that somebody cared.

All this worked only up to a point. If there was no or only little indication that someone, or the world at large, was deeply concerned about the fate of the prisoner, his ability to give positive meaning to signs from the outside world eventually vanished and he felt forsaken, usually with disastrous consequences for his will and with it his ability to survive. Only a very clear demonstration that one was not abandoned—and the SS saw to it that one received this only very rarely, and not at all in the extermination camps—restored, at least momentarily, hope even to those who otherwise by and large had lost it. But those who had reached the utmost state of depression and disintegration, those who had turned into walking corpses because their life drives had become inoperative—the so-called "Muslims" (*Muselmänner*)—could not believe in what others would have viewed as tokens that they had not been forgotten.

For those whose will to live and hope for the future had given way, the end was near. It came relatively rarely through outright suicide, because this meant to take some action, desperate as it was, and they no longer had the strength to act on their own. But there was also no need to deliberately do away with one's life. If one did not exercise great ingenuity and determination in the battle to stay alive, one was soon dead, given the conditions in the camps. Therefore if one gave up hope, one lost the ability to go on with the difficult and painful struggle survival required and so one died in a short time. Losing the will to live was the consequence of the waning of the life drives so that they became too weak for even the primary of their two tasks: to endow the self with the energy it needs to function and hope for the future. Forsaken already would be the closely related other task of the life drives: giving the individual the strength and desire to maintain emotional ties to others, which very much includes the ability to gain strength from their ties to him. This is why it was so vitally important for survival to believe that one had not been forsaken.

Since the "life drive," the "libido," the *élan vital*, or whatever term is preferred are but symbols for psychological processes, one may also elaborate on their meaning by saying that as a person loses interest in himself, his life, and his future, everybody and everything in the outside world of necessity loses interest for him, too. On the other hand, if everybody outside does lose, or seems to lose, interest in a person, then it requires unusually strong life tendencies, well-developed self-respect, and great inner security for such an individual not to soon lose interest in himself, and become ready to give up living, particularly when the circumstances of his life are extremely disagreeable and destructive.

In the camps, because of the depth of despair which so often pervaded every moment of one's existence, I experienced more keenly than ever before, and observed in most fellow prisoners, how some small sign that others indeed cared—a message from home which gave this impression, a helping gesture from another prisoner, even an item in a newspaper which suggested that the plight of the prisoners found sympathetic attention—could instantly rekindle the will to live, if one's depression had not become so deep that nothing could relieve it. The will then once again expressed itself in both its forms: as a more determined struggle to survive because one again began to hope for one's future (the direct result of the belief that others cared), and a more positive move towards others, such as some fellow prisoner.

6. Undercurrents

A PERSONAL ACCOUNT OF ELECTROSHOCK TREATMENT

BY MARTHA MANNING

A symbol of draconian psychiatric abuse to some, an unfairly maligned healing grace to others, electroshock remains the most controversial treatment for depression. In this gripping, first-person account excerpted from her book Undercurrents, *psychotherapist Martha Manning tells us how her severe and stubborn depression led her to try this "last resort" method. The author graphically describes her initial resistances, the ordeal of multiple treatments, and her ultimate return to herself and her work.*

SEPTEMBER 3, 1990

Today is the last day of summer. What a time. What a long lonely time. I never knew the days could stretch out so endlessly. Stretch so far I think they'll break, but they only heave and sag. The weight of them bears down on me mercilessly. I wake after only two hours' sleep, into another day of dread. Dread with no name or face. Nothing to fight with my body or wits. Just a gnawing, gripping fear. So hard and heavy. I can't breathe. I can't swallow.

The emptiness of the depression turns to grief, then to numbness and back again. My world is filled with underwater voices, people, lists of things to do. They gurgle and dart in and out of my vision and reach. But they are so fast and slippery that I can never keep up. Every inch of me aches. I can't believe that a person can hurt this bad and still breathe. All escapes are illusory—distractions, sleep, drugs, doctors, answers, hope. . . .

SEPTEMBER 6, 1990

I want to die. I can't believe I feel like this. But it's the strongest feeling I know right now, stronger than hope, or faith, or even love. The aching relentlessness of this depression is becoming unbearable. The thoughts of suicide are becoming intrusive. It's not that I want to die. It's that I'm not sure I can live like this anymore.

I was always taught that suicide was a hostile act, suggesting anger at the self or at others. I have certainly seen cases in which this was true. Suicide was a final retribution, the ultimate "last word" in an ongoing argument. But I think that explanation excludes the most important factor—suicide is an end to the pain, the agony of despair, the slow slide into disaster, so private, but as devastating as any other "act of God." I don't want to die because I hate myself. I want to die because on some level I love myself enough to have compassion for this suffering and to want to see it end. Like the cyanide capsule tucked in the spy's secret pocket, I comfort myself with the thought that if this ordeal gets beyond bearing, that there is a release from it all.

SEPTEMBER 8, 1990

With our combined vacations, I haven't seen my therapist Kay in almost a month. My deterioration is obvious to her. She tells me that I need "to consider ECT." "ECT?" my mind screams. "Electroconvulsive therapy? Shock therapy?" I flash to scenes of *One Flew Over the Cuckoo's Nest*, with McMurphy and the Chief jolted with electroshock, their bodies flailing with each jolt. She emphasizes the severity of this melancholic depression and reminds me that ECT has by far the highest success rate in this area. I feel like she has just told me I'm a terminal case. A lost cause.

She gives me literature to read about it. She reassures me that she is not giving up on the psychotherapy but that she believes my suffering is mostly biological and has to be addressed. "Just think about getting a consultation," she encourages. I nod, but I have absolutely no intention of doing so. I counter her concerns with a mental list of my admittedly dubious accomplishments. I still work. I still drive. I make my daughter's lunch. I pick her up from school. I answer the phone. How bad can I be?

As if sensing my silent resistance, she says, "If it was just a matter of personal strength and determination, you'd be fine. But it's not. You have to think of this as a serious illness. One that is potentially life-threatening."

When I get to my car, my hands tremble as I skim the pages of the literature she's given me. One is a recent National Institute of Mental Health consensus report that is highly favorable toward ECT for use in depressions such as mine. The side effects are scary, particularly the confusion and memory loss. Another article cites a study in which a majority of ECT patients reported that it was no more distressing than "a dental procedure." Always the empiricist, I wonder what choices were offered to the participants. "Was ECT more like having your eyes plucked out by vultures, or undergoing a simple dental procedure?"

When I tell Brian, he looks similarly horrified. "There must be other things that can be tried," he protests. "She said she thinks I'm past the point where any medicine is going to pull me out. The ECT is not a "cure" for depression, but somehow it's supposed to "reset the clock," I tell him, trying to remember all the things she told me. "She said that you can call her or make an appointment to talk about it."

OCTOBER 8, 1990
Slept one hour last night. I'm the first one at the pool, desperate for water to revive me. Each stroke is torture. I cry in the pool. I'm up against the limit of my endurance. I can't see patients today.

I think more about ECT. I'm scared about taking so much time off, losing all that money, the medical bills. The procedure scares me. The hospital scares me. Losing my memory scares me. So many parts of the body have a twin, or at least some potential for transplantation. But this is my brain. My one and only brain.

It has no counterpart. No backup.

OCTOBER 11, 1990
I clench my hands constantly, wringing them in turmoil. I pace. I rock mechanically in my rocking chair. I lay curled up on the couch. I don't know what the next step is and it scares me. There are so many choices and no guarantees. My life is a field, booby-trapped with land mines. One could go off in a place least expected and leave me in even worse shape than I am right now. God, I wish there were an answer. I am so tired.

OCTOBER 12, 1990
I am in bad shape. I call the local hospital to find the name of the doctor who does ECT. I am given the name of a Dr. Richard Samuel and the nurse says he is "very good." I'm never sure anymore what that actually means. People think I'm "very good" and I know how wrong they are. I dial the first few digits of his number and hang up. It takes me about six tries to complete the call. I set up an appointment for a consultation. He agrees to see me later today. I can't believe I'm actually doing this.

OCTOBER 16, 1990
Dr. Samuel explains ECT one more time before I give my written consent. Tomorrow morning I will be awakened at 5 A.M. for a shot of atropine used to dry secretions prior to many hospital procedures. I will change into a hospital gown and be wheeled down to a recovery room, where the treatments are

administered. I will be attached to monitors that will register the activity of my heart and my brain. A band will be fastened around my head. Because I am having unilateral ECT, several electrodes will be placed over the temporal region of my nondominant hemisphere. An oxygen mask will be placed over my nose and mouth. Through an IV, I will receive succinylcholine, which will immobilize me to prevent the breakage of bones, and methohexitol, a short-acting anesthetic. Between 80 and 170 volts will be administered for .5 to 1.0 seconds, inducing a grand mal seizure that will last for thirty to sixty-five seconds. I will awaken approximately fifteen to thirty minutes later. He warns that I may have a headache, confusion, and memory loss following the treatment.

I listen to this with the cool demeanor of a fellow professional. He asks if I have any questions and I tell him calmly that between the reading material he provided and our discussions, I feel prepared. However, on the inside I am screaming, "HOW DO I KNOW YOU'RE NOT GOING TO FRY MY BRAINS? WHAT IF THE MACHINE SHORT-CIRCUITS? WHAT IF YOUR HAND SLIPS AND YOU PUSH THE DIAL TOO FAR? WHAT IF I TOTALLY LOSE MY MEMORY? WHAT IF I DIE?" I conclude that he probably has no answers to these questions, so I spare him the hysteria. He hands me the forms to sign. My hand shakes as I take the pen. I talk to myself in my calmest, cut-the-bullshit voice. "The bottom line," I say to myself, "is that my life has already almost slipped away from me. I have two choices: I can end it or I can fight like hell to save it."

I write my name slowly and he signs it as a witness. I'm scared right down to my shoes and wonder how I'll get through the night. He anticipates my concerns and offers a mild sedative to help me sleep. I tell him that over the past year we have tried every sedative, hypnotic, and tranquilizer known to medicine in doses that would knock out an Amazon for a week. None keeps me asleep for more than two hours. He gently reminds me that even two hours would be a vast improvement over what I'm getting now.

OCTOBER 17, 1990

The night is interminable and I pace the halls again. At 4:30 someone tiptoes into my room with a flashlight and whispers that it's time for my shot. On the entire nursing staff there is one male and I have the good fortune to have him administer the shot in the butt. He leaves a hospital gown and fuzzy blue slippers and tells me to go to sleep for a while. But it's a lost cause. I hate the waiting and start to cry. Over and over, I repeat to myself the end of a Jane Kenyon poem called "Let Evening Come."

Let it come as it will, and don't
be afraid. God does not leave us
comfortless, so let evening come.

The day staff replaces the night staff. My nurse comes with a wheelchair. She must notice how frightened I am because she pats my shoulder and tells me everything will be all right. This small act of kindness makes my eyes fill up. Words stick in my throat. She wheels me through the long dark halls in silence.

The recovery room is all bright lights and shiny surfaces. There are eight beds, all empty. A group of people are assembled around a stretcher, which I assume is meant for me. Dr. Samuel introduces me to the team—two nurses and an anesthesiologist. They help me onto the stretcher and for a moment the anxiety about the ECT is replaced by the anxiety of having my bare ass visible through the open back of my hospital gown. While they uncross wires and plug in machines, I take a horizontal inventory of the room. In anticipation of Halloween, it is decorated with orange and black crepe paper. Black rubber spiders and little skeletons are suspended from the ceiling. What were these people thinking?

I am covered with hands. They take hold of different parts of me, staking out their territory. Voices tell me this is a dance done hundreds of times before, so I need not be afraid. But their casual confidence, their ease with my body, gives me no comfort. Just as I have lost so much of myself in the past year, now I lose more. I offer myself up to these strangers in exchange for the possibility of deliverance. Someone holds my hand and slips needles under my skin. Another slides down my gown and plants red Valentine hearts on my chest. Fingers anoint my temples with cool ointment and fasten a plastic crown tightly around my head. Wires connect me to machines that hum and beep, registering the peaks and valleys of my brain and my heart. They cover my mouth and nose with plastic and instruct me to breathe. For several horrible seconds, I am paralyzed before I lose consciousness. This is the nightmare that has haunted me since I was a child. I am on a beach, caught between a tidal wave and a towering sea wall. In my terror, I am frozen. I cannot run, or move, or scream. The waves slam me down and take me with them. I am drowning.

I open my eyes, squinting at the glaring white lights. A nurse smiles down and welcomes me back. She reports that I had a "good seizure," which as far as I'm concerned, belongs with other psychiatric oxymorons like "uncomplicated bereavement" and "drug holiday." My head hurts and my jaw is sore.

OCTOBER 24, 1990

Georgia, one of my favorite nurses, says that I am doing well in keeping busy, adding that it might be helpful if I give up some of my "omnipotence" about being invulnerable to the side effects of ECT. She may be right, but I refuse to give in to it. I will fight it for as long as I can and hopefully I'll know when to quit.

ECT #3. I expected that repeated exposure would desensitize me to the horror of the treatments. But they become more difficult for me over time. The hands seem rougher, the needles sharper, the band around my skull tighter, the hangover longer. Now I know how my cancer patients struggle to psyche themselves up for chemotherapy month after month. You can go through almost anything once. But to endure it each time, knowing that there will be more, and that the end is not in sight, is hard as hell.

OCTOBER 27, 1990
ECT #4. I am more hungover after each treatment. Even my legs ache. It's like having the flu for a day. I try to cover up the confusion as best I can, but it feels like I have the radio set between two stations. I give myself quizzes: "Where did you go on vacation last year?" "What was the last book you read?" And I don't know. The distant past is fine. It seems intact. But my memory for the past year is pitiful. I complain about it to a friend. He tries to reassure me. "Take it from me," he says. "You haven't missed much."

OCTOBER 30, 1990
Dr. Samuel and I review my case. I am sleeping five hours a night. I am eating. I am far less agitated. The weight of the depression has definitely eased. My brain feels like Jello, but he promises it won't last. He recommends that we stop with the next treatment. I can leave immediately afterward. He tells me not to drive a car for two weeks and not to return to work for several weeks. "Let yourself rest," he advises. I run down the hall to pack my bags.

OCTOBER 31, 1990
ECT #6. Dr. Samuel wants to get an early start on the day. A nurse from the night staff wheels me down in darkness to the recovery room. For one last time, "I let go of all holds . . ."

I stumble into consciousness through the heavy fog of anesthesia and the inevitable post ECT confusion. My nurse, Sharon, bends over me and smiles. She is dressed in a long white robe. There are gold sparkles on her face. She has wings. Her head is encircled with a halo. I blink my eyes to dispel the image. But when I open them again, she is still there. Then I panic, "Oh, my God. I'm dead!"

She wheels me back to the unit where the entire staff is dressed in costume. It is impossible to shake off the clouds with nurses going about their business dressed as witches, ghosts, and clowns. I pity any poor deluded guy who gets detained today. It would probably be saner to leave him on the streets.

The ten-minute ride to our house is filled with the miracle of so many sights I never noticed in my thousands of trips down this road. I feel like Lazarus raised from the dead. Brian reaches to unlock the front door to our house. I put my hand on his and take the keys. I haven't unlocked anything in weeks, and I fumble with them. They are foreign in my hand and I forget how to differentiate the top and bottom locks. Brian and Keara set my bags on the steps and wait with tender patience. I finally find the magic key and turn it in the right direction. The lock gives way. I open the door and step back into my life again. Brian and Keara throw their arms around me. In the warmth of their embrace, my unconscious too, welcomes me back.

OCTOBER 31, 1991

One year ago today I had my final ECT treatment and was released from the hospital. I have struggled greatly over this year with the shame of the depression, the hospital, the ECT. I've seen them as concrete signs of giving up, falling apart, getting an "F" in life. Being hospitalized on a psychiatric unit, was, for me, like crossing over into a different state. I've lost citizenship in the old place, but I haven't totally settled into the new one either. There has been a loss of innocence in it all. Some reckoning, in a real live showdown, of my own vulnerability, my capacity for unraveling, the limits of my effort and will. It is knowing that I am capable of falling, that I am fragile. That life can spin out of control for anyone is something I should have known from my work with patients. But to actually feel myself in the skid is entirely different from intellectual knowledge. To know the force of the avalanche and my powerlessness over it is to feel myself in brand-new territory.

In choosing the hospital and ECT I chose to fight for my life. Despite the continuing cycle of disquieting ups and downs, I am living the life I fought for. I know it in the joy of an ice-cold Diet Coke in a plastic cup, the fluidity of motion in swimming laps, the soft touch of Keara's breasts against mine as she seeks the same refuge she has for thirteen years. It is in the sound of my own laughter, the stirring between my legs as I feel the old wanting, the capacity to read, to watch, to follow, to listen.

For so long now I have waited to get back to baseline and return to exactly the same point from which I originally set out on these travels. My criterion for healing has been to be able to pick up right where I left off, like mid-page in a novel. I have waited and waited, but I'm still not back to that page. Kay and Lew try to tell me, in their own gentle ways, to stop waiting. I think they're trying to tell me that I'm never going to get back to that page. That I'm in an entirely new book now, most of it unwritten.

7. *The Dark Night of the Soul*

DEPRESSION AND THE VEIL OF ADDICTION

BY LINDA SCHIERSE LEONARD

We know that for many individuals and families depression and substance abuse are inseparable, each reinforcing the other's damaging effects. In this excerpt from her insightful book, Witness to the Fire, *Linda Schierse Leonard shows how an unfettered descent into the abyss of despair can engender a higher freedom that has been honored by mystics throughout the ages.*

From out of The Abyss of hopelessness and the deep collapse of the ego that Bill W.* suffered as a result of his addiction, came a powerfully creative vision of communal healing—a vision that has helped re-create the lives of over one million members in AA alone throughout the world and that has led to the formation of the twelve-step programs focused toward healing many other addictions. The impossible dilemma that Bill W. faced through his addiction, the deep ego collapse faced by addicts at the bottom of The Abyss, is fundamental to spiritual conversion and to the re-creation of one's life.

The Abyss was the place of transformation for the mystics. In its depths shone the illumination of the "divine dark," where divinity revealed itself. Dionysius the Areopagite even speaks of God as the "Divine Darkness" and sees darkness as the secret dwelling place of God. In his imagery there is a "divine progression," a ladder or chain that links ordinary mortals with the divine. Another of the great mystics, St. John of the Cross, speaks of the "secret stair" by which one descends in the dark night to meet the Beloved—the way the soul journeys into union with God. But prior to that union of ecstatic rapture with the Beloved comes the Dark Night of the Soul, that painful period of privation when one feels imprisoned in The Abyss.

* co-founder of Alcoholics Anonymous

Just as the chaos of The Abyss is an essential aspect of the creative process, so is it essential to spiritual growth. The chaos the addict experiences in the abyss of his addiction is similar to the chaos experienced by the creative person, and to the Dark Night of the Soul experienced by the mystic. Evelyn Underhill, in her classic study of mysticism, describes this as follows:

> Psychologically, then, the "Dark Night of the Soul" is due to the double fact of the exhaustion of an old state, and the growth toward a new state of conscious-ness. It is a "growing pain" in the organic process of the self's attainment of the Absolute. The great mystics, creative geniuses in the realm of character, have known instinctively how to turn these psychic disturbances to spiritual profit. Parallel with mental oscillations, upheavals, and readjustments, through which an unstable psycho-physical type moves to new centres of consciousness, run the spiritual oscillations of a striving and ascending spiritual type.[1]

The growth process requires a period of chaos that intervenes between the old state breaking down and the formation of the new state of being. We see such a state dramatically manifested in adolescence, the transition between childhood and adult life. For the great mystics, such periods of chaos and misery often lasted months or even years before the new and higher state of spirituality is reached; often the dark side is experienced before the possibility of the new is apprehended. Underhill, describing this experience, writes: "The self is tossed back from its hard-won point of vantage. Impotence, blankness, solitude, are the epithets by which those immersed in this dark fire of purification describe their pains."[2] Yet this very period of blackness is precisely that which contributes to the re-creation of character. This great period of negation in The Abyss is "the sorting-house of the spiritual life," just as it is the agonizing effort for the artist who gropes in the dark before the creative outburst. The descent experienced by the mystic and the artist is also experienced by the addict who, having reached the bottom of the soul's abyss, is faced with the inner trial by fire and the decision to accept his powerlessness, surrender his addiction, and move on toward recovery. Underhill describes this "dark night" as a threshold to a higher state. Heroism is required to endure and not succumb to the danger and the pain. The mystical journey is neither rational nor linear.

The Dark Night of the Soul refers to the common experience of the mystics whereby, after a period of great illumination, one swings back to emptiness, to pain and desolation, to impotence and helplessness, in preparation for the total self-surrender to the Divine. Having had an intense intuitive experience of God in the period of illumination, i.e., having had a spiritual awakening, the mystics describe this as a testing time, a time when one agonizes over feeling abandoned by God. It is a time of "privation worse than hell," according to Angela of Foligno. But it is also an essential time in which there is a dying to self, the necessary precondition to eternal life and union.

St. John of the Cross distinguishes between two phases of the Dark Night—the Night of the Senses in which the emotions, the imagination, the bodily senses, the lower part of the soul, are purged; and the Night of the Spirit, which entails the purgation of the intellect and will, the higher part of the soul. This latter period brings one down in the most drastic and often humiliating way before one's own disharmony and deprivation to face death, which clears the ground for humility and surrender to what is: the whole. Underhill describes it as the "naughting of the soul," directed to utter humility. The mystic Tauler described this abyss as follows: everything depends on "a fathomless sinking in a fathomless nothingness," necessary because "the Godhead really has no place to work in, but ground where all has been annihilated."[3] Thus, the whole process of transformation for the mystic requires "entering even further in, ever nearer, so as to sink the deeper in an unknown and an unnamed abyss; and, above all ways, images and forms, and above all powers, to lose thyself, deny thyself, and ever unform thyself."[4]

In the Dark Night, the soul is emptied and dried up. Just as the earthly lover fears abandonment and rejection by the beloved and can be possessed by jealousy and hatred, so the soul, in its intense thirst for love, feels forsaken and as dried up as is the lost wanderer in a desert wasteland.

In his description of this state of utter desolation, St. John cites the agony of Job, who was suddenly undone. For a time he hoped only for relief in death. He reminds us also of the hell of Jonah, swallowed by a beast of the sea and devoured in the darkness of its belly. He remembers the humiliation and imprisonment of Jeremiah, who experienced the indignation of a God whom he felt had turned against him.[5]

The deepest poverty and wretchedness are felt in the Dark Night. But through all this, the soul is being purged, and annihilated, purified in the fire. ". . . The soul is purified in this furnace like gold in a crucible," writes St. John, so that it is "conscious of this complete undoing of itself in its very substance, together with the direst poverty," and at times the consciousness of the experience is "so keen that the soul seems to be seeing hell and perdition opened."[6] The purpose of all this is that the soul may be humbled so that it may afterward be greatly exalted. "This dark night is an inflowing of God into the soul, which purges it from its ignorances and imperfections, habitual, natural and spiritual, and which is called by contemplatives infused contemplation, or mystical theology. Herein God secretly teaches the soul and instructs it in perfection of love, without its doing anything, or understanding of what manner is this infused contemplation."[7]

In The Abyss of the Dark Night one is plunged into paradox. The stress, deprivation, trials, and tribulations are part of the process of this unfathomable transformation. But there is no redemption without the cross, say the Christians. Nor, according to the alchemists, is there the transmutation of lead into gold without going through the fire. This is also the paradox of the alcoholic's "Firewater." In this very image of opposites is the paradox that can poison or redeem. Consider the alchemist's signs for the elements for Fire, (Δ) which is over our heads, and Water (∇) which is under our feet. The synthesis of fire and water gives (ϕ), a sign not only for alcohol ("burnt water"), but also for the divinity in Kabbalistic mysticism, as the combination of the Hebrew consonants for fire and water gives the word for Heaven.[8] In nature, fire and water also combine to give us the radiant rainbow.

What The Abyss asks of us, ultimately, is surrender, a Dionysian abandonment that is precisely not into the pleasures of our addictions, but rather into what some of the mystics call the "God-intoxication." This is the movement of the whole person, freely and unfettered, into the whole heart of the great "mysterium tremendum et fascinans." From the descent into The Abyss can come the gift of the humble surrendering of Love.

Theodore Roethke lived at the edge of The Abyss. Threatened by madness from manic-depression complicated by excessive drinking and spending during the phases of his mania, Roethke wrote poetry from the depths of personal suffering. His images arose spontaneously from the soul's abyss, revealing truths of the creation. The creative act seemed to be the integrating force that held him together. From his own "dark time," he gave expression to the alienation of humans and the loss of personal communion with the divine. But in The Abyss Roethke came to see the divine light of the creative. As he said in his poem "The Pure Fury":

> I live near the abyss, I hope to stay
> Until my eyes look at a brighter sun
> As the thick shade of the long night comes on.[9]

Having passed through the fire of the opposites to the place of "sunlit silence" at the bottom of the abyss, one arrives at a new place of questioning. Having faced one's limits, one encounters new possibilities. But by now one has learned that it is by "being" and by resting rather than by striving that one finally comes to "know." Meister Eckhart expresses this: "He must be in a stillness and silence, where the Word may be heard. One cannot draw near to the Word better than by stillness and silence. And when we simply keep ourselves receptive, we are more perfect than when at work."[10] The recovering addict knows this truth. In step three he turns his will and his life over to God and waits and listens for the Word of the Higher Power. In the same way the poet opens to receive the Word and transmit it to others.

The descent into The Abyss culminates in the ecstasy of union, the mystical marriage, the mystic's goal, the raison d'être of the journey. This divine wedding is also the gift the addict receives if he sees his addiction as the dark part of an individuation journey toward wholeness. If accepted and transformed, the addict is purged of neurotic guilt and the humiliation of failure and opened to the grace of the transcendent power that was always within.

In Jung's letter to Bill W., cofounder of Alcoholics Anonymous, Jung wrote of a former patient who was an addict:

His craving for alcohol was the equivalent, on a low level, of the spiritual thirst of our being for wholeness; expressed in medieval language: the union with God. . . . You see, "alcohol" in Latin is *spiritus*, and you use the same word for the highest religious experience as well as for the most depressing poison. The helpful formula therefore is: *spiritus contra spiritum*.[11]

This is the intoxicating truth of creation that the addict learns by falling into The Abyss, that the mystics learn by stepping down the "secret stairs" in the Dark Night of the Soul, and that the poet experiences by descending into the dark well of creativity.

PART TWO

Transforming Depression

8. Cognitive Therapy

A THINKING PERSON'S REMEDY FOR DEPRESSION

BY DAVID D. BURNS, M.D.

Dr. Burns presents a clear, concise, and readable account of cognitive therapy, one of the few psychotherapeutic methods that has been convincingly demonstrated to reduce depressive symptoms in a practical and cost-effective way. The author was a pioneer in developing cognitive therapy, which traces its origins to the innovative work of Dr. Aaron Beck.

A group of psychiatrists and psychologists at the University of Pennsylvania School of Medicine has reported a significant breakthrough in the treatment and prevention of mood disorders. Dissatisfied with traditional methods for treating depression because they found them to be slow and ineffective, these doctors developed and systematically tested an entirely new and remarkably successful approach to depression and other emotional disorders. A series of recent studies confirms that these techniques reduce the symptoms of depression much more rapidly than conventional psychotherapy or drug therapy. The name of this revolutionary treatment is "cognitive therapy. . . ."

Cognitive therapy is a fast-acting technology of mood modification that you can learn to apply on your own. I emphasize "fast-acting" because I believe that if you are depressed, you cannot afford a prolonged therapeutic experience which would require many months or even years to work. You need to learn to eliminate the symptoms *as rapidly as possible*. At the same time, you want to experience personal growth so you can minimize future upsets and avoid going through the emotional hell of depression again. . . .

The first principle of cognitive therapy is that *all* your moods are created by your "cognitions," or thoughts. A cognition refers to the way you look at things—your perceptions, mental attitudes, and beliefs. It includes the way you interpret things—what you say about something or someone to yourself. You *feel* the way you do right now because of the *thoughts you are thinking at this moment.* . . .

The second principle is that when you are feeling depressed, your thoughts are dominated by a pervasive negativity. You perceive not only yourself but the entire world in dark, gloomy terms. What is even worse—you'll come to believe things *really are* as bad as you imagine them to be.

If you are substantially depressed, you will even begin to believe that things always have been and always will be negative. As you look into your past, you remember all the bad things that have happened to you. As you try to imagine the future, you see only emptiness or unending problems and anguish. This bleak vision creates a sense of *hopelessness.* This feeling is absolutely illogical, but it seems so real that you have convinced yourself that your inadequacy will go on forever.

The third principle is of enormous philosophical and therapeutic importance. Our research has documented that the negative thoughts which cause your emotional turmoil nearly *always* contain gross distortions. Although these thoughts appear valid, you will learn that they are irrational or just plain wrong, and that twisted thinking is the *exclusive cause* of nearly all your suffering.

The implications are startling. Your depression is not based on accurate perceptions of reality but is the product of mental slippage: depression is *not* a precious, genuine, or important human experience. It is a phony, synthetic counterfeit. . . .

Because depression has been viewed as an emotional disorder throughout the history of psychiatry, therapists from most schools of thought place a strong emphasis on "getting in touch" with your feelings. Our research reveals the unexpected: depression is not an emotional disorder at all! The sudden change in the way you *feel* is of no more *causal* relevance than a runny nose is when you have a cold. Every bad feeling you have is the result of your distorted negative thinking. Illogical, pessimisitc attitudes play the central role in the development and continuation of all your symptoms. . . .

Your negative thoughts, or cognitions, are the most frequently overlooked symptoms of your depression. These cognitions contain the key to relief and are therefore your most important symptoms.

Every time you feel depressed about something, try to identify a corresponding negative thought you had just prior to and during the depression. Because these thoughts have actually created your bad mood, by learning to restructure them, you can change your mood. . . .

When you are depressed, you possess the remarkable ability to *believe*, and to get the people around you to believe, things which have no basis in reality. As a therapist, it is my job to *penetrate* your illusion, to teach you how to *look behind* the mirrors so you can see how you have been fooling yourself. You might even say that I'm planning to dis-illusion you! But I don't think you're going to mind at all.

Read over the following list of ten cognitive distortions that form the basis for all your depressions. Get a feel for them. I have prepared this list with great care; it represents the distilled essence of many years of research and clinical experience. When you are feeling upset, the list will be invaluable in making you aware of how you are fooling yourself.

DEFINITIONS OF COGNITIVE DISTORTIONS

1. *All-or-nothing thinking.* This refers to your tendency to evaluate your personal qualities in extreme, black-or-white categories. For example, a prominent politician told me, "Because I lost the race for governor, I'm a zero." A straight-A student who received a B on an exam concluded, "Now I'm a total failure." All-or-nothing thinking forms the basis for perfectionism. It causes you to fear any mistake or imperfection because you will then see yourself as a complete loser, and you will feel inadequate and worthless.

This way of evaluating things is unrealistic because life is rarely completely either one way or the other. For example, no one is absolutely brilliant or totally stupid. Similarly, no one is either completely attractive or totally ugly. Look at the floor of the room you are sitting in now. Is it perfectly clean? Is every inch piled high with dust and dirt? Or is it partially clean? Absolutes do not exist in this universe. If you try to force your experiences into absolute categories, you will be constantly depressed because your perceptions will not conform to reality. You will set yourself up for discrediting yourself endlessly because whatever you do will *never* measure up to your exaggerated expectations. The technical name for this type of perceptual error is "dichotomous thinking." You see everything as black or white—shades of gray do not exist. . . .

2. *Overgeneralization.* A depressed salesman noticed bird dung on his car window and thought, "That's just my luck. The birds are always crapping on *my* window!" This is a perfect example of overgeneralization. When I asked him about this experience, he admitted that in twenty years of traveling, he could not remember another time when he found bird dung on his car window.

The pain of rejection is generated almost entirely from overgeneralization. In its absence, a personal affront is temporarily disappointing but *cannot* be seriously disturbing. A shy young man mustered up his courage to ask a girl for a date. When she politely declined because of a previous engagement, he said to himself, "I'm never going to get a date. No girl would ever want a date with me. I'll be lonely and miserable all my life." In his distorted cognitions, he concluded that because she turned him down once, she would *always* do so, and that since all women have 100 percent identical tastes, he would be endlessly and repeatedly rejected by any eligible woman on the face of the earth.

3. *Mental Filter.* You pick out a negative detail in any situation and dwell on it exclusively, thus perceiving that the whole situation is negative. For example, a depressed college student heard some other students making fun of her best friend. She became furious because she was thinking, "That's what the human race is basically like—cruel and insensitive!" She was overlooking the fact that in the previous months few people, if any, had been cruel or insensitive to her! On another occasion when she completed her first midterm exam, she felt certain she had missed approximately seventeen questions out of a hundred. She thought exclusively about those seventeen questions and concluded she would flunk out of college. When she got the paper back there was a note attached that read, "You got 83 out of 100 correct. This was by far the highest grade of any student this year. A+."

When you are depressed, you wear a pair of eyeglasses with special lenses that filter out anything positive. All that you allow to enter your conscious mind is negative. Because you are not aware of this "filtering process," you conclude that *everything* is negative. The technical name for this process is "selective abstraction." It is a bad habit that can cause you to suffer much needless anguish.

4. *Disqualifying the Positive.* An even more spectacular mental illusion is the persistent tendency of some depressed individuals to transform neutral or even positive experiences into negative ones. You don't just *ignore* positive experiences, you cleverly and swiftly turn them into their nightmarish opposite. I call this "reverse alchemy." The medieval alchemists dreamed of finding some method for transmuting the baser metals into gold. If you have been depressed, you may have developed the talent for doing the exact opposite—you can instantly transform golden joy into emotional lead. Not intentionally, however—you're probably not even aware of what you're doing to yourself.

An everyday example of this would be the way most of us have been conditioned to respond to compliments. When someone praises your appearance or your work, you might automatically tell yourself, "They're just being nice." With one swift blow you mentally disqualify their compliment. You do the same thing to them when you tell them, "Oh, it was nothing, really." If you constantly throw cold water on the good things that happen, no wonder life seems damp and chilly to you!

Disqualifying the positive is one of the most destructive forms of cognitive distortion. You're like a scientist intent on finding evidence to support some pet hypothesis. The hypothesis that dominates your depressive thinking is usually some version of "I'm second-rate." Whenever you have a negative experience, you dwell on it and conclude, "That proves what I've known all along." In contrast, when you have a positive experience, you tell yourself, "That was a fluke. It doesn't count." The price you pay for this tendency is intense misery and an inability to appreciate the good things that happen.

While this type of cognitive distortion is commonplace, it can also form the basis for some of the most extreme and intractable forms of depression. For example, a young woman hospitalized during a severe depressive episode told me, "No one could possibly care about me because I'm such an awful person. I'm a complete loner. Not one person on earth gives a damn about me." When she was discharged from the hospital, many patients and staff members expressed great fondness for her. Can you guess how she negated all of this? "They don't count because they don't see me in the real world. A *real* person outside a hospital could never care about me." I then asked her how she reconciled this with the fact that she had numerous friends and family outside the hospital who *did* care about her. She replied, "They don't count because they don't know the real me. You see, Dr. Burns, inside I'm absolutely rotten. I'm the worst person in the world. It would be impossible for anyone to really like me for even one moment!" By disqualifying positive experiences in this manner, she can maintain a negative belief which is clearly unrealistic and inconsistent with her everyday experiences.

While your negative thinking is probably not as extreme as hers, there may be many times every day when you do inadvertently ignore genuinely positive things that have happened to you. This removes much of life's richness and makes things appear needlessly bleak.

5. Jumping to Conclusions. You arbitrarily jump to a negative conclusion that is not justified by the facts of the situation. Two examples of this are "mind reading" and "the fortune teller error."

MIND READING: You make the assumption that other people are looking down on you, and you're so convinced about this that you don't even bother to check it out. Suppose you are giving an excellent lecture, and you notice that a man in the front row is nodding off. He was up most of the night on a wild fling, but you of course don't know this. You might have the thought, "This audience thinks I'm a bore." Suppose a friend passes you on the street and fails to say hello because he is so absorbed in his thoughts he doesn't notice you. You might erroneously conclude, "He is ignoring me so he must not like me anymore." Perhaps your spouse is unresponsive one evening because he or she was criticized at work and is too upset to want to talk about it. Your heart sinks because of the way you interpret the silence: "He (or she) is mad at me. What did I do wrong?"

You may then respond to these imagined negative reactions by withdrawal or counterattack. This self-defeating behavior pattern may act as a self-fulfilling prophecy and set up a negative interaction in a relationship when none exists in the first place.

THE FORTUNE TELLER ERROR: It's as if you had a crystal ball that foretold only misery for you. You imagine that something bad is about to happen, and you take this prediction as a *fact* even though it is unrealistic. A high-school librarian repeatedly told herself during anxiety attacks, "I'm going to pass out or go crazy." These predictions were unrealistic because she had never once passed out (or gone crazy!) in her entire life. Nor did she have any serious symptoms to suggest impending insanity. During a therapy session an acutely depressed physician explained to me why he was giving up his practice: "I realize I'll be depressed forever. My misery will go on and on, and I'm absolutely convinced that this or any treatment will be doomed to failure." This negative prediction about his prognosis caused him to feel hopeless. His symptomatic improvement soon after initiating therapy indicated just how off-base his fortune telling had been.

Do you ever find yourself jumping to conclusions like these? Suppose you telephone a friend who fails to return your call after a reasonable time. You then feel depressed when you tell yourself that your friend probably got the message but wasn't interested enough to call you back. Your distortion?—mind reading. You then feel bitter, and decide not to call back and check this out because you say to yourself, "He'll think I'm being obnoxious if I call him back again. I'll only make a fool of myself." Because of these negative predictions (the fortune teller error), you avoid your friend and feel put down. Three weeks later you learn that your friend never got your message. All that stewing, it turns out, was just a lot of self-imposed hokum. Another painful product of your mental magic!

6. *Magnification and Minimization.* Another thinking trap you might fall into is called "magnification" and "minimization," but I like to think of it as the "binocular trick" because you are either blowing things up out of proportion or shrinking them. Magnification commonly occurs when you look at your own errors, fears, or imperfections and exaggerate their importance: "My God—I made a mistake. How terrible! How awful! The word will spread like wildfire! My reputation is ruined!" You're looking at your faults through the end of the binoculars that makes them appear gigantic and grotesque. This has also been called "catastrophizing" because you turn commonplace negative events into nightmarish monsters.

When you think about your strengths, you may do the opposite—look through the wrong end of the binoculars so that things look small and unimportant. If you magnify your imperfections and minimize your good points, you're guaranteed to feel inferior. But the problem isn't *you*—it's the crazy lenses you're wearing!

7. Emotional Reasoning. You take your emotions as evidence for the truth. Your logic: "I feel like a dud, therefore I *am* a dud." This kind of reasoning is misleading because your feelings reflect your thoughts and beliefs. If they are distorted—as is quite often the case—your emotions will have no validity. Examples of emotional reasoning include "I feel guilty. Therefore, I must have done something bad"; "I feel overwhelmed and hopeless. Therefore, my problems must be impossible to solve"; "I feel inadequate. Therefore, I must be a worthless person"; "I'm not in the mood to do anything. Therefore, I might as well just lie in bed"; or "I'm mad at you. This proves that you've been acting rotten and trying to take advantage of me."

Emotional reasoning plays a role in nearly all your depressions. Because things *feel* so negative to you, you assume they truly are. It doesn't occur to you to challenge the validity of the perceptions that create your feelings.

One usual side effect of emotional reasoning is procrastination. You avoid cleaning up your desk because you tell yourself, "I feel so lousy when I think about that messy desk, cleaning it will be impossible." Six months later you finally give yourself a little push and do it. It turns out to be quite gratifying and not so tough at all. You were fooling yourself all along because you are in the habit of letting your negative feelings guide the way you act.

8. Should Statements. You try to motivate yourself by saying, "I *should* do this" or "I *must* do that." These statements cause you to feel pressured and resentful. Paradoxically, you end up feeling apathetic and unmotivated. Albert Ellis calls this "*must*urbation." I call it the "shouldy" approach to life.

When you direct should statements toward others, you will usually feel frustrated. When an emergency caused me to be five minutes late for the first therapy session, the new patient thought, "He *shouldn't* be so self-centered and thoughtless. He *ought to be* prompt." This thought caused her to feel sour and resentful.

Should statements generate a lot of unnecessary emotional turmoil in your daily life. When the reality of your own behavior falls short of your standards, your shoulds and shouldn'ts create self-loathing, shame, and guilt. When the all-too-human performance of other people falls short of your expectations, as will inevitably happen from time to time, you'll feel bitter and self-righteous. You'll either have to change your expectations to approximate reality or always feel let down by human behavior.

9. *Labeling and Mislabeling*. Personal labeling means creating a completely negative self-image based on your errors. It is an extreme form of overgeneralization. The philosophy behind it is "The measure of a man is the mistakes he makes." There is a good chance you are involved in a personal labeling whenever you describe your mistakes with sentences beginning with "*I'm a . . .*" For example, when you miss your putt on the eighteenth hole, you might say, "*I'm a* born loser" instead of "I goofed up on my putt." Similarly, when the stock you invested in goes down instead of up, you might think, "*I'm a* failure" instead of "I made a mistake."

Labeling yourself is not only self-defeating, it is irrational. Your *self* cannot be equated with any *one* thing you do. Your life is a complex and ever-changing flow of thoughts, emotions, and actions. To put it another way, you are more like a river than a statue. Stop trying to define yourself with negative labels—they are overly simplistic and wrong. Would you think of yourself exclusively as an "eater" just because you eat, or a "breather" just because you breathe? This is nonsense, but such nonsense becomes painful when you label yourself out of a sense of your own inadequacies.

When you label other people, you will invariably generate hostility. A common example is the boss who sees his occasionally irritable secretary as "an uncooperative bitch." Because of this label, he resents her and jumps at every chance to criticize her. She, in turn, labels him an "insensitive chauvinist" and complains about him at every opportunity. So, around and around they go at each other's throats, focusing on every weakness or imperfection as proof of the other's worthlessness.

Mislabeling involves describing an event with words that are inaccurate and emotionally heavily loaded. For example, a woman on a diet ate a dish of ice cream and thought, "How disgusting and repulsive of me. I'm a *pig*." These thoughts made her so upset she ate the whole quart of ice cream!

10. *Personalization*. This distortion is the mother of guilt! You assume responsibility for a negative event when there is no basis for doing so. You arbitrarily conclude that what happened was your fault or reflects your inadequacy, even when you were not responsible for it. For example, when a patient didn't do a self-help assignment I had suggested, I felt guilty because of my thought, "I must be a lousy therapist. It's my fault that she isn't working harder to help herself. It's my responsibility to make sure she gets well." When a mother saw her child's report card, there was a note from the teacher indicating the child was not working well. She immediately decided, "I must be a bad mother. This shows how I've failed."

Personalization causes you to feel crippling guilt. You suffer from a paralyzing and burdensome sense of responsibility that forces you to carry the whole world on your shoulders. You have confused *influence* with *control* over others. In your role as a teacher, counselor, parent, physician, salesman, executive, you will certainly influence the people you interact with, but no one could reasonably expect you to control them. What the other person does is ultimately his or her responsibility, not yours.

The ten forms of cognitive distortions cause many, if not all, of your depressed states. They are summarized in Table 3-1. Study this table and master these concepts; try to become as familiar with them as with your phone number. Refer to Table 3-1 over and over again as you learn about the various methods for mood modification. When you become familiar with these ten forms of distortion, you will benefit from this knowledge all your life.

TABLE 3-1

Definitions of Cognitive Distortions

1. ALL-OR-NOTHING THINKING

You see things in black-and-white categories. If your performance falls short of perfect, you see yourself as a total failure.

2. OVERGENERALIZATION

You see a single negative event as a never-ending pattern of defeat.

3. MENTAL FILTER

You pick out a single negative detail and dwell on it exclusively so that your vision of all reality becomes darkened, like the drop of ink that discolors the entire beaker of water.

4. DISQUALIFYING THE POSITIVE

You reject positive experiences by insisting they "don't count" for some reason or other. In this way you can maintain a negative belief that is contradicted by your everyday experiences.

5. JUMPING TO CONCLUSIONS

You make a negative interpretation even though there are no definite facts that convincingly support your conclusion.

a. Mind reading. You arbitrarily conclude that someone is reacting negatively to you, and you don't bother to check this out.

b. The Fortune Teller Error. You anticipate that things will turn out badly and you feel convinced that your prediction is an already established fact.

6. MAGNIFICATION (CATASTROPHIZING) OR MINIMIZATION

You exaggerate the importance of things (such as your goof-up or someone else's achievement), or you inappropriately shrink things until they appear tiny (your own desirable qualities or the other fellow's imperfections). This is also called the "binocular trick."

7. EMOTIONAL REASONING

You assume that your negative emotions necessarily reflect the way things really are: "I feel it, therefore it must be true."

8. SHOULD STATEMENTS

You try to motivate yourself with shoulds and shouldn'ts, as if you had to be whipped and punished before you could be expected to do anything. "Musts" and "oughts" are also offenders. The emotional consequence is guilt. When you direct should statements toward others, you feel anger, frustration, and resentment.

9. LABELING AND MISLABELING

This is an extreme form of overgeneralization. Instead of describing your error, you attach a negative label to yourself: "I'm a *loser*." When someone else's behavior rubs you the wrong way, you attach a negative label to him: "He's a goddam louse." Mislabeling involves describing an event with language that is highly colored and emotionally loaded.

10. PERSONALIZATION

You see yourself as the cause of some negative external event which in fact you were not primarily responsible for.

9. *Seeking the Spirit in Prozac*

A REVIEW AND CRITIQUE OF PETER KRAMER'S
LISTENING TO PROZAC

BY JOHN E. NELSON, M.D.

This review succinctly summarizes how Prozac and its imitators can dramatically alter mood, personality, and more. The author provides fresh insights into the psychological and spiritual implications of taking medicines to restructure the self and its place in the world.

No single book published during the past few years offers a greater challenge to comfortably entrenched psychological theories—from psychoanalysis to transpersonal psychology—than does psychiatrist Peter Kramer's surprise bestseller *Listening to Prozac*.[1] It achieves this precisely because it is not at all analytic or spiritual in its tone or implications.

Kramer, who writes a respected monthly column for *The Psychiatric Times*, is a thoughtful and adroit writer who makes a compelling case that the brain and its intricate array of neurotransmitters not only regulate our mood, but also shape our temperament, character, and personality. When Kramer "listens" to Prozac, he seeks to learn what this remarkable medicine teaches us about what makes people the way they are, especially what is biologically determined from conception and what flows from experience and learning.

Prozac earned its amazing popularity (a million prescriptions a month) by selectively enhancing the effects of a single brain messenger, serotonin, which not only affects mood, but seems to regulate such traits as impetuousness, compulsivity, and our ability to censor behavior that leads to punishment. Prozac, and its two look-alike competitors, Zoloft and Paxil, are collectively referred to as SSRIs—Specific Serotonin Reuptake Inhibitors—to describe their singular affinity for this crucial neurotransmitter. Compared to their relatively crude antidepressant predecessors, SSRIs accomplish their mood-elevating mission with considerably fewer side effects and are far safer in overdose. Because they doesn't produce a quick euphoric high, they are unlikely candidates for addiction. And unlike most drugs of abuse, they enhance socially desirable traits like impulse control, self-confidence, and our ability to tune in to conversational nuance.

The implications of how Prozac and its biochemical siblings transform the human psyche strike at the heart of our fundamental sense of personal identity. For Prozac is far more than just another mood elevator cast in the mold of its less elegant forerunners. It reaches into the depths of selfhood to micromanage the way we feel about ourselves and others as no other legally available drug has done before. In molding personality the way a surgeon reshapes a crooked nose, Prozac challenges the hallowed Western notion of a substantial soul, seeming to support the Buddhist notion that there is no essential self, only a liquid stream of perceptions, emotions, and thoughts, constantly in flux, determined by events that are not only beyond the grasp of our will but largely invisible.

Through lively case studies and extensive reviews of research literature, Kramer cites evidence that Prozac can also dramatically alter such entrenched personality traits as rejection-sensitivity, novelty-seeking, risk-taking, resoluteness, and aggressiveness. He offers convincing examples of patients made "better than well" by Prozac, which seemed to dissolve lifelong hang-ups, freeing his patients to achieve career or relationship goals that had previously eluded them. Some described themselves as more poised, thoughtful, confident, and appropriately assertive, as well as less pessimistic, distractible, and—paradoxically— "more like myself."

Although Kramer unabashedly straddles the borderline between speculation and fact, he cites persuasive evidence that Prozac can reduce impulsive violence in habitually antisocial types as well as promote behavior patterns that assist a normally functioning individual to ascend through social or corporate hierarchies. Prozac is surely the harbinger of an imminent array of new "smart drugs" that enrich memory, enhance intelligence, heighten concentration, and otherwise promote behaviors associated with "alpha-males," who naturally assume leadership in any primate society. Foreseeing an escalating demand by otherwise healthy people for drugs that fine-tune personality, Kramer warns us to brace ourselves for a new era of what he calls "cosmetic psychopharmacology"—a kind of plastic surgery for the soul.

Kramer is careful not to be overly reductionistic, although he clearly focuses on neurometabolism and shows little proclivity for matters of consciousness or spirit. He avoids the temptation to overdraw his conclusions, which lends his work all the more compelling a cast. The science and careful observation speak eloquently for themselves. Kramer has simply noted—as I and many other practicing psychiatrists are observing with unsettling frequency—that Prozac can alter traits that have been thought to be either inborn or permanently fixed in early childhood, immutable components of individual selfhood.

Psychoanalysts and transpersonal theorists tend to be uncomfortable with this kind of information and exclude it from our theories and speculations. Perhaps we avoid these questions because they make us feel vulnerable, even insubstantial, or because they superficially seem to confirm the views of reductionistic philosophers who would eliminate the intangible experience of mind and consciousness from the human equation. If something as basic as our sense of well-being and our ability to make sense of the world can be radically altered by barely measurable perturbations of certain chemicals in our brain, then we might also wonder if other traits even closer to our notion of selfhood might be subject to the powerful imperialism of the biological and—to take a sinister turn—open to manipulation by outside sources.

There is also a strong inclination for transpersonal theorists to accept the Eastern view that matter occupies the lowest link in the Great Chain of Being, rendering it next to inconsequential in its effects compared to the ontologically superior force of Spirit/consciousness. As a transpersonal therapist who also practices biological psychiatry, that view seems ultimately correct to me, too. In contrast, Kramer's view seems to support the frenzy of biological materialism that holds that brain is in a superior position relative to mind, that it mysteriously *secretes* mind the way the kidneys secrete urine. Of course, this sharply challenges the core beliefs of most religions that require us to view the sentient soul as superior to the body that temporarily houses it.

It is easy to scoff at such reductionistic thinking, but it is more difficult to deny that by simply altering brain chemistry Prozac has helped a lot of people out of the stubborn morass of depression. If consciousness-oriented therapists wish to maintain our credibility and effectiveness, we must demonstrate how we can similarly use our hard-earned spiritual insights to help people who are depressed, anxious, and confused. Some of these people have inherited genes that can shift brain metabolism in ways that promote depression, schizophrenia, or manic episodes. The challenge to transpersonal psychology is not just to integrate the mysterious mind/brain interface into our theories but to bring those theories to earth in a practical way that directly helps people who are desperately struggling to improve their lives.

As we seek ways to integrate Spirit with Prozac, we might begin by reviewing some of the highlights of Kramer's book.

THE GENESIS OF PROZAC

Prior to 1953, the only antidepressants were opium and amphetamines, which enjoyed a long but checkered popularity among depressed people and recreational users alike. Both afford a brief respite from depression, but they have obvious shortcomings that preclude long-term use.

Then the first modern, effective antidepressant, Imipramine (Tofranil) was developed serendipitously from noticing the beneficial mental effects of an anti-tuberculosis medicine that has a similar chemical structure. Imipramine was the first "tricyclic antidepressant," a class of drugs that gained great popularity in treating an otherwise untreatable group of people, despite a number of toxic side effects that caused many who took them to decide that they would rather be depressed.

Attempts over the next few decades to improve on the tricyclics included *monoamine-oxidase inhibitors* (MAOIs), and trazodone. But the former agents could be life-threatening if certain dietary restrictions were not strictly maintained, and the latter proved to be so sedating at therapeutic doses that people complained about a "zombie effect" similar to that associated with antipsychotic medicines. All medicines have side effects, but before Prozac, antidepressants were among the "dirtiest" drugs, more like hurling a beanbag than a dart.

Because depression is so prevalent, and modern cultures are less willing to endure chronic misery than those of past eras, the wealthiest pharmaceutical companies were happy to fund large-scale research into better medicines to treat depression. Throughout history, most common drugs were discovered in nature, usually as alkaloids from plants or fungi that had been used medicinally by pretechnological cultures. Some modern medicines are natural constituents of our bodies. But Prozac is a true designer drug, not so much discovered as planfully created through the efforts of a large drug company, Lily, using state-of-the-art animal and cellular models, all processed through a vast array of supercomputers that compared millions of chemical configurations to determine which would work in certain types of brain cells. This technique is called "rational drug design," and it is the wave of the future.

What Lily's scientists came up with is a drug that is far less "dirty" than its predecessors in that it exclusively affects the neurotransmitter serotonin, and does not affect dopamine, nor-epinephrine, or acetylcholine as do virtually all the other antidepressants that preceded it. This allowed doctors to use Prozac freely on patients who could not before be treated because of their vulnerability to side effects. Many physicians who never before prescribed antidepressants now felt free to give Prozac. Because it is relatively benign in overdose, it was also safer in the hands of suicidal patients. It is not especially sedating, and patients no longer complained of feeling drugged.

After its 1986 debut, Prozac's popularity was nearly instantaneous; it enjoyed the fastest acceptance of any psychotherapeutic medicine ever. Doctors now write about 650,000 prescriptions a month for Prozac, and by now more than 10 million people worldwide have taken it. From the *Today Show* to *Nightline*, television commentators reveled in its controversial aspects, fueled by frenzied Scientologists who find evil incarnate in rival psychiatric ministries. Not once, but twice did a giant Prozac capsule radiate its green and white promise of happiness and success from the cover of *Newsweek*.

Although Prozac's noteworthy effects on mood were easy to recognize and quantify, a few years passed before psychiatrists began noticing its more subtle but no less remarkable effects on personality. Kramer's genius was to be the first to gather these anecdotes in a coherent way and present them to the public. Although it is beyond the scope of this essay to detail the numerous ways that Prozac can alter deep-seated personality traits, we can gain a feel for the process by focusing on three: rejection sensitivity, dysthymia, and leadership.

REJECTION SENSITIVITY

Rejection sensitivity is not a diagnosis in itself, but a personality trait that everyone experiences to one degree or another. In its extreme and most pervasive form, it is associated with so-called Borderline Personality Disorder, an unfortunate instability of the core sense of selfhood that predisposes an individual to an extraordinary variety of life difficulties. These people simply seem to be physiologically wired to be deeply wounded by rejection. On experiencing a loss, they suffer more and become more depressed than do most men and women.

An older name for this trait is *hysteroid dysphoria*, a term that characterizes people with an extreme appetite for attention and a marked fear of abandonment, a desperate emotional state that results in a constellation of behaviors that amount to an exaggerated caricature of femininity, which for many makes it even less palatable when we observe it in a man.

These people are extremely brittle, their moods rapidly ranging from giddy elation to desperate unhappiness in response to external sources of admiration and approval, often several times a day. They feel devastated when a love affair terminates, but when they find a new source of approval, they again feel elated within a few days. When they are gratified by another, they minimize and deny the shortcomings of the relationship and idealize all love objects. When depressed, they rapidly become desperate for attention and often suicidal.

These love-intoxicated people tend to be egocentric, narcissistic, vain, and clothes-crazy. They are provocatively seductive, manipulative, superficially charming, and think emotionally and illogically. Unsavory individuals find them easy prey to flattery and compliments. In an intimate relationship they are clinging, demanding, withholding, and foreplay-oriented. If a romantic partner frustrates them, they become bitterly reproachful, abusive, and vindictive, often seeking solace in alcohol or other drugs. For hysteroid dysphorics, the agony of rejection is so surpassing, and the fleeting elation following approval so intense, that their quest for outside support becomes a full-time task.[2]

Although at first contact hysteroid dysphorics may resemble people with classical or major depression, their mood is far more responsive—too responsive—to external events. Another difference is that such people usually do not respond to tricyclic antidepressants as do most people with major depression, and they usually complain bitterly about side effects. Before the advent of Prozac and other SSRIs, psychiatrists found that some of these people benefited from MAOIs, despite the obvious difficulties in giving these potentially lethal agents to a group of patients who tend to be binge eaters and impulsively suicidal.

Kramer cites preliminary evidence that Prozac is a more desirable alternative to the MAOIs for borderlines and hysteroid dysphorics, stabilizing their mood and rendering them relatively impervious to abandonment scenarios. Like the MAOIs, it seems to home-in on maladaptive personality attributes, only with fewer and less severe side effects. In my experience, SSRIs are the first physical agents that practically offer a measure of relief to a large number of chronically distressed people whom most psychotherapists find too personally demanding to treat.

The prospect of a medicine that reduces such a seemingly learned aspect of personality as rejection sensitivity opens a new era of speculation about the physiological underpinnings of human nature. It now seems possible to manipulate brain chemistry in a way that achieves what once only psychotherapy did— to reframe particular elements of personality, trait by trait. As managed care systems insidiously undermine the financial practicality of individual psychotherapy, we can only expect such quick fixes to grow in popularity.

DYSTHYMIA

Dysthymia is a state of chronic low-grade depression, sometimes called the depressive personality or *minor* depression. It differs from major depression in that it does not wax and wane in noticeable cycles, but tends to be an enduring facet of a person's life, although it is not so profoundly disabling. Compared with nondepressed people, dysthymics have significantly fewer friends, their incomes tend to be lower, and they live in smaller homes. Their temperamental characteristics—social discomfort and lack of flexibility—result in a restricted life with few social rewards. Kramer suggests that dysthymics were constitutionally timid and avoidant of stimulation from an early age.

Women tend to be overrepresented in any population of dysthymics. Dysthymic women are the classic "women who love too much," their faulty self-esteem locking them into abusive relationships far past the point that most other women would leave. Their tendency to persevere in hopeless tasks generates conditions conducive to a chronically disappointed, morose, and deprived life-style. Modern technological society demands us to adopt extroverted behaviors, expend high degrees of energy, take risks, firmly assert our needs, and respond flexibly to rapidly changing situations.

No wonder that many who feel out of tune with the demands of modern life flock to psychiatrist's offices hoping to find a social panacea in a pill. Evidence is mounting that Prozac and other SSRIs are effective in reducing dysthymic traits in a way that more traditional antidepressants were not. In fact, Prozac may be more effective in these chronic, low-grade depressions than in relieving more serious melancholia, for which some psychiatrists are returning to the tricyclics.

SEROTONIN AND LEADERSHIP

Perhaps no other boon of Prozac and other serotonin-boosters equals their reputed ability to foster advancement in corporate hierarchies. The evidence cited in Kramer's book comes from research on captive Vervet monkeys.

In any troop of monkeys, social hierarchies quickly form, with a dominant alpha-male rising to a position of leadership. Other male monkeys make submissive gestures when near the alpha-male, who usually ends up with the most food and the largest harem. Alpha-males do not need to be violent to achieve this position. On the contrary, they are purposeful in their behavior, seldom seeking fights, but able to respond assertively, even aggressively when challenged. They tend to be socially well-integrated and engage in numerous affiliative activities with both other males and females, whose approval seems especially necessary for them to maintain dominance. Conversely, fighting with females signals low-hierarchy and leads to ostracism from the troop.

When researchers measured serotonin levels in these monkey troops, the alpha-male was inevitably the highest. When for some reason a monkey lost his dominant status to another, his serotonin level dropped dramatically while that of the new leader rose by almost 40 percent, indicating a biological preference for incumbency that may apply to political human beings as well. To make matters more interesting, researchers then removed the alpha-male from the troops, causing other males to compete to fill the vacuum. Monkeys with naturally high serotonin usually prevailed in this power struggle. Not surprisingly, giving Prozac or another drug that raises serotonin levels to an individual monkey enhanced his chances of achieving dominance over those without the social lift from modern neuroscience.[3]

Other research on humans suggests that recidivistic criminals and people who commit suicide have lower serotonin levels than normal. Kramer also cites evidence that serotonin levels in both humans and monkeys are under genetic influence, with some individuals endowed with higher levels that dispose them to engage in behaviors—affiliation with females seems particularly important— that help them assume a dominant role.[4]

The list of character traits once thought to be learned early in life that now appear to be under the sway of serotonin by no means stops here. This powerful brain chemical also plays a role in modulating self-esteem, assertiveness, diligence, seriousness, risk-taking, novelty-seeking, aggressiveness, impulsiveness, introversion, clarity of thought, and our ability to experience pleasure in everyday life. While some theorists argue that the evidence in Kramer's book proves that the physical realm is superior to the mental, that we are little more than mechanistic servants of the incredibly complicated interplay of various neurohumors in the brain, there is a far deeper implication.

IS THERE SPIRIT IN THE CAPSULE?

Ancient shamans knew that certain fungi, leaves, bark extracts, roots, and cacti have a powerful effect on consciousness, which they equated with Spirit. Unfettered by dualist philosophies that have dominated Western thought since the seventeenth century, they devised a simple but elegant solution to the conundrum of how a mere *physical* substance could so radically affect non-material Spirit. They believed that the Spirit of the plant cordially merged with the Spirit of the person who ate it, naturally altering—and sometimes healing—both.

We have much to learn from these venerable technicians of the sacred. Transpersonal psychology may be unique in its efforts to unite modern science with the "perennial philosophy" that holds that a divine, universal consciousness pervades the realm of things, lives, and minds, itself existing on a higher plane than matter, which it *ensouls*. This view allows for free will, creativity, intuitive insight, collective consciousness, emergence of novelty, and paranormal capabilities as potentials inherent in sentient life.

Modern neuroscience may be catching up with this idea as it discovers how thinking, learning, and choosing can alter the architecture and chemical balance of the physical brain. Kramer agrees that when Prozac affects a change that helps a person to tolerate rejection or bolster self-esteem, it chemically mimics the interior milieu of someone exposed to a more benign world in childhood. In this vein, many philosophers confirm that it is no less heuristic to argue that the *mind creates the brain* than to maintain the more common opposite view, although both sides may be misrepresenting the question.

To affirm the ontological superiority of Spirit in its transient form of the human mind or soul, I would agree with Kramer that nothing we learn about our neurophysiology or our animal nature will deny the possibility of transcendence. But I would add that it was our human minds that had the insight, ingenuity, and will to develop Prozac in the first place, just as it is our minds that prescribe it to our patients, just as it is our patient's minds that choose or not choose to take it.

We human beings *invented* Prozac, using our unique creativity, resourcefulness, and ingenuity, at least partly motivated by our compassionate desire to alleviate a major form of suffering that has long bedeviled the human condition. Here we have biology doubling back on itself, consciousness evolving the capacity to control itself from *underneath*, by manipulating its physical vehicle, the brain. This new feedback loop enhances our capacity for self-regulation and frees us to progress along higher paths of personal and spiritual growth. Because something of inferior status could hardly take control of something of superior status, the reasonable conclusion is that consciousness is on a higher plane of being than matter. And we might expect this evolutionary trend toward ever greater degrees of control to continue.

So when we "listen" to Prozac, we hear the tale of our minds, hearts, and singular Spirit once again asserting their hegemony over the material and biological, reaffirming our highest evolutionary imperative and transpersonal vision. If materialists argue that the individual personality is more determined by chemistry than karma, we might offer the riposte that it may simply be the individual's evolutionary karma to reap the benefits of Prozac.

10. Prozac and Personality

THE CASE OF TESS

BY PETER D. KRAMER, M.D.

Author of the best-selling book Listening to Prozac, *psychiatrist Peter Kramer is widely respected as a thoughtful and compassionate columnist who balances body and mind in his astute inquiries into human nature. Through a timely case history from his book, Kramer illustrates how the controversial antidepressant Prozac alters more than mood.*

Two weeks after starting Prozac, Tess appeared at the office to say she was no longer feeling weary. In retrospect, she said, she had been depleted of energy for as long as she could remember, had almost not known what it was to feel rested and hopeful. She had been depressed, it now seemed to her, her whole life. She was astonished at the sensation of being free of depression.

She looked different, at once more relaxed and energetic—more available— than I had seen her, as if the person hinted at in her eyes had taken over. She laughed more frequently, and the quality of her laughter was different, no longer measured but lively, even teasing.

With this new demeanor came a new social life, one that did not unfold slowly, as a result of a struggle to integrate disparate parts of the self, but seemed, rather, to appear instantly and full-blown.

"Three dates a weekend," Tess told me. "I must be wearing a sign on my forehead!"

Within weeks of starting Prozac, Tess settled into a satisfying dating routine with men. She had missed out on dating in her teens and twenties. Now she reveled in the attention she received. She seemed even to enjoy the trial-and-error process of learning contemporary courtship rituals, gauging norms for sexual involvement, weighing the import of men's professed infatuation with her.

I had never seen a patient's social life reshaped so rapidly and dramatically.

Low self-worth, competitiveness, jealousy, poor interpersonal skills, shyness, fear of intimacy—the usual causes of social awkwardness—are so deeply ingrained and so difficult to influence that ordinarily change comes gradually if at all. But Tess blossomed all at once.

"People on the sidewalk ask me for directions!" she said. They never had before.

The circle of Tess's women friends changed. Some friends left, she said, because they had been able to relate to her only through her depression. Besides, she now had less tolerance for them. "Have you ever been to a party where other people are drunk or high and you are stone-sober? Their behavior annoys you, you can't understand it. It seems juvenile and self-centered. That's how I feel around some of my old friends. It is as if they are under the influence of a harmful chemical and I am all right—as if I had been in a drugged state all those years and now I am clearheaded."

The change went further: "I can no longer understand how they tolerate the men they are with." She could scarcely acknowledge that she had once thrown herself into the same sorts of self-destructive relationships. "I never think about Jim," she said. And in the consulting room his name no longer had the power to elicit tears.

This last change struck me as most remarkable of all. When a patient displays any sign of masochism, and I think it is fair to call Tess's relationship with Jim masochistic, psychiatrists anticipate a protracted psychotherapy. It is rarely easy to help a socially self-destructive patient abandon humiliating relationships and take on new ones that accord with a healthy sense of self-worth. But once Tess felt better, once the weariness lifted and optimism became possible, the masochism just withered away, and she seemed to have every social skill she needed.

Tess's work, too, became more satisfying. She responded without defensiveness in the face of adamant union leaders, felt stable enough inside herself to evaluate their complaints critically. She said the medication had lent her surety of judgment; she no longer tortured herself over whether she was being too demanding or too lenient. I found this remark noteworthy, because I had so recently entertained the possibility that unconscious inner conflicts were hampering Tess in her dealings with the labor union. Whether the conflicts were real or illusory, the problem disappeared when the medication took effect. "It makes me confident," Tess said, a claim I since have heard from dozens of patients, none of whom had been given a hint that this medication, or any medication, could do any such thing.

Tess's management style changed. She was less conciliatory, firmer, unafraid of confrontation. As the troubled company settled down, Tess was given a substantial pay raise, a sign that others noticed her new effectiveness.

Tess's relations to those she watched over also changed. She was no longer drawn to tragedy, nor did she feel heightened responsibility for the injured. Most tellingly, she moved to another nearby town, the farthest she had ever lived from her mother.

Whether these last changes are to be applauded depends on one's social values. Tess's guilty vigilance over a mother about whom she had strong ambivalent feelings can be seen as a virtue, one that medication helped to erode. Tess experienced her "loss of seriousness," as she put it, as a relief. She had been too devoted in the past, at too great a cost to her own enjoyment of life.

In time, Tess's mother was given an antidepressant, and she showed a modest response—she slept better, lost weight, had more energy, displayed a better sense of humor. Tess threw her a birthday party, a celebration of the mother's survival and the children's successes. In addition to the main present, each child brought a nostalgic gift. Tess's was a little red wagon, in memory of a time when the little ones were still in diapers, and the family lived in a coldwater flat, and Tess had organized the middle children to wheel the dirty linens past abandoned tenements to the laundromat many times a week. Were I Tess's psychotherapist, I might have asked whether the gift did not reveal an element of aggression, but on the surface at least the present was offered and received lovingly. In acknowledging with her mother how difficult the past had been, Tess opened a door that had been closed for years. Tess used her change in mood as a springboard for psychological change, converting pain into perspective and forgiveness.

There is no unhappy ending to this story. It is like one of those Elizabethan dramas—Marlowe's *Tamburlaine*—so foreign to modern audiences because the Wheel of Fortune takes only half a turn: the patient recovers and pays no price for the recovery. Tess did go off medication, after about nine months, and she continued to do well. She was, she reported, not quite so sharp of thought, so energetic, so free of care as she had been on the medication, but neither was she driven by guilt and obligation. She was altogether cooler, better controlled, less sensible of the weight of the world than she had been.

After about eight months off medication, Tess told me she was slipping. "I'm not myself," she said. New union negotiations were under way, and she felt she could use the sense of stability, the invulnerability to attack, that Prozac gave her. Here was a dilemma for me. Ought I to provide medication to someone who was not depressed? I could give myself reason enough—construe it that Tess was sliding into relapse, which perhaps she was. In truth, I assumed I would be medicating Tess's chronic condition, call it what you will: heightened awareness of the needs of others, sensitivity to conflict, residual damage to self-esteem—all odd indications for medication. I discussed the dilemma with her, but then I did not hesitate to write the prescription. Who was I to withhold from her the bounties of science? Tess responded again as she had hoped she would, with renewed confidence, self-assurance, and social comfort.

I believe Tess's story contains an unchronicled reason for Prozac's enormous popularity: its ability to alter personality. Here was a patient whose usual method of functioning changed dramatically. She became socially capable, no longer a wallflower but a social butterfly. Where once she had focused on obligations to others, now she was vivacious and fun-loving. Before, she had pined after men; now she dated them, enjoyed them, weighed their faults and virtues. Newly confident, Tess had no need to romanticize or indulge men's shortcomings.

Not all patients on Prozac respond this way. Some are unaffected by the medicine; some merely recover from depression, as they might on any anti-depressant. But a few, a substantial minority, are transformed. Like Garrison Keillor's marvelous Powdermilk biscuits, Prozac gives these patients the courage to do what needs to be done.

11. *Depression in Borderline Personalities*

USING EMPATHY TO HEAL THE WOUNDED SELF

BY BEVERLY LOCKWOOD-CONLAN, L.C.S.W.

People with "borderline personality" experience alterations of mood that differ significantly from other common forms of depression. In this essay, a uniquely gifted psychotherapist shares the fruits of her experience in working intimately with people whom many consider too needy and demanding for orthodox psychotherapy.

No group of severely depressed people are more shunned by professional psychotherapists than those that bear the diagnosis of Borderline Personality Disorder. Many otherwise dedicated therapists consider them too emotionally damaged to treat, too demanding of their time and energy, or too likely to breach comfortable therapeutic boundaries for ordinary psychotherapy.

Even biological psychiatrists tend to avoid these people, believing that such deep-seated personality disturbances are beyond the reach of medications, or fearing that patients will use their prescriptions in impulsive suicide gestures. Borderlines—as they are often called—find themselves referred from therapist to therapist, often "dumped" on inexperienced younger therapists in public clinics, growing more bitter and disillusioned as they grow older.

The borderline personality defies efforts at precise definition. Not really psychotic but more severely disturbed than classical neurotics, their faulty ego functioning spawns severe relationship problems and difficulties navigating through life. Borderlines experience extreme instability of mood, difficulty maintaining self-identity, chaotic relationships involving intense attachment and dependency, lingering abandonment fears, childlike clinging behavior, and a habit of alternately idealizing and devaluing people who try to get close to them. They long to attach to people stronger than themselves but communicate more primal needs than most are willing to meet, provoking the very abandonment that they so fear. They use others to shore up their shaky sense of selfhood, often rejecting those unable to perform this function.

It is not surprising, then, that many psychotherapists avoid these patients who, in their state of deprivation and desperation, can be insistently demanding, angry, devaluing, and manipulative. The primitive feeling-states of these patients resonate with unresolved primal issues in the therapist—fears about her own neediness for example—engendering fear, anger, contempt, disgust, disbelief, and occasionally impulsively cruel responses. The therapist's unrecognized feeling may be: "How dare you be so primitive and remind me that I myself have these feelings. I will reject this part of you, deny this part in myself, and therefore feel better." Yet the ultimate expression of empathy is being able to remain connected to the other's feeling-state even when being personally attacked, flowing with the process rather than fighting it.

As an exercise in empathizing with borderline depression, imagine yourself feeling internally shattered like broken glass because of a casual but insensitive comment. You lose track of who you are and anticipate that something terrible could happen at any moment. You feel devoid of boundaries, as though your skin is disappearing. Your inner emptiness can only be filled by intimate contact with another, and you experience utter desolation without it. Rage about not being understood overwhelms you, along with deep psychic pain that makes you wish to end your life, or at least take enough pills to numb the misery for a while. The intensity of the pain might lead you to seek solace in alcohol or drugs, starve yourself, induce vomiting, or superficially cut your skin to salve the unbearable inner-mounting tension.

This agonizing state calls for a psychotherapist to place herself inside the other's being, to walk this desolate inner world in twinship with her, much as a loving mother would instinctively recognize her child's pain and help her deal with it. For instance, one of my patients, who had been repetitively humiliated for expressing her basic human needs, felt such shame after she impulsively revealed that she needed me that she huddled in a corner on the floor and cried inconsolably. This required my understanding affirmation that her need was natural and acceptable. I could then help her mourn the loss of what will never be—being a child with a good-enough mother—and reassure her that I would be there to meet her needs in every way I could. Some patients may require a therapist to spend long hours with them in empathic union while they cry away the grief that prevents them from speaking the unspeakable.

Depression in borderlines is unique in that their emotional states are more changeable than those of most depressed people. Clinical depression in other types of patients usually manifests as an enduring melancholic mood persisting for months. But borderline depression is fleeting, changing from hour to hour, responding to seemingly trivial incidents that trigger emotions that can be outside their awareness. A chance word or action on the part of spouse or friend will be experienced as such overwhelming rejection as to render them nonfunctional. One of my patients commented, "I can't bear to have anyone throw stones at my glass house." She described this state as literally "losing myself."

We can usually trace triggering events of these fleeting depressions to two causes: loss of the other (abandonment) or loss of self (identity diffusion, fragmentation). Abandonment depression follows any actual or threatened loss of a significant other that deals a devastating blow to an incompletely solidified ego, which requires an external source for sustenance. This other person provides functions for the borderline that she cannot provide for herself—soothing, affirmation, stability, and affect regulation. Without these functions, her psychic life is in danger, as she could "fall apart." The fear is of going crazy, losing one's foothold in the world, ceasing to exist. With these dangers lurking, she might do literally anything to avoid abandonment. And when abandonment occurs, it is painful beyond words, leading to overpowering depression and impulses to remove herself from the world.

Loss of self-identity is equally traumatic to the borderline. A chance word, an unexpected situation, may suddenly jerk her shaky psychic structure out from under her, leaving her struggling to regain equilibrium and a sense of security. The world and who she is in it, how she fits, and what her position and value are remain uncertain. One of my patients described this as a state in which she felt as though her skin was dissolving and she no longer existed. The resulting depression and disorientation remain until her inner sense of self is at least partially restored.

One of my patients, a middle-aged married woman with a three-year-old son, arrived for therapy in an acute state of fragmentation, feeling suicidal but without a clue as to why she suddenly became so depressed. Exploring the matter further, I learned that she had just learned that she was not pregnant again, as she had hoped. This revived her loss of an early infant-mother union, which she never experienced consistently with her own mother. She had attempted to repair this loss to some extent with her son, but as he grew older this was losing its ability to gratify her, and she was again beginning to feel her original loss as permanent and irretrievable.

Through my empathizing with her original loss, she re-created in our relationship the longed-for early mother-child union, which she experienced as relieving her depression. She left the session feeling less alone and more able to bear the possibility of never having another child. This is an example of abandonment depression arising very suddenly and rapidly relieved within the therapeutic relationship. This is a common characteristic of borderline depression— rapid self-fragmentation and suicidal depression from which the person quickly reconstitutes when provided an adequate holding environment.

ORIGINS OF THE BORDERLINE PERSONALITY

At the core of the borderline syndrome is a weakly constructed self resulting from failure to form adequate self/other boundaries during early childhood. The borderline makes a desperate attempt to maintain the integrity of her fragile selfhood by overidealizing others with the unspoken goal of merging with them. Most people with this diagnosis have suffered neglect, deprivation, or physical and sexual abuse in childhood.

To illustrate with a typical case, Sara, a thirty-six-year-old woman who had an alcoholic mother and a father who abandoned the family, was beaten frequently and severely by her mother, treated like a servant, harshly criticized, and locked alone in a room for hours. Her mother habitually left home for a day or longer, causing Sara to react with feelings of panic and helplessness, followed by numbness and dissociation. When she was eight, her mother married her stepfather, who repeatedly sexually molested her. By age thirteen, she was so withdrawn that her school recommended counseling. She was sent to a child guidance clinic where for several years her psychiatrist used her as servant, companion, and occasional sex object. This derailed the normal adolescent development that should have occurred during that time and prevented her from consolidating a firm sense of selfhood. She experienced incapacitating depression, desperately clinging to harmful relationships, and resorting to self-mutilation when they went awry.

Contemporary developmental research has shown that infant and childhood attachment patterns persist into adulthood. Three forms of attachment are commonly noted: (1) a secure attachment, (2) an anxious-ambivalent pattern in which people show insecure clinging behavior, and (3) an avoidant pattern in which people become emotionally withdrawn and isolated. Most borderlines fall into the second category and need repetitive reassurance to maintain even an ephemeral sense of secure attachment. This is why so many borderlines keep toy animals, teddy bears, and dolls, which represent the surrogate parent to a child.

Without parental attunement to her feelings and needs, the borderline person is unable to negotiate the essential developmental stages of trust, autonomy, identity, and intimacy necessary to become a mature adult. She remains stuck at a primitive stage of development, hating herself for being a small child in an adult body. She feels humiliated at her predicament but incapable of modulating her feelings or behaving as a rational adult. She feels she is living a lie, pretending to be a competent adult even with close friends or lovers, who may never see her true self. The trusted therapist may be the only person in her life who sees her authentic inner being.

It is, after all, through relationship with her mother that a young child first comes to know who she is, defining herself through her mother's mirroring feedback. If she eventually develops autonomy, it is because her mother was a reliable source of soothing comfort, wisdom, and strength, who encouraged her to incorporate these functions into her own selfhood as she grew older. If she avoids splitting others into categories of all good or all bad, it is because capable parenting imparted enough cognitive flexibility to see herself and others as a mix of positive traits and weaknesses. Her consistent internal image of her caring mother prevents her from feeling abandoned when she is temporarily alone. She bears forever within her the union that keeps her safe from the terror of total aloneness.

For healing to begin, the therapist must recognize, accept, and love the child in the adult body. It is often this "child's" reactions that cause so much trouble in the adult world. After all, it is acceptable for a two-year-old to throw a tantrum or be self-centered to the exclusion of others' feelings. We do not expect good judgment, rational behavior, or facility in handling powerful emotions from a two- or three-year-old, but we do expect this from adults. However, even experienced therapists may err by expecting a much higher level of functioning from regressed borderline patients than they are capable of. The more regressed and wounded the patient, the more the therapist must take on a mothering role to repair the damaged self.

HOW EMPATHY HEALS DEPRESSION

Relationship as healer underlies many scientific and philosophical theories of healing throughout history. The concept of relationship itself as the primary healing force in illness is implicit in shamanic healing practices of ancient societies, healing chants of Tibetan Buddhist monks, sweat lodges of Native Americans, and faith healing of fundamentalist Christian communities. Freud knew that relationship is central to the "talking cure" of modern psychoanalysis.

Whether the connection is with a shamanic spirit guide or a real human being seated nearby, healing flows from interconnectedness, which is also the key to healing depression in borderline personalities. Relationship with an empathic therapist who takes on the substantial commitment of reparenting can foster stability, health, and even survival. There must be a unique quality to this relationship that heals the inner loneliness and relationship-hunger that destabilizes the borderline's self.

The more regressed and wounded the patient, the more the therapist must assume the mothering function that was lacking in childhood. With very regressed patients, the psychotherapeutic relationship must take on an aspect of a "real" relationship. The patient must come to know that the love given is genuine and unconditional, and that there are true maternal feelings on the part of the therapist toward her. The therapist embodies some of the qualities of a real mother—subordinating her own needs to those of the patient, attending to the patient's well-being, promoting her growth, suffering with her in psychic pain, rejoicing in successes, guiding her through the vicissitudes of life, and helping her come into fullness as a person. This reparenting becomes a powerful force that helps the patient internalize the strength and coherent internal structure that her own mother never fostered.

In time, the patient gradually internalizes not only the functions of the therapist but also her person. More than most, this patient expresses a strong need to know what is behind the persona of the therapist—how she lives her life, what her values are. Selectively sharing some aspects of one's personal life can be helpful to a borderline patient who previously lacked a reliable exemplar on which to model her own life, although she must feel free not to adopt the therapist's pattern of living. For example, the patient may have little idea how to celebrate holidays, how to spend leisure time, how to cultivate friendships, or how to develop hobbies and interests. Knowing something of the therapist's life helps advance these crucial aspects of living that fortify her sense of self.

The therapist must be both mother and therapist to the patient. The patient needs the mother she never had to cure her inner loneliness, but because of the early damage, she needs more than *just* a mother. She simultaneously needs a trained professional who can objectively understand her current dilemma, help her work through the longing, grief, and pain of early trauma and loss, and repair the past through therapeutic work. She also needs more than a therapist who maintains a professional and detached distance, reviving the withholding and abandoning experiences of her past. She needs relationship with a person who will provide a living emotional interaction that is vital and authentic without losing her own center.

Many therapists believe that the best strategy with a regressed borderline is to shore up ego boundaries, keep her functioning in an adult mode if possible, and avoid rekindling feelings left over from an earlier stage of life. This may be an appropriate strategy for time-limited therapy. However, this ignores the vulnerable and wounded "child" who lives within a thin facade of adulthood. If this frightened child can be revealed to the "therapist/mother" to be comforted and cared for, a deeper healing of inner loneliness takes place.

The therapist should not take this course, however, without the most profound commitment and sense of responsibility to the patient. There are pitfalls in encouraging regression that demand more time, involvement, and attention than many therapists are willing or practically able to commit. Activating regressive states can feed the relationship-hunger of the patient, and the therapist must be available to cope with the primal longings that may emerge. The therapist should not expect the patient to adhere to firm personal boundaries until she has moved beyond the small child stage. This approach may be too demanding and personally disturbing for most therapists, who may be unable to restrain destructive acting-out of such volcanic emotions.

The following illustrates how relationship hunger can be first activated, then contained within the therapeutic relationship. Sara, who was mentioned earlier, could not tolerate being away from the therapeutic relationship on weekends in the early stages of therapy because of her abandonment fears. Her terror was so great that in order to "hold" her during this time, I made a tape of my voice talking to her. I gave her a small toy animal that she could cuddle. We also created, through guided imagery, a little fantasy world where only she and I existed, to which she could retreat for comfort when she was alone. These measures served to fortify her through painful times of separation.

The therapist must provide not only empathy but actually *share* the emotional state of the patient, reducing her inner loneliness. To accomplish this without losing herself in the patient's chaotic world, the therapist must possess sufficient ego-strength to withstand intense emotional states as she helps integrate the experience by translating it both verbally and nonverbally in a way that is tolerable and coherent. The therapist must take in the person's pain, rework it inside herself, then project it back into the patient in a more palatable form. Once she feels understood, the patient invests the therapist with power to respond to her particular constellation of unmet developmental needs. She allows the therapist to hold parts of her self that cannot function autonomously. The therapist becomes the guardian of these fragments in order to help the patient integrate them into a whole person. The patient's loneliness becomes more tolerable as she begins to process deep feelings in the context of the relationship.

In this light, it is essential for the therapist to be comfortable with her own experiences with abandonment and loss of self. We have all experienced abandonment feelings in early childhood and identity issues in adolescence; recalling these helps us understand how borderline patients feel. For example, a patient's need for me to call her in the evening to provide soothing that she could not provide for herself triggered a memory of my own urgent need as a child to receive my working mother's telephone call each evening, which I required like a lifeline on a sinking ship. Therapists who are strongly defended against such needs might not wish to work with borderline patients.

The way a child's emotional experience becomes organized is governed by mutual feedback and affect attunement within the mother/child dyad. Early emotional experiences are, for the most part, *physical* sensations rather than psychologically elaborated feelings, and the caregiver demonstrates her emotional resonance through affectionate holding and warm sensory contacts with the infant's body. Similarly, affect attunement in psychotherapy requires a therapist to immerse herself into the inner world of the patient so that she can help contain disturbing feeling-states.

As the therapist takes in the pain and processes an experience for the patient, she resembles a mother interpreting an emotionally wrenching event for a small child so that it accrues a meaningful context within the social and family environment. This diminishes abandonment depression by providing a relationship in which to work through whatever abandonment experience or relationship loss the person has suffered. The therapeutic relationship also allays depression that follows "loss of self," fortifying the patient's ego by providing internal structure that she cannot provide for herself. Ideally, the patient incorporates self-soothing skills and learns to provide them for herself.

These interpersonal transactions extend beyond resolving the impact of parental limitations on the child's emerging self, and they also provide more than a "corrective emotional experience." They include the *intersubjective field*—the playing ground on which two unique selves interact to form a new whole, which then provides the patient an internal working model in future relationships. This temporarily merges therapist with patient, which can simultaneously be a terrifying, fascinating, and uniquely human experience. One way to feel whole is to feel part of another person, and thus part of all human beings. The self discovered is every self; it is universal—the human self. Intersubjectivity keeps alive a common humanity, without which an individual self flounders.

A Wintu shaman from Northern California heals through "feeling with" the patient in a way that exemplifies the spirit of healing in a psychotherapeutic relationship:

I feel for the sores, the aches, and the pains. When I put my hand over the body, I can feel every little muscle and every little vein. I can feel the soreness. It hurts me. If they have heart trouble, my heart just beats. Any place they are hurting I hurt. I become a part of their body.[1]

Such merger/fusion experiences in shamanic healing or psychotherapy are akin to the mother-infant union and lead to a kind of spiritual transcendence in which we feel ourselves as part of a force greater than ourselves. The spiritual nature of the caregiving relationship demonstrates that one thing is not separate from another, that we exist in patterns of mutuality and interconnectedness. This can have a quality of connecting to each other on another dimension.

Plumbing the depths of the human psyche has all of the qualities of seeking to grasp the unknowable that accompany exploring the mysteries of outer space, the ocean depths, or the world where spirit resides. As a psychotherapist who would heal the dark sickness of the soul, one must be willing to walk through the storm of fire, there to encounter the depths of soul and emerge unscathed, empowered to embody more of the humanity of which it is our sacred privilege to be a part.

In *On Listening*, Carl Faber states that there are those therapists who

> . . . listen in the deepest way of the healing traditions—the true midwives of the human spirit. These are the helpers who are willing to go "there," to the boundaries of their understandings and identities day after day. Like the shamans, they are ready to listen to stories that bring them to the edge of freedom, creativity, the pulse of instinct, experiences of overwhelming conflict, suicide, and the abyss of insanity. They are ready to follow the souls wherever they go. They respect the mystery. They know that it is only at the edge of the Pit that healing wells up from the soul. And, frequently, the listeners as well as the talkers must be in jeopardy before Orpheus plays his sweet songs. These are women and men who nourish the tender plants of fragile, injured individualities into the trees that change families, institutions, and aesthetic and cultural traditions. Instead of being the entertainers of the rich, they live at the eye of personal and social revolution.[2]

12. Alternative Medical Treatments for Depression

WHAT YOUR DOCTOR DOESN'T KNOW CAN HURT YOU

BY HYLA CASS, M.D.

For some people, depression can be traced to physical abnormalities that mimic its symptoms, including chronic fatigue syndrome, hormone imbalances, and food and drug sensitivities. If the underlying disorder is promptly recognized, antidepressant medications or lengthy psychotherapy may be avoided. In this essay, psychiatrist Hyla Cass sheds light on several common conditions often overlooked by physicians and nonmedical therapists alike. Her unorthodox remedies represent the avant-garde of the newly emerging field of nutritional medicine.

Anxiety and depression are a price we pay for our complex life-styles. We feel pressured to keep up with jobs, family, and the myriad responsibilities of everyday life. Any *extra* stressors become just too much to handle, and symptoms drive us to seek psychotherapy or counseling. Compounding these psychological symptoms, there are often underlying *physical or metabolic problems*, usually undetected and underdiagnosed by physicians, that can be the root cause of *emotional problems*. Once properly diagnosed, these disorders can be effectively treated by alternative medical means, either through an enlightened health practitioner or by an educated patient.

While psychotherapy has an important role, we are mind-body organisms, and we cannot expect the brain to work without the rest of the body being in proper balance. Every disorder or deficiency in the body affects the brain, which is extremely sensitive to imbalances caused by such physical insults as low blood sugar, water retention, or oxygen deprivation. Some depressed patients do not respond well to psychotherapy. However, when their conditions are properly—metabolically—diagnosed and treated, the process accelerates. The individual is more able to be present and to retain and integrate the material learned in therapy.

INFECTIOUS CAUSES

In my own psychiatric practice, I prefer to begin psychotherapy only after excluding an underlying physical cause. This can run the gamut from hypoglycemia, to viral and fungal infections, hormonal imbalances, allergies, sensitivities, toxic chemical or metal overload, and deficiencies of vitamins, minerals, or amino acids.

Chronic Fatigue Syndrome

Catherine, a successful thirty-two-year-old professional woman, described herself in desperate terms: "I feel like I'm losing my mind. I'm absentminded, simple tasks overwhelm me, and I'm in tears at the drop of a hat. I'm exhausted most of the time. I can barely get up in the morning. All day there's a constant struggle to stay awake. I feel my life is over at thirty-two!" Although she did have an obvious problem with workaholic habits, a high stress level, and a driving need to be a successful professional like her father, Catherine's medical history revealed other, unaddressed explanations for her desperation.

Eight months earlier, Catherine had the flu. Despite her apparent recovery within a month, she never fully regained her former strength and energy. For one thing, she could no longer exercise as before and found that it depleted rather than energized her. She drank coffee to boost her energy, but after a while even that did not work. Based on her history, I ordered several blood tests. These revealed a number of problems, any one of which could cause fatigue, anxiety, and depression: *iron-deficiency anemia, elevated viral antibodies, and hypoglycemia.* Except for anemia, for which I prescribed an iron supplement, orthodox physicians, do not typically diagnose or treat these conditions. Alternative practitioners, however, are able to treat them with diet and a variety of nutritional supplements.

Catherine's flu turned out to be Epstein-Barr virus, a chronic, relapsing form of infectious mononucleosis, and part of a syndrome called Chronic Fatigue Syndrome (CFS)[1]. It appears to be caused by one of a group of viruses that can lie dormant for months or years at a time, then be reactivated by physical or emotional stress. Symptoms include depression, extreme fatigue, nonrestorative sleep, impaired memory and concentration, anxiety attacks, intermittent low-grade fevers, sore throat, swollen lymph glands, muscle aches and pain (*fibromyalgia*), and allergies.

One feature that distinguishes CFS from depression or other causes of fatigue is a *negative response to exercise.* While most individuals feel energized after exercise, chronic fatigue patients feel *worse.* A special brain scan called SPECT demonstrates a clear difference in the cerebral blood patterns before and after exercise, clarifying the two diagnoses.[2]

Despite orthodox physicians' propensity to ignore CFS or advise their patients that "You just have to get a lot of rest and learn to live with it," there are specific remedies for this syndrome. Nature provides us with a variety of herbs such as astragalus, licorice, echinacea, and goldenseal that boost the immune system, helping it to fight viral invaders. Catherine began to take these herbs, plus megadoses of vitamins and minerals, and amino acids, especially lysine and cysteine.

Candidiasis

Presenting a similar picture to both CFS and hypoglycemia is a systemic yeast infection called *chronic candida albicans*, systemic candidiasis, or Candida hypersensitivity syndrome.[3,4] Candida albicans is a yeast that inhabits the gastrointestinal tract, kept in balance by friendly bacteria that aid in digestion, such as *acidophilus, bifidus, and bulgaricum.* Antecedent factors may include stress, and long-term use of antibiotics, birth control pills, or steroids. Mercury dental fillings have been implicated in its etiology, and their removal has led to reversal of candidiasis.[5] Symptoms may include depression, mood swings, fatigue, PMS, impaired memory and concentration, food cravings, nasal congestion, vaginal yeast infections, abdominal bloating and gas, constipation or diarrhea, recurrent fungal infections, and urinary tract infections.

Candida is a controversial diagnosis in orthodox medical circles, usually acknowledged only in severely debilitated patients. Nonetheless, its constellation can be diagnosed by a specific lab test for anti-candida antibodies, then treated with dietary changes, antifungal herbs and/or drugs, and an immunity-enhancing support program.

HORMONAL IMBALANCES

Sex Hormones

Laura, a forty-year-old secretary, was referred to me by her psychotherapist to explore the possibility of an underlying physical imbalance. Despite a year of weekly therapy sessions, some with her husband in a couples' group, Laura was still depressed, anxious, irritable, tired. She was dissatisfied with her job, her family, and life in general. She argued daily with her husband and teenage daughter. She had severe Premenstrual Syndrome (PMS). Although she had been told by her gynecologist that she was nowhere near menopause and that her problems were all psychological in origin, her psychological state resembled that induced by shifting female hormones. When her blood levels of the sex hormones estrogen, progesterone, and DHEA (dehydroepiandrosterone) were checked, the last two were low. Progesterone deficiency can lead to depression, PMS, water retention, and weight gain.

To smooth out these imbalances, I prescribed natural progesterone, a derivative of the Mexican wild yam. This product also helps to prevent *osteoporosis*, a form of bone loss associated with menopause. It is supplied either in capsule form or as a skin cream that is applied to fatty areas of the body such as the abdomen and thighs. The hormone is then absorbed transdermally into the system. This is not the synthetic hormone, Provera, used in pharmacological hormone therapy, which has many negative side effects and few if any positive ones. In addition, I gave Laura some herbal combinations, *dong quai* and *vitex* among them, to further simulate progesterone naturally. Lastly, I prescribed DHEA, an adrenal hormone produced by both men and women. DHEA peaks in a person's twenties and diminishes after that. It is a precursor of both male and female hormones (testosterone and estrogen) and is useful for depression, weight loss, diabetic control, life extension, and immune function. A likely reason for its lack of general usage in the medical world is that it cannot be manufactured as a drug and thus is not potentially profitable to the pharmaceutical industry. Additional treatment for Laura's PMS included vitamin B6, magnesium, and evening primrose oil.

Laura's response to the program was gratifying. Not only did her PMS resolve, but so did her depression and irritability. Then, the DHEA improved her energy level and sexual desire. Needless to say, all this had a positive effect on her relationship. Laura's was another case of physical imbalance causing emotional imbalance. Addressing the physical problem had a positive effect on her emotions.

She did not require estrogen replacement therapy (HRT), which is generally provided by a pharmaceutical derivative of pregnant mare's urine. The most commonly used drug for HRT is Premarin, which is high in estradiol and is proven to promote cancer growth in susceptible individuals. In addition, the collection of urine from pregnant mares is one more unnecessary and inhumane abuse of our animal friends. The pregnant mares are kept immobilized in cramped stalls for continuous urine collection, and their foals sold for slaughter. The mares are immediately impregnated to repeat the cycle until they are no longer useful for this purpose.

Alternative physicians use natural forms of estrogen or *phytoestrogens* derived from plant sources such as the soybean. These derivatives are high in estriol, a portion of the estrogen complex that not only does *not* encourage cancer but actually protects against it! Estriol has been widely used in Europe for many years but is available in the U.S.A. by prescription only through special pharmacies. The combination of natural estrogen, natural progesterone, and DHEA (all based on laboratory measures), plus other herbal, vitamin, and mineral supplements more effectively prevent symptoms of menopause, which erroneously are thought to be an inevitable part of aging. In countries such as Japan where soy is a dietary staple, there is a very low incidence of menopausal symptoms and of breast and uterine cancer. This same population, when exposed to the typical American diet, loses this protection, indicating that this is not a genetic propensity.

Is there a corresponding male menopause? I believe so. Men who complain of such problems as fatigue, weight gain, and loss of sexual interest or function may be deficient in male sex hormones, the androgens. Testosterone and DHEA levels can be measured and supplemented, leading to a reversal of these difficult symptoms, thereby giving these men a new lease on life.

Thyroid Imbalance

The following case is yet another example of the mood-hormone connection. Jennifer came to see me, depressed, tired, unable to get up in the morning to attend her college classes, and feeling overwhelmed by her graduate-level course work. Jennifer's history revealed that she was often cold, especially her hands and feet (she even wore socks to bed), had thinning hair, dry skin, constipation, and was losing the outer part of her eyebrows. I suspected an imbalance in her thyroid, the energy-generating gland located below the Adam's apple. When I asked about thyroid disease, she said that it had been suspected before, but her tests had been normal. I checked her thyroid hormones, including thyroid antibody levels. An underactive thyroid can often hide behind "normal" blood tests. Dr. Broda Barnes's technique of monitoring thyroid function through body temperature is used by many alternative practitioners. If the temperature is consistently low, these physicians treat the patient with thyroid replacement therapy, monitoring progress both by clinical signs and symptoms and rise in temperature.[6]

Although Jennifer's thyroid hormone levels were normal, she did in fact have *antithyroid antibodies* in her bloodstream, confirming a diagnosis of *Hashimoto's Thyroiditis*. This is an autoimmune disease, treatable with thyroid hormone, antioxidants, and adrenal support. Her signs were those of *hypo*thyroidism, suggesting that the circulating hormone was being rendered ineffective. With this condition, there are often intermittent signs of *hyper*thyroidism—overactive thyroid, such as irritability or heart palpitations. I prescribed thyroid hormone from natural sources and asked her to monitor her body temperature so I could adjust her dosage. She asked whether this would suppress her own thyroid function and whether she would need it for the rest of her life. The answer was no on both counts. The treatment actually supported her own gland, allowing it to heal. Within ten days of starting the program, she was feeling alive again. Her mood and energy lifted, as did the gloomy fog of her mornings past.

Hypoglycemia

Let us next address Catherine's *hypoglycemia*—low blood sugar. This disorder is often related both to stress and to poor eating habits, both of which affect the adrenal glands. Although doctors may diagnose other glandular deficiencies, *low adrenal function*, which is related to hypoglycemia, remains a medical orphan. Our tiny (but very important) adrenal glands prepare us for fight or flight. Many of us live in a constant state of emergency. When a person is under stress, the adrenals secrete the hormone cortisol, which raises blood sugar temporarily, only to plummet over and over again until these overtaxed glands are exhausted—and so are we. Catherine's coffee drinking was an attempt to boost her blood sugar—and give her a quick shot of energy—by stimulating her already tired glands. It was like beating a dead horse.

As mentioned, hypoglycemia can also result from poor eating habits, particularly in people genetically predisposed to this condition. The disorder can present in a variety of ways: depression, irritability, anxiety, panic attacks, fatigue, "brain fog," headaches, including migraines, insomnia, muscular weakness, and tremors, all of which may be relieved by food. There may be cravings for sweets, coffee, alcohol, or drugs. In fact, many addictions are related to hypoglycemia. Coffee and sugar consumed by recovering addicts only prolongs their problem, though in a less dangerous, more socially acceptable form. It is interesting to note the large amount of these substances consumed at Alcoholic's Anonymous meetings and on psychiatric wards. Patients can often overcome coffee, drug, and alcohol addiction through correcting their hypoglycemia *with minimal withdrawal symptoms or later cravings*. For recovering alcoholics, for example, I recommend the hypoglycemic regimen described below plus the amino acid glutamine, which is particularly useful when a craving strikes.

For Catherine's hypoglycemia, I prescribed a program designed to both strengthen her adrenals and maintain adequate blood sugar levels. This included: elimination of refined carbohydrates (sugar, white flour), coffee, and alcohol; eating small, frequent meals of complex carbohydrates, high fiber, and protein;

daily supplementation with chromium, manganese, potassium, B vitamins, pantothenic acid (B-5), and vitamin C.

Catherine responded well to the nutritional program. Within three months she was feeling like herself again—active, enthusiastic, optimistic, and no longer depressed. She continued the hypoglycemic diet and remained on a maintenance dose of supplements to sustain her immune function. As we can see, Catherine had both a metabolic disturbance—hypoglycemia—and an immune problem, both of which superficially *appeared strictly psychological* in origin. While therapy together with specific stress reduction techniques would have been useful, the underlying pathology had to be addressed first.

FOOD AND CHEMICAL SENSITIVITIES

Food and chemical sensitivities are often present in individuals with some or all of the above conditions. We generally think of allergies as manifesting by a rash, hives, nasal congestion, or gastrointestinal problems. These reactions are mediated by the classically recognized *IgE* (immune globulin E) protein component of the immune system. However, food and chemical sensitivities mediated by another component, IgG (immune globulin G), can produce a great variety of symptoms such as depression, anxiety, "brain fog," fatigue, hyperactivity, attention deficit disorder, joint pains, migraines, irritable bowel syndrome, and food cravings, mimicking many other illnesses in the process.

Alternative medical practitioners often recommend specific diagnostic and treatment programs for this food and chemical sensitivity syndrome. A common approach is "rotation and elimination" whereby the patient avoids the offending substance, then gradually reintroduces it until it is tolerated. This food can then be eaten on a rotating basis, no more than every four days, to avoid further sensitivity. Disadvantages of this technique include nutritional limitations, personal inconvenience, and inability to avoid some common substances, particularly airborne pollutants and allergens.

The desensitization technique that I prefer is NAET—Nambudripad's Allergy Elimination Technique. Diagnosis is by muscle testing (Applied Kinesiology), using an indicator muscle to determine if a particular substance causes weakness in the individual's energy field.[7] Treatment is with acupuncture or acupressure. After a twenty-five-hour period of avoidance, the patient can often go back on the offending food or be exposed to the chemical *with no further problem*. While this may sound impossible, just as acupuncture once seemed, the results are compelling. The process may be explained in the same way as acupuncture, in which treating subtle energy channels can affect physical processes.

AMINO ACID DEFICIENCY

In some cases when depression remains unresponsive, the physician can check the patient's plasma *amino acid* levels.[8] Brain chemicals called *neurotransmitters* carry messages of stimulation or inhibition between nerve cells. If these messengers are in short supply, depression can result. By increasing the level of *precursors—amino acids* that the body converts to neurotransmitters—it is possible to reverse depression. For example, the amino acid precursors tyrosine and phenylalanine produce norepinephrine, and tryptophan becomes serotonin. Antidepressant medicines work in a similar way. That is, they increase neurotransmitter levels by inhibiting their breakdown, thereby elevating mood. If a patient is already on antidepressant medication, she can remain on it while balancing her chemistry. She may later be able to discontinue the medication.

VITAMIN AND MINERAL DEFICIENCIES

A simple and often overlooked cause of depression is a lack of specific vitamins and minerals that are essential to metabolic processes. The body is run by a myriad of chemical reactions as it digests, absorbs, and utilizes the raw material that we put into it in the form of food. Vitamins and minerals are essential *cofactors* or chemical helpers in metabolic processes. If through nutritional deficiency or poor absorption these are not available, metabolism is impaired, causing symptoms. For example, a common condition in women who regularly lose blood in their menstrual cycle is *iron deficiency anemia*. This chronic loss of iron, as seen in our first case, Catherine, impairs the oxygen-carrying capacity of the red blood cells. Her depression and fatigue might have been detected much earlier and treated with iron supplements, thereby aiding her immune system, which was compromised by the low iron.

A similar cause of these symptoms, especially in older individuals, is vitamin B-12 deficiency, which is easily detected by a blood test and corrected by supplementation. B-12 is best given by injection, since the problem often results from poor intestinal absorption of this particular vitamin. Women taking birth control pills can have deficiencies of vitamins B6, B12, folic acid, and vitamin C, leading to depression, fatigue, confusion, and irritability. It is of note that vitamin C can act as a natural tranquilizer. Doctors Hoffer and Osmond reported patients' responding to 10 grams of vitamin C daily when tranquilizers had been found ineffective. Magnesium deficiency can produce anxiety, irritability, and hypersensitivity to noise, all of which can be rapidly reversed with magnesium supplementation.

Deficiencies in almost any of the vitamins and minerals can present with emotional or cognitive symptoms—depression, anxiety, impaired memory and concentration—the very symptoms we saw in our case examples. The treatment is either by determining the specific deficiencies through laboratory tests (blood and urine) followed by appropriate supplementation, or by taking a combination megavitamin/mineral supplement. Because lab tests can be costly, I most often recommend the latter. The "RDA"—Required Daily Allowance of vitamins and minerals—advocated by the orthodox dietitians and the FDA is meaningless. The recommended levels are not nearly sufficient for good health maintenance, but only for preventing serious, end-stage deficiency disease, such as scurvy (vitamin C deficiency) or pellagra (vitamin B1 deficiency). Of interest is that the average American diet is generally *deficient even in the RDA!*

What causes these deficiencies? We need only consider the high-sugar, low-fiber, additive-preserved food that many people "live" on, combined with the impaired absorption that accompanies such poor nutrition. It is no wonder that we are a nation of stressed, depressed, fatigued individuals with learning disabilities and degenerative diseases in all the body systems. We are overfed and undernourished. A poorly nourished body contains a malnourished brain.

ANTIDEPRESSANT MEDICATION

Some people prefer taking medication for their depressed mood. If there is no glaring metabolic illness, antidepressant medication can be very effective. For example, James, a fifty-year-old salesman, had been depressed for at least a year. He was unproductive in his work, had trouble making decisions, and could not motivate himself to exercise, although he knew it could help raise his mood. When he asked for an antidepressant, I prescribed one from the newest class of antidepressants, the selective serotonin reuptake inhibitors. These work by allowing serotonin to accumulate in the space between the neurons, correcting a deficiency of this "feel-good" neurotransmitter. The best known drug in this category is Prozac, but there are others, each with its own pattern of effects and side effects. Two weeks later James was—both by his word and my observation—a changed man. He was organized, productive, exercising daily, energized—and happy.

Do I have any qualms about going the chemical route? There certainly are risks of unwanted side effects as I explained to James. The choice was then up to him. In his case, the medication caused a dry mouth and a decrease in sex drive, but he felt it was worth the trade off. Although a natural "metabolic balancing" approach to diagnosis and treatment seems preferable, there is a place for antidepressant medication. However, anyone taking these must be carefully monitored for negative effects and have blood tests to determine baseline and follow-up levels for any organ or system likely to be affected, such as the liver, kidneys, or blood cells.

CONCLUSION

A psychiatrist can be not only a healer but an educator and facilitator as well, helping people to make choices in life-style, diet, supplements, and medications. Rather than *curing* depression, the goal is *balance*, in *body* as well as in mind and spirit. The physical imbalances can run the gamut from hypoglycemia, to viral and fungal infections, hormonal imbalances, allergies, sensitivities, toxic chemical or metal overload, and deficiencies of vitamins, minerals, or amino acids. Imbalance in one area is reflected in problems in other areas, and the weakest link shows first.

Ideal treatment is holistic: evaluate the whole person and treat each imbalance accordingly, being aware that the body/mind seeks homeostasis. Address as many areas—physical, emotional, and spiritual—as possible, thereby encouraging shifts that move the individual toward balance and health.

Postscript to the reader: Please consult your physician before following the suggestions for treatment described in this chapter.

13. *The Energy Dynamics of Depression*

HEALING DEPRESSION THROUGH BODYWORK

BY ALEXANDER LOWEN, M.D.

Alexander Lowen is the founder of Bioenergetics, a system of releasing pent-up emotions that take refuge in various systems of the body. In this excerpt from his book Depression and the Body, *the author introduces his revolutionary theory that suppressing negative feelings and impulses armors and devitalizes the body, blocking the flow of energy that allows us to function in a life-affirming way.*

THE DEPRESSIVE CONDITION

The word "depression" is loosely used today to describe any low mood. But not all low moods are depressed states, and a clear distinction must be drawn between them. If we fail to make this distinction, we will fall into the error of regarding the depressive reaction as normal under some conditions. For example, we will assume that it is perfectly natural for a person to become depressed when he suffers a loss, financial, personal, or otherwise. Long John Nebel took this position during a radio interview with me on NBC. He asked, "Don't you consider it normal for a person to become depressed when a job promotion which he has anticipated for some time falls through?"

He was surprised when I answered, "No. The normal reaction to this situation is disappointment."

"What is the difference between them?" he asked.

The depressive reaction immobilizes a person. He is unable to muster the desire or the energy to carry on his usual activities. He feels defeated, is pervaded by a sense of hopelessness, and as long as the depressive reaction continues, he doesn't see any use of further effort. Disappointment may leave a person feeling sad, but it doesn't immobilize him. He can talk about his disappointment and otherwise express his feelings, something the depressed person cannot do. As a result of his disappointment he may reevaluate his aspirations or find other means to realize them. He does not have the sense of hopelessness that characterizes the depressed person. Neither his interest in life nor his energy is seriously affected.

In contrast to disappointment there is often no apparent reason for the depressive reaction. In many cases it occurs when everything appears to be going well, sometimes just at the point when the person is on the verge of or has just realized his ambition. For instance, one man became depressed when he sold his business for more than $1,000,000. This had been his goal for a number of years, and he had worked energetically to achieve it. Yet when the sale was consummated, depression set in. . . .

The apparent contradiction between success and depression can be explained if we assume that success was not the person's real goal. If it was love, for example, and the achievement was unconsciously conceived as a means of obtaining love, it is clear that the failure to do so could result in a severe disappointment. But since these people are not grounded in their bodies and are out of touch with their feelings, they fail to sense their disappointment. Being unable to express any feeling, they go into a depression. . . .

We experience many low states in life which are not depressive reactions. In addition to disappointment, one can be dejected by a refusal or disheartened by an unfortunate event. Each has an emotional tone of sadness distinguishing it from the depressed state. If one is out of touch with this feeling, one gets depressed. A simple illustration is the following: A patient will often answer my initial inquiry, "How do you feel?" with the response, "I feel depressed." Looking at him, however, I observe that his face is sad, sometimes close to tears. When I point this out, he may say, "Why, yes. I *do* feel sad." Surprisingly, the recognition and acceptance of a feeling changes the quality of the mood. The patient no longer feels as depressed as he did when he blocked his awareness of the feeling of sadness.

Psychotherapists have long known that getting a patient to cry or to become angry breaks the grip of the depressive reaction. Crying is the more appropriate emotion, since the depressive reaction is linked with a sense of loss. . . . I have found that it matters little which emotion is expressed. The expression of *any* emotion is sufficient in most cases to lift the person out of his depressive mood.

Since depression is caused by the suppression of emotion, it cannot itself be regarded as one. It represents the absence of emotion. It is not a true feeling; one doesn't "feel" depressed, and it should not be confused with a real feeling, such as feeling "blue," a state embracing elements of sadness and loneliness. Feelings and emotions are organismic responses to events in the environment; the depressed state is a *lack* of responsiveness. Feelings change as the outside situation changes, causing a different response from the organism. The proper company, for example, can lift a person out of his blue mood; the individual in a depressed state, however, remains unresponsive.

Depression is a loss of an organism's internal force comparable in one sense to the loss of air in a balloon or tire. This internal force is the constant flow of impulses and feeling from the vital centers of the body to the periphery. Actually, what moves in the body is an energetic charge. This charge activates tissues and muscles in its path, giving rise to a sensation or feeling. When it results in action, we call it an impulse—a pulse from within. In the depressed state impulse formation is sharply reduced both as to number of impulses and their strength. This diminution produces a loss of feeling on the inside and a loss of action on the outside. We can speak therefore of depression being an internal collapse, meaning that the ability of the organism to respond with appropriate impulses to environmental events has greatly diminished.

Thinking in terms of impulses and the force they exert clarifies our understanding of the nature of depression. Impulses exert an outward pressure and normally result in some form of expression. Expression literally means outward-moving force. Behind every desire, feeling, or thought is an impulse, which may be defined as an energetic movement from within the organism to the outer world. Each impulse that carries through to the outside represents a desire, evokes a feeling, is associated with a thought, and ends in an action. Thus, for instance, when we have the impulse to strike someone, it represents the desire to stop that person from causing us pain; it carries with it the feeling of anger; it is associated with thoughts relating to the situation that provoked the impulse; and it ends in a blow.

An impression is the opposite of an expression. When an impulse affects another person, he receives an impression. The impulse need not be a blow; it may be a look, a gesture, or a word. The impression is the result of an external force acting on the body. In a living organism, impressions evoke some response from the organism which constitutes a recognition of the impression. Inanimate objects do not generally react to external forces. I can, for example, press my thumb into a ball of putty and leave an impression, but the putty does not sense the impression and does not react to it. For an object to react, it must contain some internal force. An inflated balloon will react to the pressure of my thumb because it contains such a force. It will first become distorted, then resume its original shape after the pressure is removed. A deflated balloon will not do this. This oversimplified analogy helps explain why the depressed person does not react like a normal person to the stimuli proceeding from his environment. He may sense them like any normal person, but his undercharged body and deflated spirit render him incapable of responding.

THE SUPPRESSION OF FEELING

We do not express all our impulses all the time. In the course of growing up we learn which to reveal and which to hold back. We also learn when certain impulses can be expressed and also the proper manner of their expression. The conscious holding back of an impulse is done by the voluntary muscular system of the body, which is under the control of the conscious mind or ego. It occurs at the surface of the body just before the impulse is released in action. Actually the muscles that would be involved in expression are set to act but are blocked by a command from the mind. The inhibitory command does not affect the other components of the impulse. We remain conscious of the desire, in touch with the feeling, and aware of the thought. It is only the action that is blocked.

The suppression of impulses is another matter. All components of an impulse are blocked when suppression occurs. The word "suppression" means that the impulse is pushed down under the surface of the body, below the level at which perception occurs. One is no longer conscious of the desire or in touch with the feeling. When the memory or thought of the impulse is pushed back into the unconscious, we speak of repression. Memories and thoughts are repressed, impulses and feelings are suppressed. The suppression of impulses is not a conscious or selective process like the act of holding back their expression. It is the result of the continual holding back of expression until that holding back becomes a habitual mode and an unconscious body attitude. In effect, the area of the body that would be involved in the expression of the impulse is deadened, relatively speaking, by the chronic muscular tension that develops as a consequence of the continual holding pattern. The area is effectively cut off from consciousness by the loss of normal feeling and sensation in it.

The deadening of part of the body has an effect on its overall functioning. Each area that becomes deadened reduces the vitality of the whole organism. It limits to some degree the body's natural motility, and it acts as a restriction on the function of respiration. Thus it decreases the organism's energy level and indirectly weakens all impulse formation.

In situations where the expression of an impulse would evoke a threat to a child from his environment, the child will consciously try to suppress that impulse. He can do this by decreasing his motility and limiting his breathing. By not moving and by holding one's breath one can cut off desire and feeling. In effect, in a desperate maneuver to survive, one deadens the whole body.

The suppression of feeling creates a predisposition to depression, since it prevents the individual from relying on his feelings as a guide to behavior. His emotions do not flow in sufficient strength to give him a clear direction; that is, he lacks what it takes to be an inner-directed person. He loses faith in himself and is forced to look to the outside world for guidance. He was conditioned to do this by his parents, whose love and approval he needed. As an adult he makes every effort to gain love and approval from the outside world and he does this by proving that he is worthy of the response he seeks. The effort will be a tremendous one, for the stakes are high, and the individual's total energies will be mobilized and committed to this undertaking. . . .

On the conscious level the depressed person is saying, *"I can't respond"* while proclaiming at the same time his desire to get well. In his unconscious there are deeply buried resentments which add up to an *"I won't respond."* Being unaware of these resentments, he cannot express them. On the surface he presents himself as a person who would do anything to get out of his depression. But he is like a swimmer with an anchor attached to his leg. No matter how hard he struggles to rise to the surface, the anchor drags him down. The suppressed negative feelings with their accompanying weight of guilt are like the anchor in the analogy. Release the swimmer from his anchor and he will rise naturally to the surface. Release the suppressed negative feelings in a depressed person and his depressive reaction will be over.

Are there suppressed negative feelings in every case of depression? My unequivocal answer is yes. These feelings could be demonstrated in every case I have seen. Demonstrating their existence, however, is very different from releasing them, and only their release has a positive effect on the depressive condition.

The presence of these negative feelings in a person's unconscious is responsible for the collapse of his self-esteem because they undermine the foundations of a solid self-awareness. Every depressed person has previously operated on the basis of a denial of his negativity. He has invested his energy in the attempt to prove himself worthy of love. Whatever self-esteem he built up rested on perilous foundations. The collapse was inevitable. At the same time, the energy that went into the effort to realize the illusion was diverted from the real goal of living—pleasure and satisfaction in being. The process of energy renewal which depends on pleasure was greatly weakened. In the end the person finds himself without a base to stand on and without the energy to move.

THE LACK OF ENERGY

Depression is marked by the loss of energy. This must be recognized if we are to understand and treat it. The depressed person complains of a lack of energy, and most observers agree the complaint is valid.

Everything about the patient indicates his impoverishment. All major organismic functions, those involving the whole body as opposed to single organ systems, are depressed. The quantity and extent of movement are reduced. Cinematic studies support this observation, revealing a marked decrease in body movement in the depressed as compared with the normal individual. This decrease is clearly evident in the severely depressed person who just sits most of the time, barely moving. But even in the less depressed person there is a noticeable diminution in spontaneous gestures and a visible lack of facial change. The depressed face droops and the skin seems to sag as if it lacked the energy to maintain its tone. The normal play of facial movement—eyes, mouth, brow, and so on—is absent.

This low energy level can be directly related to a decrease in his metabolism. I mentioned earlier the loss of appetite common in the depressed state. More important, however, is the decrease in oxygen intake due to marked diminution in respiratory activity. Not only is the patient's breathing restricted by his underlying neurotic or schizoid personality, but it is further diminished by the depressive reaction. The relation between depressed mood and depressed breathing is so direct and immediate that any technique which activates breathing loosens the grip of the depressive mood. It does so by actually increasing the body's energy level and by restoring some flow of bodily excitation. Generally the increased breathing will lead sooner or later to some form of emotional release, either to crying or anger. . . .

Therapeutically, it is easier and more effective to work with a patient from the physical or energetic side of the personality than from the psychic or interest side. Anyone who has lived with or treated a depressed person knows how difficult it is to activate him by arousing his interest. His resistance to taking an active interest in the world is enormous. In part this is due to a deep negative attitude of which he is unconscious and which must be uncovered and worked through for a lasting result. But in large part his resistance stems from a sense of depletion and exhaustion arising from his lack of energy. If the depressive tendency is not too strongly structured in the personality, there is often a spontaneous recovery of energy and, with it, of interest. Generally this recovery is only temporary unless the person can find ways to sustain his energy and maintain his interest. . . .

I have pointed out that the collapse ushering in the depressive reaction can be due to a disillusionment, sometimes produced by an event which shatters the person's dream. But such cases are less frequent than those in which the depressive reaction cannot be traced to a specific event, and here the energy factor is most apparent.

Martin, for instance, was referred to me because of a severe depressive reaction. He sat in his house all day unable to do any work or to respond to his surroundings. Before Martin became depressed, he was a hardworking man, a house painter by occupation. He told me that he was one of the best, that he could work ten hours a day "like a machine." Driving himself, he saved money, which he invested in real estate. As if this wasn't enough for one man, he spent nearly every evening at fraternal and church meetings, where he was intensely active. It was, consequently, quite a shock to his friends when he suddenly lost interest in all activity.

Martin could offer no reason for his collapse, and in the course of treatment I could not find the specific event that triggered it. Very likely it was something small. It only takes the slightest prick of a pin or the touch of a lighted cigarette to burst a balloon. But in view of Martin's history the specific event would not be all-important. He had maintained his intense pace for almost eighteen years. How long *could* he have gone on? A man is not a machine, which needs only a constant fuel supply to keep it operating. A man needs pleasure and a feeling of satisfaction in his life. Pleasure was alien to Martin. He knew only work. Even sex had lost its appeal long before his depression struck. Over the years he had shown progressively less interest in his wife and family. The other pleasures men seek— boating, fishing, bowling, and so on—Martin disdained.

He was a compulsive worker, not a creative one. In a culture that values productivity, Martin would pass for normal, despite the fact that during his working years his emotional life was quite depressed. When we assume that such a person is energetic, we ignore the fact that it takes more energy to be emotionally alive than to function as a machine. Whatever self-esteem Martin had prior to his depression was not a self-esteem based on being a person. If he had prided himself on his working capacity, he now faced the realization that this is not the true measure of a man.

Something was radically amiss, and I believe Martin's depression was inevitable. A pattern of self-denial began early in his life associated with a need to prove his worth through work. Despite his religious affiliation, he lacked faith, and despite his solid citizenship, he was not a grounded individual. To me the surprising thing was that he had not collapsed sooner.

I believe it a fair assumption that depression occurred when Martin, the machine, ran out of steam. He had exhausted his vital reserve in the effort to maintain an impossible image. I believe that if he had had more energy available, his depressive reaction would merely have been postponed. He was like a man who runs until he collapses from exhaustion and then lacks both the energy and the desire to get up again. And Martin looked that way.

Regardless of the catalyst to the depressive reaction, it does not occur until the person has reached a breaking point. If an individual has not arrived at that point, I don't believe he will give up his struggle to realize his illusion. Proof of this is that when the individual recovers his energy and asserts his interest in life again, it is still oriented toward the pursuit of the elusive goal. Thus just as interest is tied to a high energy level, disillusionment and loss of interest are related to a low one.

Helping a person regain his energy is a first step in the treatment of depression. Yet even when a person's normal level of energy is restored, he is not free from his tendency to depression—only from the depressive reaction itself. Whatever that "normal energy level" is, it cannot be regarded as the equivalent of health. It falls short of the requirement for healthy living and functioning. It provides enough force to power the ego drives, but it does not sustain the pleasure motivation. It can keep the upper half of the body activated, but it fails to extend into the legs and ground. It takes energy to stay up, it takes real energy or vitality or inner strength to keep one's spirits constantly up, and the person who tends to depression doesn't *have* that kind of energy.

14. *The Dark Hero*

A JUNGIAN CASE HISTORY

BY FRANCOISE O'KANE

Jungian analyst Francoise O'Kane illustrates the negative pole of the hero archetype in the form of a haunting case history. The dark hero is a sinister and desperate rebel who expresses his depression and hopelessness through destructive aggression. His masked depression surfaces as he shares his emotional reactions to the threatening power expressed in his art, offering hope of salvation.

As a child, Patrick had been the black sheep of a bourgeois family; too often, he had also played the role of scapegoat. His artistic nature, his talent for painting and writing, did not fit in with his parents' academic ambitions for their children. They spent a great deal of time and energy trying to "convert" him. But the more pressure they put on him, by comparing him to his better behaved and more successful brothers, the more Patrick defied them. Yet, underneath his bravado he felt lonely and tearful, a marginal figure in his own family. As a reaction, he gradually developed a violent hatred toward his parents and kept trying to provoke and hurt them.

Vicious circles, of course, and a case that is far more complex than this brief summary would indicate. What is clear is that Patrick never managed to develop a stable ego. His parents' disapproval, which on the surface he sneered at, had been deeply hurtful. He was a sensitive child and easily hurt. By the time he reached adolescence, he was convinced that no one could love him for who he was and that he would have to buy love by doing what others asked of him—which he refused to do.

Thus, instead of adapting to the demands of others, real or imagined, Patrick began a career in anarchy. He projected onto society as a whole his parents' "nastiness" and decided to take revenge. During the following years he was involved in a series of misdemeanors, violent demonstrations, and grandiose provocations; he spent some time in jail and later lived as a drop-out with other marginal people. At that time, he went through a very deep crisis and attempted suicide, almost succeeding. But, paradoxically, his rebellion contributed to giving him a degree of stability: "alone against all others," he felt strong and his rage carried him.

During all these years, Patrick kept painting in an autodidactic manner, finding relief in his art. He sold a first picture almost by chance and gradually gained a reputation as an artist. A gallery organized exhibitions of his work, and he made some money. His attitude toward this success was ambivalent: the fact that his art was valued by others gave him more self-confidence, but he was convinced that no one really understood his message. This message may be summarized in one sentence: "Just look and see how rotten the world is!" Patrick paints end-of-the-world landscapes, dark, desperate scenes, full of haunted, persecuted creatures. He says he wants to "shake people up," to "draw them away from their little bourgeois, blind happiness"—which he unconsciously envies.

In the course of the analysis, the depression Patrick had managed to transform into aggression slowly emerged. His dreams were a continuous series of brutal scenes, catastrophes, and deaths. The violent figures of his paintings followed and attacked the ego. The ego normally managed to defend itself, but it could never quite get rid of its attackers. Patrick's aggressiveness, which manifested among other things in a need always to dominate and control others (and brought various relationships with women to an end), was in fact an expression of a total feeling of helplessness toward the nefarious fate that seemed to keep destroying his life. It was also an expression of a deep feeling of being a victim of the "radioactivity" and the "sterility" he projected onto the world and that could attack him at any time in the shape of a disease: Patrick is a hypochondriac.

Every time he feels threatened by a situation or by a person, Patrick becomes terribly aggressive. But the aggression that he channels into his art leaves him totally helpless. The pictures are a direct cry from the unconscious, and while he is working he is totally flooded, almost in a trance; and as soon as a painting is finished, he panics. He then gets into his car and drives for hundreds of miles, without a specific aim—another way of running away from depression.

Our long analytic relationship was characterized by a progressive passage from aggression to depression: during a first phase, Patrick's despair erupted in the form of violent tirades directed at me and at the analysis. When a number of chance events precipitated a crisis by shaking his precarious balance, the sessions became the container in which he could let go and safely express his despair. He discovered that he need not panic when violent forces attacked him. He let his depression get the better of him and learned that in time a less threatening phase would come. During that period he also talked about his paintings; this gave him some distance from them, and he was better able to work actively on them.

In any case, for Patrick the analysis was aimed more at learning to cope than at working on symbolic material. He refused to talk about his dreams and was not interested in trying to discover their meaning. Simply bringing them into the *temenos* of my office seemed to somewhat depotentiate their threatening energies. The analytic process took place purely on an emotional level. By sharing with me his emotional reactions to the threatening power expressed in his drawings and deep depression, he gradually learned that he could live despite his despair. The analysis did not cure his depressions—and I don't think he expected it to—but it did help him come to terms with them.

As a result of this kind of process, another passage has taken place. Patrick has stopped running away from a fate he experienced as incredibly dark; he feels more responsible for his own destiny, for his own life. Instead of being only a victim, he has become an actor, and this allows him hope.

It was hope that impelled Patrick to find an analyst, and later to keep coming to the sessions, despite the fact that, through them, the depression he had been stubbornly avoiding was brought to the surface. The feeling that something was happening, even if not a cure in the traditional sense, led him to give up his plan of committing suicide. He says, almost with sarcasm, that his hope is nothing but an illusion, a chimera, since tomorrow will be no better than today. But he also believes that if he gave up hope, he would simply die.

At a deeper, more emotional level, Patrick's hope is genuinely alive. It was well expressed at the very beginning of our work in a dream image that became very precious to him. In the dream he was on a raft floating in between deep, black straits; there was a storm and icy rain was falling. The raft was caught in turbulence and he had trouble not being thrown into the water. But in the distance, where the river flowed, he could see a lake with a small fishing harbor on its shore.

This was the first dream with a positive tone to it that Patrick could ever remember having.

15. Sadness: The Enemy of Depression

SEEKING HAPPINESS THROUGH WHOLENESS

BY ERIC FROMM

Can we be truly happy without first knowing sadness? Can wholeheartedly embracing the inevitable sorrows of life be an antidote for depression? Existential philosopher and psychiatrist Eric Fromm explores these knotty questions in this excerpt from his book The Sane Society.

What is meant by happiness? Most people today would probably answer the question by saying that to be happy is to have "fun," or "to have a good time." The answer to the question, "What is fun?" depends somewhat on the economic situation of the individual, and more, on his education and personality structure. Economic differences, however, are not as important as they may seem. The "good time" of society's upper strata is the fun model for those not yet able to pay for it while earnestly hoping for that happy eventuality—and the "good time" of society's lower strata is increasingly a cheaper imitation of the upper strata's, differing in cost but not so much in quality.

What does this fun consist in? Going to the movies, parties, ball games, listening to the radio and watching television, taking a ride in the car on Sundays, making love, sleeping late on Sunday mornings, and traveling, for those who can afford it. If we use a more respectable term, instead of the word "fun," and "having a good time," we might say that the concept of happiness is, at best, identified with that of pleasure. We can define the concept somewhat more accurately as the pleasure of unrestricted consumption, push-button power, and laziness.

From this standpoint, happiness could be defined as the opposite of sadness or sorrow, and indeed, the average person defines happiness as a state of mind which is free from sadness or sorrow. This definition, however, shows that there is something profoundly wrong in this concept of happiness. A person who is alive and sensitive cannot fail to be sad, and to feel sorrow many times in his life. This is so, not only because of the amount of unnecessary suffering produced by the imperfection of our social arrangements but because of the nature of human existence, which makes it impossible not to react to life with a good deal of pain and sorrow. Since we are living beings, we must be sadly aware of the necessary gap between our aspirations and what can be achieved in our short and troubled life. Since death confronts us with the inevitable fact that either we shall die before our loved ones or they before us—since we see suffering, the unavoidable as well as the unnecessary and wasteful, around us every day, how can we avoid the experience of pain and sorrow? The effort to avoid it is only possible if we reduce our sensitivity, responsiveness, and love, if we harden our hearts and withdraw our attention and our feeling from others, as well as from ourselves.

If we want to define happiness by its opposite, we must define it not in contrast to *sadness* but in contrast to *depression*.

What is depression? It is the inability to feel, it is the sense of being dead, while our body is alive. It is the inability to experience joy, as well as the inability to experience sadness. A depressed person would be greatly relieved if he could feel sad. A state of depression is so unbearable because one is incapable of feeling anything, either joy or sadness. If we try to define happiness in contrast to depression, we approach Spinoza's definition of joy and happiness as that state of intensified vitality that fuses into one whole our effort both to understand our fellow men and be one with them. Happiness results from the experience of productive living, and the use of the powers of love and reason which unite us with the world. Happiness consists in our touching the rock bottom of reality, in the discovery of our self and our oneness with others as well as our difference from them. Happiness is a state of intense inner activity and the experience of the increasing vital energy which occurs in productive relatedness to the world and to ourselves.

16. Despair Work

HEALING THE SELF THROUGH HEALING THE PLANET

BY JOANNA MACY

In this far-reaching chapter from her book World as Lover, World as Self, *Joanna Macy argues that psychic pain and despair may be an appropriate reaction to our failure to recognize the world and its creatures as nothing less than extensions of ourselves. Healing flows from compassionate acceptance of the interconnectedness between our own destiny and that of future generations who will dwell in our lengthening shadow.*

We are bombarded by signals of distress—ecological destruction, social break-down, and uncontrolled nuclear proliferation. Not surprisingly, we are feeling despair—a despair well merited by the machinery of mass death that we continue to create and serve. What is surprising is the extent to which we continue to hide this despair from ourselves and each other. If this is, as Arthur Koestler suggested, an age of anxiety, it is also an age in which we are adept at sweeping our anxieties under the rug. As a society we are caught between a sense of impending apocalypse and an inability to acknowledge it.

Activists who try to arouse us to the fact that our survival is at stake decry public apathy. The cause of our apathy, however, is not mere indifference. It stems from a fear of confronting the despair that lurks subliminally beneath the tenor of life-as-usual. A dread of what is happening to our future stays on the fringes of awareness, too deep to name and too fearsome to face. Sometimes it manifests in dreams of mass destruction, and is exorcised in the morning jog and shower or in the public fantasies of disaster movies. Because of social taboos against despair and because of fear of pain, it is rarely acknowledged or expressed directly. It is kept at bay. The suppression of despair, like that of any deep recurrent response, produces a partial numbing of the psyche. Expressions of anger or terror are muted, deadened as if a nerve had been cut.

The refusal to feel takes a heavy toll. Not only is there an impoverishment of our emotional and sensory life—flowers are dimmer and less fragrant, our loves less ecstatic—but this psychic numbing also impedes our capacity to process and respond to information. The energy expended in pushing down despair is diverted from more creative uses, depleting the resilience and imagination needed for fresh visions and strategies. Furthermore, the fear of despair can erect an invisible screen, selectively filtering out anxiety-provoking data. In a world where organisms require feedback in order to adapt and survive, this is suicidal. Now, when we urgently need to measure the effects of our acts, our attention and curiosity slacken as if we are already preparing for the Big Sleep. Many of us doggedly attend to business as usual, denying both our despair and our inability to cope with it.

Despair cannot be banished by injections of optimism or sermons on "positive thinking." Like grief, it must be acknowledged and worked through. This means it must be named and validated as a healthy, normal human response to the situation we find ourselves in. Faced and experienced, its power can be used as the frozen defenses of the psyche thaw and new energies are released. Something analogous to grief work is in order. "Despair work" is different from grief work in that its aim is not acceptance of loss—indeed, the "loss" has not yet occurred and is hardly to be "accepted." But it is similar in the dynamics unleashed by the willingness to acknowledge, feel, and express inner pain. From my own work and that of others, I know that we can come to terms with apocalyptic anxieties in ways that are integrative and liberating, opening awareness not only to planetary distress, but also to the hope inherent in our own capacity to change.

INGREDIENTS OF DESPAIR

Whether or not we choose to accord them serious attention, we are barraged by data that render questionable the survival of our culture, our species, and even our planet as a viable home for conscious life. These warning signals prefigure, to those who do take them seriously, probabilities of apocalypse that are mind-boggling in scope. While varied, each scenario presents its own relentless logic. Poisoned by oil spills, sludge, and plutonium, the seas are dying; when the plankton disappear (by the year 2010 at present pollution rates, according to Jacques Yves Cousteau), we will suffocate from lack of oxygen. *Or* carbon dioxide from industrial and automotive combustion will saturate the atmosphere, creating a greenhouse effect that will melt the polar icecaps. *Or* radioactive poisoning from nuclear reactors and their wastes will accelerate plagues of cancer and genetic mutations. *Or* deforestation and desertification of the planet, now rapidly advancing, will produce giant dustbowls, and famines beyond imagining. The probability of each of these perils is amply and soberly documented by scientific studies. The list of such scenarios could continue, including use of nuclear bombs by terrorists or nation states—a prospect presenting vistas of such horror that, as former Soviet Premier Nikita Khruschev said, "The survivors will envy the dead."

Despair, in this context, is not a macabre certainty of doom or a pathological condition of depression and futility. It is not a nihilism denying meaning or efficacy to human effort. Rather, as it is being experienced by increasing numbers of people across a broad spectrum of society, despair is *the loss of the assumption that the species will inevitably pull through.* It represents a genuine accession to the possibility that this planetary experiment will end, the curtain rung down, the show over.

SYMPTOMS AND SUPPRESSIONS

In India, at a leprosarium, I met a young mother of four. Her leprosy was advanced, the doctor pointed out, because for so long she had hidden its signs. Fearing ostracism and banishment, she had covered her sores with her sari, pulled the shoulder drape around so no one would see. In a similar fashion did I later hide despair for our world, cloaking it like a shameful disease—and so, I have learned, do others. At the prospect of the extinction of a civilization, feelings of grief and horror are natural. We tend to hide them, though, from ourselves and each other. Why? The reasons, I think, are both social and psychological.

When the sensations aroused by the contemplation of a likely and avoidable end to human existence break through the censorship we tend to impose on them, they can be intense and physical. A friend who left her career to work as a full-time anti-nuclear organizer says her onslaughts of grief come as a cold, heavy weight on the chest and a sense of her body breaking. Mine, which began years ago after an all-day symposium on threats to our biosphere, were sudden and wrenching. I would be at my desk, alone in my study translating a Buddhist text, and the next moment I would find myself on the floor, curled like a fetus and shaking. In company I was more controlled; but even then, in those early months when I was unused to despair, I would be caught off guard. A line from Shakespeare or a Bach phrase would pierce me with pain as I found myself wondering how much longer it would be heard, before fading out forever in the galactic silences.

In a culture committed to the American dream, it is hard to own up to despair. This is still the land of Dale Carnegie and Norman Vincent Peale, where an unflagging optimism is taken as the means and measure of success. As commercials for products and campaigns of politicians attest, the healthy and admirable person smiles a lot. The feelings of depression, loneliness, and anxiety, to which this thinking animal has always been heir, carry here an added burden: one feels bad about feeling bad. One can even feel guilty about it. The failure to hope, in a country built and nurtured on utopian expectations, can seem downright un-American.

Despair is tenaciously resisted because it represents a loss of control, an admission of powerlessness. Our culture dodges it by demanding instant solutions when problems are raised. My political science colleagues in France ridiculed this, I recall, as an endemic trait of the American personality. "You people prescribe before you finish the diagnosis," they would say. "Let the difficulties reveal themselves first before rushing for a ready-made solution or else you will not understand them." To do this would require that one view a stressful situation without the psychic security of knowing if and how it can be solved— in other words, a readiness to suffer a little.

"Don't come to me with a problem unless you have a solution," Lyndon B. Johnson is quoted as saying during the Vietnam War. That tacit injunction, operative even in public policy-making, rings like the words my mother said to me as a child: "If you can't say something nice, don't say anything at all."

In our culture the acknowledgment of despair for the future is a kind of social taboo, and those who break it are considered "crazy," or at least "depressed and depressing." No one wants a Cassandra around or welcomes a Banquo at the feast. Nor are such roles enjoyable to play. When the prospect of our collective suicide first hit me as a serious possibility—and I know well the day and hour my defenses against this despair suddenly collapsed—I felt that there was no one to whom I could turn in my grief. If there were—and indeed there was, for I have loving, intelligent friends and family—what is there to say? Do I want them to feel this horror too? What can be said without casting a pall, or without seeming to ask for unacceptable words of comfort and cheer?

To feel despair in such a cultural setting brings a sense of isolation. The psychic dissonance can be so acute as to seem to border on madness. The distance between our inklings of apocalypse and the tenor of business as usual is so great that, though we may respect our own cognitive reading of the signs, we tend to imagine that it is we, not the society, who are insane.

Psychotherapy, by and large, has offered little help for coping with these feelings, and indeed has often compounded the problem. Many therapists have difficulty crediting the notion that concerns for the general welfare might be acute enough to cause distress. Assuming that all our drives are ego-centered, they tend to treat expressions of this distress reductionistically, as manifestations of private neurosis. In my own case, deep dismay over destruction of the wilderness was diagnosed by a counselor as fear of my own libido (which the bulldozers were taken to symbolize), and my painful preoccupation with U.S. bombings of Vietnam was interpreted as an unwholesome hangover of Puritan guilt. Such "therapy," of course, only intensifies the sense of isolation and craziness that despair can bring, while inhibiting its recognition and expression.

Some of the biggest money-makers in the film industry, as Andrée Conrad points out in *Disaster and the American Imagination*, are movies that feature cataclysmic events and violent mass death. Earthquakes, rampaging sharks and killer bees, blazing skyscrapers and doomed craft in air and sea, loaded with panicked passengers, vie in imageries of terror. Contrived with technical brilliance, these films draw large crowds and large profits. Their appeal, indeed their fascination, stems from an inchoate but pervasive sense of doom in the American public. The scenarios they present give structure and outlet to unformulated fears of apocalypse, and in so doing provide catharsis. But it is a dangerous catharsis, Conrad observes.

Hooking our anxieties onto isolated and unlikely emergencies, frequently handled with technological heroics, these entertainments give their audience, sitting safely in a comfortable theater, the illusion of having dealt with what is bothering them. On fictitious, improbable themes they air and exercise our dread, while habituating us to prospects of mass death and raising our horror threshold another notch. They blur the boundaries between fantasy and reality, making the next day's news seem like more of the same—alarms to be passively watched until the credits appear and we can stop for a beer on our way to bed.

These entertainments constitute a new version of what Geoffrey Gorer in the 1950s called our "pornography of death." He pointed out that, just as the repression of sex in our puritanically conditioned culture produces debased expressions of it, so is our repression of the reality of personal death released in fascination with sadistic violence. By analogous reasoning, disaster films can be seen as pornographies of despair. In the same way that X-rated "adult" flicks cheapen the sexual hungers they trade on, the towering infernos and devouring jaws dull and divert us from the true dimensions of our despair.

Until we get in touch with them, our powers of creative response to planetary crisis will be crippled. Until we can grieve for our planet and its future inhabitants, we cannot fully feel or enact our love for them. Such grief is frequently suppressed not only because it is socially awkward. It is also denied because it is both painful and hard to believe. At the root of both inhibitions lies a dysfunctional notion of the self. It is the notion of the self as an isolated and fragile entity. Such a self has no reason to weep for the unseen and the unborn, and such a self, if it did, might shatter with pain and futility.

So long as we see ourselves as essentially separate, competitive, and ego-identified beings, it is difficult to respect the validity of our social despair, deriving as it does from interconnectedness. Both our capacity to grieve for others and our power to cope with this grief spring from the great matrix of relationships in which we take our being. We are, as open systems, sustained by flows of energy and information that extend beyond the reach of conscious ego.

VALIDATING DESPAIR

You can hold yourself back from the suffering of the world: this is something you are free to do, . . . but perhaps precisely this holding back is the only suffering you might be able to avoid.

—FRANZ KAFKA

The first step in despair work is to disabuse ourselves of the notion that grief for our world is morbid. To experience anguish and anxiety in the face of the perils that threaten us is a healthy reaction. Far from being crazy, this pain is a testimony to the unity of life, the deep interconnections that relate us to all beings.

Such pain for the world becomes masochistic only when we assume personal guilt for its plight or personal responsibility for its solution. No individual is that powerful. Certainly by participation in society each shares in collective accountability, but the acknowledgment of despair, like faith, is a letting go of the manipulative assumption that conscious ego can or should control all events. Each of us is but one little nexus in a vast web. As the recognition of that interdependence breaches our sense of isolation, so does it also free our despair of self-loathing.

Our religious heritages can also serve to validate despair and attest to the creative role of this kind of distress. The biblical concept of the suffering servant, as well as an array of *Old Testament* prophets, speaks to the power inherent in opening ourselves to the griefs of others. In Christianity the paramount symbol of such power is the cross. The cross where Jesus died teaches us that it is precisely through openness to the pain of our world that redemption and renewal are found.

The heroes and heroines of the Mahayana Buddhist tradition are the bodhisattvas, who vow to forswear nirvana until all beings are enlightened. As the *Lotus Sutra* tells us, their compassion endows them with supranormal senses: they can hear the music of the spheres and understand the language of the birds. By the same token, they hear as well all cries of distress, even to the moaning of beings in the lowest hells. All griefs are registered and owned in the bodhisattva's deep knowledge that we are not separate from each other.

POSITIVE DISINTEGRATION

The process of internalizing the possibility of planetary demise is bound to bring some psychic disarray. How to confront what we scarcely dare to think? How to think it without going to pieces?

It is helpful in despair work to realize that going to pieces or falling apart is not such a bad thing. Indeed it is as essential to evolutionary and psychic transformations as the cracking of outgrown shells. Polish psychiatrist Kazimierz Dabrowski calls it "positive disintegration." It is operative in every global development of humanity, especially during periods of accelerated change, and, he argues, permits the emergence of "higher psychic structures and awareness." For the individual who, in confronting current anomalies of experience, allows positive disintegration to happen, it can bring a dark night of the soul, a time of spiritual void and turbulence. But the anxieties and doubts are, Dabrowski maintains, "essentially healthy and creative." They are creative not only for the person but for society, because they permit new and original approaches to reality.

What "disintegrates" in periods of rapid transformation is not the self, of course, but its defenses and ideas. We are not objects that can break. As open systems, we are, cyberneticist Norbert Wiener said, "but whirlpools in a river of everflowing water. We are not stuff that abides, but patterns that perpetuate themselves." We do not need to protect ourselves from change, for our very nature is change. Defensive self-protection, restricting vision and movement like a suit of armor, makes it harder to adapt. It not only reduces flexibility but blocks the flow of information we need to survive. Our "going to pieces," however uncomfortable a process, can open us up to new perceptions, new data, new responses.

ALLOWING OURSELVES TO FEEL

The second requirement in despair work is to permit ourselves to feel. Within us are deep responses to what is happening to our world, responses of fear and sorrow and anger. Given the flows of information circling our globe, they inhere in us already by virtue of our nature as open systems, interdependent with the rest of life. We need only to open our consciousness to these profound apprehensions. We cannot experience them without pain, but it is a healthy pain—like the kind we feel when we walk on a leg that has gone asleep and the circulation starts to move again. It gives evidence that the tissue is still alive.

As with a cramped limb, exercises can help. I have found meditational exercises useful, particularly ones from the Buddhist tradition. Practices designed to increase the capacity for loving-kindness and compassion, for example, are effective in getting us in touch with those concerns in us that extend beyond ego.

In one workshop I led, entitled "Being Bodhisattvas," we did a meditation on compassion, adapted from a Tibetan *bodhicitta* practice. It involved giving oneself permission to experience the sufferings of others (in as concrete a fashion as possible), and then taking these sufferings in with the breath, visualizing them as dark granules in the stream of air drawn in with each inhalation, into and through the heart, and out again.

Afterwards one participant, Marianna, described her experience in this meditation. She had been resistant, and her resistance had localized as a pain in her back. In encouraging the participants to open themselves to their inner awareness of the sufferings of others, I primed the pump with some brief verbal cues, mentioned our fellow beings in hospitals and prisons, mentioned a mother with dried breasts holding a hungry infant . . . That awoke in Marianna an episode she had buried. Three years earlier she had listened to a recording by Harry Chapin with a song about a starving child; she had, as she put it, "trouble" with it. She put away the record never to play it again, and the "trouble" remained undigested. With her recollection of her experience with the song, the pain in her back moved into her chest. It intensified and hardened, piercing her heart. It seemed for a moment excruciating, but as she continued the exercise, accepting and breathing in the pain, it suddenly, inexplicably, felt right, felt even good. It turned into a golden cone or funnel, aimed point downwards into the depths of her heart. Through it poured the despair she had refused, griefs reconnecting her with the rest of humanity.

Marianna emerged from this with a sense of release and belonging. She felt empowered, she said, not to *do* so much as to *be*—open, attentive, poised for action. She also said that she believed she permitted this to happen because I had not asked her to "do" something about the griefs of others, or to come up with any answers, but simply to experience them.

What good does it do to let go and allow ourselves to *feel* the pain of our planet's people? For all the discomfort, there is healing in such openness, for ourselves and for our world. To accept the collective pain reconnects us with our fellow beings and our deep collective energies.

ALLOWING IMAGES TO ARISE

To acknowledge our pain for the world and tap its energy, we need symbols and images for its expression. Images, more than arguments, tap the springs of consciousness, the creative powers by which we make meaning of experience. In the challenge to survival that we face now, a strong imagination is especially necessary because existing verbal constructs seem inadequate to what many of us are sensing.

At a week-long meeting of college teachers and administrators, I chaired a working group on issues of planetary survival, and began to explore ways we could share our concerns on an affective as well as cognitive level. I asked the participants to offer, as they introduced themselves, a personal experience or image of how in the past year the global crisis had impinged on their consciousness. Those brief introductions were potent. Some offered a vignette from work on world hunger or arms. A young physicist simply said, very quietly, "My child was born." A social worker recalled a day her small daughter talked about growing up and having babies; with dull shock she encountered her own doubt that the world would last that long. Some offered images: fish kill washed up at a summer cottage, strip mines leaching like open wounds. Most encompassing in its simplicity was John's image: the view from space of planet Earth, so small as it glittered there that it could be covered by the astronaut's raised thumb. That vision of our home, so finite it can be blotted out by a single human gesture, functioned as a symbol in our week's work. It helped us cut through the verbiage of reports and the temptations of academic one-upmanship to the raw nerve in us all—desperate concern.

In the sharing of despair that our imagery had permitted, energy was released. As pent-up feelings were expressed and compared, there came laughter, solidarity, and resurgence of commitment to our common human project.

In that same working group on planetary survival, John showed slides of a trek up Mount Katahdin with some of his Yale students. On a ridge between two peaks was a narrow, knife-edge trail they had to cross. It was scary and dangerous because fog had rolled up, blanketing out the destination and everything but the foot-wide path itself. That picture of the trail, cutting through the clouds into the unknown became a strong symbol for us, expressing the existential situation in which we find ourselves, and helping us proceed with dogged patience, even though we cannot see more than a step at a time.

Recognizing the creative powers of imagery, many call us today to come up with visions of a benign future—visions which can beckon and inspire. Images of hope are potent, necessary: they shape our goals and give us impetus for reaching them. Often they are invoked too soon, however. Like the demand for instant solutions, such expectations can stultify—providing us with an escape from the despair we may feel, while burdening us with the task of aridly designing a new Eden. Genuine visioning happens from the roots up, and these roots for many are shrivelled by unacknowledged despair. Many of us are in an in-between time, groping in the dark with shattered beliefs and faltering hopes, and we need images for that in-between time if we are to work through it.

The first despair work I can recognize as such occurred on a spring weekend toward the end of our military actions in Vietnam. Although I had been active in anti-war protests, I felt sapped that day by a deep sense of futility. To give form to feeling, and tired of words, I worked with clay. As I descended into the sorrow within me, I shaped that descent in the block of clay—cliffs and escarpments plunging into abysses, dropping off into downward-twisting gullies, down, down. Though I wept as I pushed at the clay with fingers and fists, it felt good to have my sense of hopelessness become palpable, visible. The twisted, plummeting clay landscape was like a silent scream, and also like a dare accepted in bitter defiance, the dare to descend into nothingness.

Feeling spent and empty, the work done, my mind turned to go but then noted what my fingers had, of themselves, begun to explore. Snaking and pushing up the clay cliffs were roots. As they came in focus, I saw how they joined, tough and tenacious, feeding each other in an upsurge of ascent. The very journey downward into my despair had shaped these roots, which now thrust upward, unbidden and resilient. For long moments I traced them, wonderingly, with eyes and fingers.

Quaker-style meetings, where a group sits and shares out of open silence, can let images appear and interact. In one I remember Humpty-Dumpty was evoked. Poor old Humpty-Dumpty, falling and breaking and all the king's men cannot put him together again. So it is with our outmoded paradigms, our egos and self-concepts: it felt good to give imaginative form to the sense of fragmentation in our time. As we ruminated on that, a voice among us slowly spoke, adding what she saw: from the shattered shell, a bird rose into the air. Eggshells break to reveal new life, I had forgotten that. The very imagery that expressed our pain pointed to the possibility of hope.

Sometimes it takes a while, in the slow alchemy of the soul, for hope to signal, and longer for it to take form in concrete plans and projects. That is all right.

I said to my soul, be still, and wait
without hope,
For hope would be hope of the
wrong thing.

—T.S. ELIOT

WAITING

So we wait; even in our work, we wait. Only out of that open expectancy can images and visions arise that strike deep enough to summon our faith in them. "The ability to wait," wrote William Lynch, "is central to hope."

Waiting does not mean inaction, but staying in touch with our pain and confusion *as* we act, not banishing them to grab for sedatives, ideologies, or final solutions. It is, as a student of mine quoted, "staying in the dark until the darkness becomes full and clear." The butterfly, I am told, eats its way out of the cocoon. In despair, if we digest it, is authenticity and energy to fuel our dreams.

In my own feelings of despair, I was haunted by the question, "What do you substitute for hope?" I had always assumed that a sanguine confidence in the future was as essential as oxygen. Without it, I had thought, one would collapse into apathy and nihilism. It puzzled me that, when I owned my despair, the hours I spent working for peace and environmental causes did not lessen but rather increased.

One day I talked with Jim Douglass, the theologian and writer who had left his university post to resist nuclear weapons. Jailed repeatedly for civil disobedience in this effort, he was leading the citizens' campaign against the Trident submarine base. He had said he believed we had five years left before it was too late— too late to avert the use of our nuclear arsenal in a first strike strategy. I reflected on the implications of that remark and watched his face, as he squinted in the sun with an air of presence and serenity I could not fathom. "What do you substitute for hope?" I asked. He looked at me and smiled. "Possibilities," he said. "Possibilities . . . you can't predict, just make space for them. There are so many." That, too, is waiting, active waiting—moving out on the fog-bound trail, though you cannot see the way ahead.

COMMUNITY

Despair work is not a solo venture, no matter how alone one may feel. It is a process undertaken within the context of community, even if a community of like-minded others is not physically present. Just knowing that one's feelings are shared gives a measure of validation and support.

Many kinds of community can provide the environment for the kind of sharing that despair work involves. The necessary openness and trust can be found in groups devoted to personal or spiritual growth, and also in groups organized for social action. The "affinity groups" that have emerged in the peace and safe-energy movements, and that are based on strategies of nonviolence, set a high priority on mutual support.

My son had a dream one night about the affinity group he belonged to in the anti-nuclear movement in New England. It conveys something of the sense of strength generated in such community. In the dream he and his affinity group are standing together looking out over a darkened city. All is black and cold. Through their linked hands he feels the current of the group's energy. They chant and the current grows stronger; lights begin to appear and soon the city is aglow, empowered by the energy of their trust and commitment. That, in and of itself, seems a fulfillment.

When we face the darkness of our time, openly and together, we tap deep reserves of strength within us. Many of us fear that confrontation with despair will bring loneliness and isolation, but—on the contrary—in the letting go of old defenses, truer community is found. In the synergy of sharing comes power. In community, we can find our power and learn to trust our inner responses to our world.

PART THREE

Embracing Depression

17. Chaos Theory and Depression

DISINTEGRATING INTO A NEW LIFE

BY ANDREA NELSON, PSY.D.

This sophisticated original article brings Chaos theory down from the lofty heights of theoretical mathematics into the practical sphere of everyday psychology. The author shows how personal growth and transformation in depressed people is related to universal principles underlying the mysterious ways that order arises from Chaos.

Passionate advocates of Chaos theory herald it as the third great scientific revolution of the twentieth century, following relativity theory and quantum mechanics. The essence of Chaos theory is that a hidden order underlies chaos. The new tools of Chaos mathematics reveal patterns of order deeply embedded in the tempest seething around us. It rekindles an ancient idea of creative tension between order and chaos that dates to early Greek philosophers and to diverse creation myths that invoke a primordial state of chaos from which all things spring forth.

The Greek roots of the word *chaos* convey a sense of an empty space or abyss—a formlessness that contains the seeds of creativity. This transformative quality is lost in our modern usage where chaos has come to mean confusion, disorder, randomness, a complete lack of structure and organization, and even anarchy. Order, on the other hand, conveys a feeling of comfort and security—a sense that we are in control of a meaningful system. Chaos theory has reinfused creativity into our understanding of chaos.

Chaos theory focuses on the dynamics of the system as a whole, on what the parts are doing *all together*, rather than individually. It challenges us to see the universe as a spontaneous, flowing, whole process, an interconnecting web of relationships. Such a world view discourages us from seeing depression as an isolated, totally undesirable symptom to be alleviated as soon as possible. Instead we are compelled to wonder how depression fits into the overall process of change. In the human psyche, tempestuous emotional states generate a creative tension between chaos and order that is vital to the richly complex process of human psychological growth.

A multitude of life events, such as loss, illness, transitions, and conflicts within and between human beings, can disturb and destabilize our lives. We may be stricken with paralyzing anxiety and struggle to avoid the dread associated with chaos. However, chaos resisted does not disappear; it may manifest as depression or other psychological symptoms.

When we accept the transformative potential of chaos, we often find that our original difficulties were caused by our clinging inflexibly to our habitual way of ordering our world. We seek security in order, but often such a prevailing order is intolerant of new input and rejects chaos that threatens to bring disorder to our psyche. When we protect ourselves from chaos we cut ourselves off from the flow of life. Eventually this may precipitate depression. Learning to face chaos is an integral step on the way to transforming depression into a new, more adaptive order.[1]

Depression is like a prison we create for ourselves by clinging to an inflexible sense of order that evolves as a defense against chaos. In exchange for a false feeling of security and control, we sacrifice our potential for growth, our freedom, and our range of options. Yet, despite our fear, we are fascinated with the formlessness of chaos and its unknown and unpredictable possibilities. Order without chaos is lifeless.

If, during the emotional crisis of depression, a person either consciously enters or is cast into the creative abyss of chaos, her old emotional patterns and habits break down. By facing uncomfortable feelings engendered by such fertile disorder, she creates fresh emotional patterns that are more complex and appropriate to her new circumstances. She encounters previously unconscious material in the melancholic abyss and, by bringing it into consciousness, integrates it into a new order of the psyche.

PRIGOGINE'S THEORY OF DISSIPATIVE STRUCTURES

To grasp how Chaos theory can help us understand the growth potential of depression, we must first review a few basic principles of this expanding discipline. Under the broad umbrella of Chaos theory, we find Ilya Prigogine's theory of dissipative structures for which he was awarded the 1977 Nobel prize in chemistry.[2] Although his theory describes how order arises out of chaos at a simple chemical level, his principles have wide application across many disciplines, including psychology.

Prigogine questions whether change, whereby things take form and dissolve, is imposed from the outside on inert matter, or whether change comes from within, the result of intrinsic and independent activity of matter. Prigogine proposes a new sense of order that intrinsically transforms chaos. Order does not need to be imposed externally, by God, society, science, or therapists. Order emerges internally. When disorder, or chaos, increases in a given system—whether it be biological, chemical, social, or psychological—*spontaneous* self-reorganizations to higher levels of organization can occur.

These questions are important to a psychotherapist because they profoundly influence her view of the role that depression, turmoil, and chaos play in psychological growth. Prigogine's research strongly supports the answer that growth, or becoming, is inherent in matter. He views matter not as the passive substance described in the mechanistic world view but as being associated with spontaneous activity. If order arises spontaneously out of chaos, even at the level of simple chemical reactions, how true this must be at the complex level of human consciousness. Chaos plays a critical role in transformation: "most of reality, instead of being orderly, stable, and equilibrial, is seething and bubbling with change, disorder, and process."[3]

FAR-FROM-EQUILIBRIUM CONDITIONS

Prigogine discovered a radical new property of matter: the capacity for self-organization, through which order arises "spontaneously" out of chaos. Dissipative structures—Prigogine's term for open systems—form in high-energy environments that are described as being far-from-equilibrium or chaotic. For example, a vortex forms in a fast-flowing, turbulent river, not a placidly trickling stream. Similarly, a new-born infant requires an optimally stimulating environment to thrive.

Assuming that a similar, although more complex, process operates at the psychological level implies that as open systems, human beings maintain a stable life process and a coherent state of consciousness by continuously generating and capturing energy and information through their interaction with their physical and social worlds. The human self-system has inherent self-organizing properties by which the self shapes its own development by actively exchanging energy and dissipating energy/information with the environment. Increasingly complex structures of consciousness emerge from this interaction. A self-system changes when fluctuations of energy—for example, the chaos of an emotional crisis—

disrupt an existing psychological structure so that its elements contact each other in new ways and make new connections. Given optimal conditions, the self-system reorganizes this structure into a new whole.

A psychological dissipative structure, such as the self-system, maintains its identity by remaining continually open to the flux and flow of energy with its environment, including dissipating wasted energy or entropy; for example, through fluctuations of mood. The stability and continued existence of the self depends on this continued exchange of energy, which occurs through activities like talking with a friend, reading a newspaper, fighting with a neighbor, painting a picture, acting in a play, communing with nature, or debating an issue. Moods that fluctuate in response to environmental conditions may dissipate emotional energy which, in turn, helps the self remain stable and flexible.

Mood fluctuations that are responsive to the environment facilitate exchanges of energy between the self-system and the environment. Dynamically chaotic mood fluctuations may efficiently dissipate the effects of the environment and facilitate the most effective organism/environment interaction. For example, a person feels immediately angry in response to being insulted at a social gathering and reacts assertively to handle the situation. Her mood is flexible and responsive to her environment. She dissipates her anger directly through her assertive behavior. On the other hand, another individual's mood is not flexibly responsive to her environment. She does not immediately feel any anger and takes no action. However, later in the evening she continues to brood over the insult, repeatedly berates herself for not defending herself, and becomes depressed.

Chronically depressed individuals lack a healthy chaotic and responsive quality in their moods, which instead are limited to repetitive cycles of restricted, negative affect. Their emotional life is stagnant, they feel hopeless and helpless, and they are unable to envision a better future.

A depressed person functions more like a closed system than an open system and does not take in fresh energy from the environment. As an individual becomes depressed, she typically withdraws, drastically reducing her contact with the environment. She has no energy or motivation to get out of bed in the morning. She may not even watch television or read a book. She feels mentally shut down and may continuously ruminate over the same foreboding thoughts. This further reduces her energy exchange with the environment so that fresh energy is not taken in, and wasted energy, or entropy, is not dissipated back into the environment. Instead, entropy accumulates in the depressed self and further drains it of energy. William Styron, writing about his own depression, describes this well: "The madness of depression is . . . a storm of murk. Soon evident are the slowed-down responses, near paralysis, psychic energy throttled back close to zero. Ultimately, the body is affected and feels sapped, drained."[4]

If an individual's self-system is sensitive, flexible, and open to influences from the world around her and from her inner emotional life, she will adapt to new circumstances by spontaneously evolving a new optimal order. However, the less open an individual's self-system, the more rigid will be her way of ordering her view of the world. Her self-image will be narrow, and she will not integrate unacceptable emotions and rejected aspects of her personality into her self-system. A depressed person's world is static, maladaptive, and closed. She may be so withdrawn and isolated from life that she rarely experiences chaos because she is defended against it. She drains herself of energy through her desperate efforts to avoid and reject experiences of chaos. By rejecting the realities of human existence and withdrawing emotionally, she restricts the full development of her personality. Such a person is limited in her awareness of what is happening both inside and outside herself. She is less in touch with her needs and desires and, therefore, less able to satisfy them. These conditions perpetuate depression.

A depressed person has drastically reduced her energy exchange with her environment and experiences minimal spontaneous internal fluctuations of energy. Life events, such as a suicide attempt, a natural catastrophe, falling in love, childbirth, or psychotherapy, can create an intense fluctuation of energy that perturbs the self-system to a critical point where the emotional upheaval can not be dampened by the system through negative feedback, but instead triggers a transformation in the system. Existential psychologist Irvin Yalom describes a confrontation with one's own death as "an event, an urgent experience, that propels one into a confrontation with one's existential 'situation' in the world" and "acts as a catalyst that can move one from one state of being to a higher one."[5]

A state of depression contains within it the potential for growth. When a depressed person is confronted with the turmoil of a life crisis, she is, willingly or unwillingly, immersed in the far-from-equilibrium conditions that are ripe for a spontaneous shift to a higher level of integration. While she is destabilized psychologically and emotionally, a bifurcation point is reached in which her rigid way of ordering her world is shaken. Irresistible chaos erupts, and she may feel anchorless, panicky, or overwhelmed. If she is able to flow with these feelings and confront the chaos, she may evolve a more flexible and adaptive way of ordering her world. Accepting chaos is enlivening and is the first step to naming its parts and understanding how it works.

When depression erupts as a symptom, it draws our attention to aspects of ourselves that we have ignored because they are unacceptable or too painful. When we face the chaos of these emotions, we pass through a stage in our evolution toward a self-system with its own unique order, and we leave behind an outmoded, more constrained sense of self. As a person actualizes her unique self-system, her way of ordering the world becomes dynamic, flexible, and adaptive. She stands on a foundation that is broader and more stable. This ordering strengthens her sense of self.

As an open system, a person is linked with her environment in a multitude of complex and interconnected ways. Each transformation to a higher level of organization and complexity creates more points of contact both within a person and between her and the environment. As an individual's sense of self becomes more complexly organized, she has access to wider and deeper ranges of environments from which to draw energy and into which to dissipate wasted energy or entropy. There is a greater flow of energy through the system. She is more engaged in the world and more aware of her inner experiences; therefore, she is more open to perturbations that destabilize her self-system and trigger further growth.

Transformation expands boundaries that constrain our behavior and our ways of defining ourselves as we break out of old restricting attitudes and qualities. We may experience a transformative experience as a loss of security or equilibrium and a venture into the unknown that can be frightening if not understood. Growth is frequently a struggle as we let go of old patterns and viewpoints before risking a new way of being in the world. A person may fight against, rather than nurture change. Unfortunately, this turmoil and struggle is sometimes misunderstood as psychopathology instead of a harbinger of transformation.

A Therapy Example

Brian felt anxious, guilty, and consumed with self-blame when a significant love relationship ended. He initially coped with his feelings by frenetic activity at work. However, one day his boss yelled at him unfairly, which cast him into a deep depression and was the last straw that finally propelled him into therapy. He soon discovered in therapy that his recent loss rekindled feelings of shame, inadequacy, and a distorted, negative self-image that began in early childhood when he was severely abused. His current crisis involved an influx of intense emotional energy that catapulted Brian into a chaotic state—fertile ground for transformation.

Brian's depression and inner turmoil were positive signs that his old pattern of psychological organization was breaking down. He had been trapped in an established order and never questioned his negative view of himself. Psychotherapy involved helping Brian accept, face, and eventually understand the chaos of his emotional crisis. Therapy supported conditions that challenged his restricted and static sense of self in a way that was difficult for him to reject. This fresh input triggered an expansion of his sense of self, and he began to see the world and himself differently. However, he often felt anchorless and unable to connect with his habitual patterns of coping. He was frightened by this at times but was also encouraged to trust that this chaos could open new possibilities. As he began to integrate a more complexly organized and healthy self-image, he felt less damaged, and his sensitivity to criticism and rejection diminished. He felt less anxious and guilty, and he was able to initiate more meaningful relationships in his personal life and at work.

Therapy for depression is a flow between optimal states of chaos and order. By first accepting chaos, we can then work to discern previously hidden patterns in this chaos. In Brian's case, he was able to see how his early experiences of abuse had distorted and restricted his view of himself and his world. His self-image was static, maladaptive, and unquestioned until the chaotic crisis of the breakup of his relationship propelled him into therapy. By understanding the causes of the chaos and its meaning in his life, he brought new order out of his chaos.

CHAOS THEORY'S IMPLICATIONS FOR PSYCHOTHERAPY

We usually label a state of mind psychopathological because it is maladaptive for an individual in society and/or because it causes painful symptoms like depression. Traditionally, we have viewed depression negatively as something to be alleviated as soon as possible, and equate clinical improvement with its reduction. Frequently we combat depression with medication and/or by techniques like cognitive restructuring.

In contrast, if we think in terms of a chaos model of psychological growth, we view symptoms positively as indicators of far-from-equilibrium states that foreshadow transformative change. Their intensity may indicate profound healing. Depression is seen as less of a problem when it provokes us to look more deeply into ourselves. When we merely suppress symptoms, we dampen energy fluctuations in the self-system and stabilize it at a lower level of functioning, thereby destroying the conditions necessary for transformation to a higher level of functioning. The chaos view of depression fosters healing by supporting an individual's turmoil. A therapist who appreciates the transformative power of chaos understands that healing and a new more integrated and expanded self-system can emerge from a crisis.

This view of depression also calls forth an affirming attitude from the therapist who would not label clients as avoiding, denying, or resisting unconscious and repressed parts of themselves, but as behaving consistently with how they have come to organize their experiences in the world. A person responds to and perceives her environment according to her inner structure and level of organization, and a therapist's primary responsibility is to obtain as clear an idea of her client's inner structure as possible.

Effective therapists use empathic attunement to enter the subjective world of the client to understand how she organizes her experiences. A client is usually not aware of how she constitutes her reality, but by exploring her inner world with her, a therapist gradually increases her awareness. Furthermore, a client entering therapy is frequently closed to fresh sources of external energy and locked into a rigid and limited way of organizing the world. Through a variety of interventions—reframing, education, interpretations, confrontations, and clarifications—a therapist can provide external energy that triggers far-from-equilibrium fluxes of psychic energy in the client. By adding new input, these interventions destabilize the client's habitual ways of thinking and may lead to a spontaneous reorganization of her self at a new and more adaptive level.

CONCLUSION

As therapists, we must also face the dark abyss of our own chaos. When we confront the stormy and irrational powers at the depth of our being we may then transform them into something meaningful and begin to accept these powers in others. We may measure our psychotherapeutic efficacy by how deeply we enter into chaos with a client. Our task involves supporting the client's descent into the creative abyss of chaos as well as ensuring conditions conducive to the timely integration of new insights and ways of being.

Modern science often confirms ancient wisdom. Plato valued "ritualized madness, where chaotic and seemingly insane experiences and behavior lead to deeper levels of order." Similarly, if we value the chaos underlying depression, we may creatively unfold deeper, richer realms of our psyche.

18. Transpersonal Psychology and Depression

BY JOHN E. NELSON, M.D.

As we broaden our focus to include the bodies, minds, and spirits of depressed people, we must not neglect those same essential aspects of therapists who work with them. Through a unique perspective that blends the rational and intuitive, transpersonal psychology offers techniques for transforming the healer's sacred wounds into a regeneration in spirit for both therapist and patient.

Physician, heal thyself.

—LUKE 4:23

Transpersonal psychology is a vital, thirty-year-old international movement that is leading the way toward reintegrating spirit—the essence of consciousness and selfhood—into modern healing practices. Its success in challenging the powerful resistances of entrenched materialism and religious dogmatism speaks for the hunger in Western societies to return psychology to its ancient roots as a *logos* of the *psyche*, a path to knowing the soul.

When I accepted the task of editing an anthology on depression that includes a transpersonal perspective, I expected to find a wealth of thoughtful articles generated by the sensitive and creatively articulate people who lead the transpersonal movement. As the project nears its completion, however, I am left to speculate why this most common of psychiatric diagnoses receives so *little* attention from a discipline whose techniques aim to foster compassion and deep healing of the psyche. Although speakers at transpersonal meetings inveigh against doctors who do no more than push pills at depressed people, they seldom offer alternatives that are more likely to reduce suffering or redirect deeply depressed individuals toward a path of spiritual growth.

Yet the transpersonal approach to healing would seem to be ideally suited as a method of training therapists who are uncommonly sensitive to the pain of depression, which might be envisioned as a spiritual crisis that alienates one from his deepest spiritual roots. What sets transpersonal psychology apart from orthodox psychiatry and psychology is its focus on the higher aspirations of humankind, our common desire to seek unity with a common, everyday, divine presence. Its founders' intuitions about the unrealized potentials of humankind naturally drew them to place the "perennial philosophy" at the core of their discipline.

The perennial philosophy, first articulated by the German philosopher Leibnitz, was brought into modern times by novelist Aldous Huxley, who described it as:

> ...a metaphysic that recognizes a divine Reality [within] the world of things and lives and minds; the psychology that finds in the soul something similar to, or even identical with, divine Reality; the ethic that places man's final end in the knowledge of the immanent and transcendent Ground of all being...[1]

Guided by such an ideal, the transpersonal movement naturally indulged its passion for exploring the higher reaches of human experience by researching ways to expand consciousness through Gnostic contemplative techniques, esoteric Yoga and Buddhist practices, shamanic journeys, and breath-control methods designed to remove early-life impediments to self-realization. These methods move an individual beyond the constraints of ordinary ego-based consciousness toward a grander perspective that gradually reveals the subtler meanings of life to those willing to practice them with discipline.

The overriding aim of these transpersonal techniques is essentially fourfold: (1) To open the compassionate heart to recognize one's own authentic self, which leads to empathic acceptance of the uniqueness, yet common spirit, of others; (2) To foster creativity by gaining access to recurring archetypal myths that guide humanity to greater wisdom; (3) To open the intuitive "inner eye" that lifts an individual beyond the constraints of his ordinary senses, opening the visionary capacity latent in us all; (4) To expand consciousness to the point that an individual directly experiences identity with a universal divine Presence. Those familiar with esoteric Eastern philosophy may note that these steps correspond with the four higher chakras of Tantric yoga, which I have discussed in previous works.[2]

Because a depressed person seems to be moving in the opposite direction from the aspirations of transpersonal psychologists who may treat him, some may conclude that he is beyond reach of methods that require commitment to a spiritual path. A deeply depressed individual loses touch with his spiritual roots, with a corresponding devitalization of his inner world. He becomes so wrapped up in his personal distress that he is no longer capable of feeling love for himself, much less others. It is a daunting task to foster creativity in a person who lacks energy to get out of bed, who joylessly and inattentively watches TV from morning to night. Cultivating intuition or awareness of one's essential divinity seems impossibly abstract and irrelevant to a person who is so fixated on a hopelessly lost relationship or career goal that he cannot read the morning paper.

Yet if consciousness-oriented practitioners wish to remain relevant as healers and true to their goal of fostering spiritual growth, they must broaden their range of therapeutic approaches to include persons who have lost their connection to spirit. This may mean temporarily directing therapy towards egoic or pre-egoic levels. For severely depressed persons, a truly holistic healer will forfeit his aversion to biological treatments and work hand in hand with an enlightened physician who may search for hormonal factors or prescribe antidepressant medications to restore balance to brain metabolism. For persons with less severe depressions, an *artful* healer will search for ego-based impediments to growth that lead to arrested development, to personal stagnation so characteristic of the depressed psyche.

Here is where the idea of "spiritual growth" can benefit from closer inspection. As transpersonal philosopher Ken Wilber points out, we are fundamentally constructed of spirit. Spirit is not something we can attain to, but something we *are:*

> ... the Absolute is both the highest state of being and the ground of all being; it is both the goal of evolution and the ground of evolution; the highest stage of development and the reality or suchness of *all* stages of development; the highest of all conditions and the Condition of all conditions; the highest rung in the ladder *and* the wood out of which the ladder is made.[3]

Growth in spirit, then, can occur at any stage of life as we expand awareness of self, others, and the world. It is just as growth-producing to teach a small child or severely regressed schizophrenic how to brush his teeth or tie his shoelaces as it is to enhance intuition in an accomplished artist. There is just as much upward movement when we help a person lost in a solitary fantasy world to regain touch with consensual reality as there is in uncovering latent creativity in a healthy, loving mother. The important point is that a healer's therapeutic response must be tailored to the specific level of his patient's consciousness rather than to his own preconceptions of what it means to advance on a spiritual path.

This is not to say that we should forfeit our noble ambition to lead those who come to us for help beyond ego-based modes of attachment and aversion that so often lead to depression. It is just that we may have to deal with lower-level considerations first. This not only includes focusing on ego-based attachments to other people, ambitions, or objects, but even manipulating neurotransmitters that regulate brain function. When we do so, we do not reduce consciousness to mere physical activity; we simply affirm that matter and spirit are intertwined, and this fusion is especially apparent in that form of matter known as the brain.

As is made clear in other chapters of this anthology, some forms of depression are primary brain diseases, at least partially genetically driven. It is important to discern these from milder depressions that usually follow from a perceived loss, or those that are personality based. Biologically driven depressions are likely to recur in cycles, sometimes alternating with manic episodes, and be accompanied by "vegetative" signs like early-morning awakening, slowing of thinking and responses, and a pervasive loss of energy and vitality. Mood swings tend to come and go with their own rhythm, not necessarily triggered by negative life events, or perhaps brought on by a disappointment that the person would usually shake off.

Although modern, enlightened treatment of such major depression should include medication, such persons also desperately need spiritually-sensitive counseling to help them maintain their life perspective as they reconstruct a sense of meaning and purpose for their existence. An attuned therapist can motivate them to avoid self-destructive acts by encouraging empathic reflection of the effects that their suicide might have on others who care about them. It may be of benefit to remind that person of his past accomplishments that helped others and of the tragic loss of his unique capabilities for helping people in the future. Transpersonal training uniquely prepares a therapist for such "heart-work."

When working with a person with major depression, an artful therapist will focus on revivifying his forsaken goals. Even the best of modern antidepressant medications may take weeks to ply their effects, during which time a person feels cut off from his long-term ambitions for education, career advancement, or personal growth. Along with this is a feeling of alienation from others, even those who are truly concerned and committed to them. Here is where the nondemanding structure of an I-Thou therapeutic relationship can help overcome their desire to withdraw and maintain a necessary connection to others.

In treating milder depression—the kind that follows loss of a romantic relationship, a career goal, or health—a transpersonally trained therapist is again in an ideal position to help. From study of Eastern psychology, he knows that this kind of suffering naturally and inevitably follows from *desire*, from attachment to specific outcomes, from an inability to surrender to the natural flow of change intrinsic to all worldly existence. Helping a patient let go of his maladaptive attachments and cultivate equanimity is a dynamic, mutual learning process between therapist and patient, as the therapist inescapably confronts his own attachments that he projects upon the depressed patient. The Buddha never taught that overcoming desire is easy, only that it is *possible*.

BECOMING A TRANSPERSONAL HEALER

One of the great insights of transpersonal psychology and the perennial philosophy is that sentient beings share a common Ground of being, within which energy and information constantly resonate from mind to mind, usually beneath the threshold of ordinary awareness. In medical school, I was taught by learned scientists how modern medicines and surgical techniques heal disease in the body and mind. Later, during my specialty training in psychiatry, I learned how a caring relationship heals a wounded self through sincere empathy, good listening, sensitive interpretation, and personal respect. These were valuable lessons that served me well.

But nowhere in all those years of arduous training did my teachers mention the most important element in any healing process: *the state of mind of the healer*. If a physician prescribed an antibiotic, it mattered little if he was hung-over, constipated, or unhappy with his wife; the medicine fought the infection unaided. In psychoanalysis, the therapist is remotely ensconced at the end of a couch, where he may be furious at a colleague, worried about the stock market, or even sound asleep. No matter; the cure will come forth after a series of timely interpretations. It is axiomatic that the analyst is not a real person to the patient anyway, only a fantasy figure constructed from the patient's projected needs.

Insights from modern consciousness research are rapidly changing that view. The emerging idea that we all participate in a transcendent, universal ground of consciousness structured like a holographic field suggests that we are more vulnerable to each other than most of us dare to admit.[4] Patient and healer meet each other in the midst of a field of consciousness in which both actively participate, sometimes "vibrating" in harmony, sometimes in discord. Beneath and beyond the surface communications are subtle *sub rosa* exchanges that affect both in ways not immediately accessible to awareness.

This subliminal rapport between therapist and patient dominates every aspect of the healing situation. R. D. Laing once pointed out that it is not merely what the patient says but also *how the therapist listens*, that determines how close they get or how far apart they remain.[5] Healing requires more than transferring chemicals from pharmacy to brain, more than transmitting wisdom from tongue to ear. These are important aspects of healing, but even more essential is an exchange of *spirit* from healer to patient and back again. Once activated, this resonance acquires a self-fortifying momentum, operating beyond the momentary awareness of the participants, as if it had ends of its own. The great healing traditions agree that this exchange of energy is mediated through the heart, through the medium of universal love.

A modern mental health practitioner commands immensely powerful tools, from medicines that alter the delicate metabolic pathways of the brain, to refined psychotherapeutic techniques that plumb the depths of the soul. Wielded by clumsy or uncaring hands, these can destroy a vulnerable depressed person as easily as heal. The technical proficiency requisite to artful healing comes from dedicated scientific study. But equally important is the healer's commitment to his own spiritual growth, to clearing the debris of ego-attachment that insulates him from the painful reality of those he seeks to heal. To be effective, the healer must relinquish his defensive armoring against the pain of life, his indulgence of activities that constrict awareness, and the arrogance that prevents him from learning from his patients.

This is not to say that a healer must have all these attributes to be effective, only that he must value them as personal goals. In this regard, he would do well to emulate his predecessors, the shamanic medicine men of earlier times. Author Michael Harner described the willingness of the shaman to join his patient in a mutual search for the power that heals:

> Through his heroic journey and efforts, the shaman helps his patients transcend their normal, ordinary definition of reality, including the definition of themselves as ill. The shaman shows his patients that they are not emotionally and spiritually alone in their struggles against illness and death.
>
> The shaman shares his special powers and convinces his patients, on a deep level of consciousness, that another human is willing to offer up his own self to help them. The shaman's self-sacrifice calls forth a commensurate emotional commitment from his patients, a sense of obligation to struggle alongside the shaman to save one's self. Caring and curing go hand in hand.[6]

By the time a prospective healer of the psyche completes advanced scientific study, he is likely to have mastered many of the tasks of the ego-based world. Yet the rigors of professional training can retard his ongoing spiritual growth—the shamanic vocation—by forcing him into rigid patterns of linear logic, demanding unbending conformity to orthodoxy, rejecting radical deviations from "normal" emotions, and numbing his natural compassion for the sake of objectivity. In the West, spiritual considerations are systematically excluded from scientific training and actively discouraged afterwards. To remedy this gap in his education, the first task of a would-be healer upon completing formal training is to set out on a disciplined spiritual path.

Spiritual growth is no more than expanding personal consciousness upward from the present stage of development toward the next higher level. For most of us, this means mastering the ego-based strivings of early adulthood, then clearing away impediments against opening the compassionate heart. Orthodox psychotherapy can be fairly effective in resolving stubborn blockages left over from painful childhood experiences, freeing the self for natural growth. Most of the better training programs for mental health professionals wisely insist that they engage in individual psychotherapy before graduation.

The day has come, however, when orthodox psychotherapy focused on personal biography is no longer sufficient to fuel self-realization. Indeed, a healer cannot be fully effective until he experiences universal love as a personal reality. This implies that he has transcended his ego's need for excessive wealth and prestige as ends-in-themselves, and so frees the best of his energies to be in the service of others. For most people, this task requires specific spiritual practice.

If a healer is unable to make contact with a depressed person, this is simply a reflection of his inability to move freely into other systems of feeling and thinking. Once a healer frees himself from attachment to a specific way of knowing, he will encounter no state of mind, no shadowy mood beyond his understanding. That is not to say that he should get stuck where his patients are stuck. Intuitive knowing requires the most careful checking against self-deception. This means that he must become expert at the ruthless art of honest introspection.

So prepared, the artful healer knows he cannot force a depressed person to change his mood or attitudes. Instead, he seeks to understand, accept, nurture, and finally to allow natural and inevitable change to acquire its own impetus. Every living organism has a built-in drive toward health, toward adaptation to its surroundings. But fear and anxiety—fear of fear—undermines that drive. The revolutionary task of the artful healer is to teach his depressed patients to navigate with courage in their often bleak and forbidding internal environment as he has learned to do. Then he can lead his patient—not back to endless chains of frustrated longings but to willingly surrendering his rigid attachments to specific outcomes, realigning with the flow of an ever-changing world.

For all sentient beings, quality of life is identical to quality of consciousness, the condition of the soul. Those who understand this equation, usually through some form of daily introspection or meditation, learn to direct the healing power of spirit through themselves toward the goal of reducing suffering. Compassion infuses and informs every genuine act of healing, from lifting a scalpel, to writing a prescription, to sharing the seemingly endless anguish of depression.

Of the many techniques of meditation that have evolved from the world's contemplative traditions, introspective meditation such as the Buddhist *Vipassana* is especially suited to the healer's art. By intently observing the ever-changing forms of consciousness ebbing and flowing within his awareness, an artful healer learns mindfulness, and with it insight into his inner nature that allows him to bring to others this same realization.[7] The particular religious form of the healer's meditation—even thoughtful agnosticism—matters little, for it is the conditioning of the compassionate heart, which inevitably follows from conscientious meditation, that empowers his healing touch.

I am not saying that it is impossible to be effective in treating depressed people without practicing meditation, only that meditation can make any healer more sensitive and perceptive. The mindfulness gained from regular meditation enables a healer to live with fullness and presence in each moment. By attending carefully to fluctuations of feeling and mood without immediately reacting to them, the healer receives each experience free from judgment or aversion. He freshly perceives his depressed patient's immediate reality, without analysis, comparison, or interpretation, and so gains a clear understanding of how that person creates his world view. No matter how wrenching a session with a melancholic patient may be, or how much pain the healer absorbs, a moment of mindfulness restores calm and balance and allows him to respond in a caring and heartfelt way.

Severe depression insidiously erodes the dynamic relationship between individual consciousness and the spiritual ground of our being. It is, therefore, through the medium of consciousness that healing takes place. So a healer's primary task is to observe the state of consciousness of his depressed patient, using empathic awareness as his primary tool. He strives to know his patient through what Heinz Kohut called *vicarious introspection*—a form of meditative mindfulness in which he creates within himself an internal image of his patient's moment-to-moment experience.[8]

In this way, the healer practices impeccability—in the sense that the Yaqui *brujo* Don Juan taught Carlos Castaneda—conducting his art with personal centeredness, clarity of purpose, and sharply focused will.[9] At every moment he is thoroughly *here* for anything that might take place, no matter how unexpected or beyond the pale. Impeccability, Don Juan taught, is the capacity to experience the ego's worldly frame of reference side by side with its greater subconscious underpinnings without getting lost in either. This dual perspective allows the healer to respond flexibly from a position halfway between the rational and intuitive. Poised midway between everyday awareness and immersion in the dark subconscious, he enters his patient's disintegrating world as if it were his world, yet still keeps one foot firmly planted on the path back to his own everyday reality.

This is no easy task. It requires personal familiarity with how pain emerges from attachment and aversion, how mindless desire disposes one to the hopeless agony of defeat. To empathize with a depressed individual involves training of a very different sort from the aloof objectivity taught in professional schools. This suggests that most healers adept at working with depressed people have themselves at some time undergone a spiritual crisis, a *sacred wound* that alienated them from their authentic self, followed by a hard-won regeneration in spirit. Once a healer personally experiences the effects of losing his intimate relationship with his own spiritual roots, he gains a feeling for others caught up in a similar process.

The heart of the depressed person lies within our heart; his pain rests sorely within us. Even to pretend competence in meeting such an individual, we must seek within ourselves the wellsprings of all human thought and feeling. We must learn by impeccably exploring our deepest selves that every thought, every shifting mood, no matter how hideous or exalted, lies within our own capability. Once we *feel* this through and through, and also lovingly accept it as our birthright, we will be ready to encounter the source of our own suffering and that of those we seek to heal. The depressed can be our teachers.

19. The Path of the Dragon

PSYCHEDELIC AND EMPATHOGENIC TREATMENT OF DEPRESSION

BY SHYLOH RAVENSWOOD

For more than three decades, the search for legitimate uses for psychedelic drugs has been embroiled in controversy. This original article outlines the potential benefits and pitfalls of integrating these potent, consciousness-altering agents into our therapeutic armamentarium.

To live outside the law, you must be honest.

—BOB DYLAN

For millennia, spiritual seekers in pretechnological societies gained healing and insight from ingesting certain botanical preparations under the guidance of shamans specially trained to prepare and administer them wisely. Although modern Western cultures have declared many of these agents illegal, when used in this healing context, they are far from the equivalent of street drugs of abuse, but are truly *medicines.*

Psychedelic medicines used in ancient times were gathered from the wild and usually taken by eating the whole plant, such as the *Peyote* cactus and *psylocybin* mushroom used by Greater American high-plains Indians. Others were extracted from their plant sources under ceremonial conditions, such as the potent *Auyasca* used by tropical rain forest peoples, and the mysterious Iboga, which central African shamans used to access collective tribal myths and archetypal memories. These substances bonded tribal peoples during ritual celebrations, or facilitated healing, especially of what are now called psychiatric disorders. Using these drugs mindfully and in sacred context seemed to immunize the indigenous users against abuse or addiction.

In modern decades, synthetic variants of these venerable medicines are in vogue in all social strata despite costly efforts to suppress them. LSD and a burgeoning variety of "designer drugs" mimic the subjective effects of their botanical forerunners. Some, like MDMA (Ecstasy) and other "empathogens," alter feeling and mood in ways that may have been unknown to ancient peoples. Unfortunately, today's technological cultures have turned away from their shamanic roots, and so provide no meaningful guidance for the uninitiated, other than authoritarian injunctions simply not to use them under any circumstances.

Not surprisingly, contemporary efforts to suppress psychedelics are as widely disregarded as those of an earlier generation to ban alcohol. Their unfortunate effect is to deprive users of time-honored inner technologies that enabled our "primitive" ancestors to benefit from these medicines in ways that fostered individual and cultural benefit. Our forebearers recognized that human beings have a natural, innate drive to alter consciousness for state-specific tasks, including spiritual exploration.[1] We should search for safer ways to regulate our inner states rather than dictating which states of consciousness are socially acceptable and which are not.

THERAPY WITH PSYCHEDELICS

Illegal though they may be, an expanding variety of psychedelic medicines remain available through underground channels. Using models from American Indian and other tribal cultures, modern "shamans"—often trained psychiatrists and psychologists—assume the considerable risk of operating outside orthodoxy to integrate psychedelics into their therapeutic armamentarium, or to exercise the venerable medical tradition of disciplined self-experimentation. A few courageous experimenters publish their results, and their encouraging findings have motivated the federal government again to allow a few open experiments, some with grants.[2]

But for now, we must turn back to earlier experiments performed in the 1950s and 1960s before the federal government banned even carefully designed research. More than one thousand clinical papers describing forty thousand patients who had engaged in psychedelic therapy were published during that time. Lester Grinspoon, a respected psychiatric research scientist, summarized these in a controversial 1979 book in which he outlined two basic ways to use LSD and similar psychedelics in therapy.[3] One method is to administer a single, heavy dose with the aim of jarring an individual out of his habitual world view and fostering a mystical or conversion experience that dramatically restructures his values and relationships. This method may be best for treating alcoholics and criminals.

Another method—dubbed *psycholytic* ("mind-loosening")—holds promise for treating depression and personality disorders. Psycholytic therapy involves relatively small doses of LSD or its equivalents administered over several sessions, usually a week apart. This dose is sufficient so that most people definitely feel alterations in perception, emotion, and cognition, but are not so overwhelmed as they may be with higher doses. Although research methods into these kinds of therapy do not always meet exacting standards of proof, and many reports are simply anecdotal, advocates claim dramatic improvements that persist long after treatment ends.

One overview of forty-two papers describing psycholytic therapy with severely depressed patients reported 62 percent were improved initially, following about fourteen treatments on average. A follow-up of fifteen of these patients two years later indicated about six in ten remained improved or stayed the same, and 30 percent were worse. Only a few relapsed to their pretreatment state.[4] This figure is comparable to the *acute* effects of most standard antidepressant medications, which seldom maintain their beneficial effects two years after a person stops taking them.

In most of these reports, the therapists did not merely administer psychedelics and passively observe the results, but used them to enhance intensive psychotherapy. In a 1986 article, Grinspoon emphasized that it would be an error to consider psychedelic drug therapy as a form of chemotherapy, such as lithium or traditional antidepressant medications. Instead, it is more like, "a hybrid between pharmacotherapy and psychotherapy."[5]

One case was especially dramatic. After administering 100 mcg. of LSD, the psychiatrist suggested that the patient entertain a fantasy about castrating his father:

> The effect was electric. He exploded with laughter. The feelings and fantasies about his father came pouring out, as though Moses had smote the rock. For the balance of the afternoon we reveled in an exchange of fantasies about his father. From that day he was a changed man. Previously he had been a Milquetoast at work whom everyone pushed around. Now he became self-assertive and positive. He no longer let advantage be taken of him. He was poised and comfortable . . . During the next LSD sessions . . . he was able to continue the work of the preceding session. With the dread of his father laid to rest . . . he expressed for the first time the desire for a girl. In the months following, astounding changes developed. He developed a sense of humor; he became efficient; he began to date; he made plans to leave his job and set up his own business, and this he actually accomplished. He enjoyed dating and experienced intense sexual feelings . . . In seventeen years of practicing psycho-

therapy, I have never seen as much change in an individual with a rigid obsessional character. The change has been permanent.[6]

Such stories of dramatic alterations in one's core sense of self-in-the-world recall the amazing personality changes attributed to the modern antidepressant medicine Prozac, which seems to enhance character traits like impulsivity, novelty-seeking, risk-taking, and assertiveness.[7] This link between psychedelics and "new-generation" antidepressants like Prozac may be through their common effects on a primary brain neurotransmitter, *serotonin*. Unfortunately, such desirable changes tend to fade after an individual stops taking Prozac, unlike the more deep-rooted changes initiated by psychedelic therapy.

As valuable as these biological speculations may be, studying the way psychedelics and empathogens affect the brain may not lead us to understand how they can transform the psyche in such profound ways, even after a single experience. They appear to act more like intensive psychotherapy than like antidepressant medications in that they highlight and clarify life's "big" questions. Who am I? What is my true path in life? How can I access my spiritual roots? In this way, ancient shamans taught that their sacred medicines were *teachers*, as well as healers.

THERAPY WITH EMPATHOGENS

Another class of generally illegal medicines with significant potential for enhancing treatment of depression is the empathogens, a name that reflects their ability to open the core self to powerful feelings of empathy and compassion without causing vivid visions characteristic of other psychedelics. This class includes the rarely encountered MDA (Eve) and the more popular MDMA that gained notoriety in the underground "Rave" scene both in the United States and abroad.

Although many consider MDMA to be a modern "designer drug" cleverly crafted to circumvent drug laws, it was discovered in 1912 by scientists at the German pharmaceutical firm Merck, who never developed its potential. It lay fallow until the 1970s when several adventuresome California psychiatrists began integrating it into therapy. Because of the sense of blissful communion with others that it can induce, it grew in popularity as a recreational drug, some using it recklessly, with undefined intention in suboptimal settings.

Of course any substance from coffee to vitamins can be abused, but MDMA soon fell under the gaze of militant guardians of the national consciousness who summarily declared it illegal in 1985. For political considerations, the Drug Enforcement Administration dislikes people using drugs that expand consciousness, and they often grasp for reasons, however scientifically questionable, to forbid their use. In the case of MDMA, they justified their ban by citing a single research project with MDA, a similar drug that seemed to decrease serotonin receptor sites in rat brains.

Several thoughtful scientists have now criticized this judgment as derived from contrived reasoning, pointing out that the observed decrease of serotonin receptor sites is demonstrably temporary, with ambiguous implications. They argue that brain *change* is not necessarily brain *damage* and may simply reflect the physical concomitant of a radically altered world view.[8] For instance, an improved mood, an enhanced self-image, and a falling away of outworn fears and habits would certainly be reflected in physiological changes. Other authors who recently conducted an exhaustive search of the medical literature were unable to find a single report of a life-threatening event induced by MDMA in a therapeutic setting.[9]

Having observed the profoundly life-enhancing benefits of empathogens, many physicians and other healers continue quietly to explore the potential of these medicines to open the compassionate heart to oneself and others. What they are finding is that MDMA can, in carefully selected individuals, stimulate people to evaluate previously unexamined habits and self-denying attitudes that engender depression, and especially suicide.

One common feeling that leads people to consider suicide is alienation, of perceiving oneself to be an exile. Many suicidal people feel isolated, uniquely chosen by fate to endure hardships and deprivations without help or appreciation. Finding it burdensome to cope with a solitary and thankless struggle, they withdraw into private, lonely worlds, feeling unworthy and justly abandoned. Such individuals may engage in psychotherapy, but they may find it difficult to talk about emotionally laden issues, needing weeks or months to warm up to a therapist—a luxury that may be interrupted by a suicide attempt.

Here is where MDMA may play a vital role in establishing the bond of trust necessary for self-disclosure. If *artfully* used in a timely intervention, it can quickly overcome alienation by fostering a sense of deep interconnectedness with friends, family, and humanity as a whole. Unless a therapist authentically deserves this trust by being caring and empathic, the feeling is likely to wear off with the medicine. But given favorable circumstances, it can buy enough time to make the difference between choosing life or death.

One therapist estimated that a single, five-hour session with MDMA could activate and process psychic material that normally takes five months of weekly sessions. One of her patients described the kind of open-heartedness that typically emerges from this kind of work:

MDMA helped me look at my suffering, to see my life as a whole and understand it better. It gave me the courage to face my fears instead of ignoring them, to know that the most important thing is to struggle to trust myself. I don't know what my life will be like now, or how much I want to live, but I do know that the experiences I have gone through, even though painful, have also been full of tenderness and trust, and there is no longer this feeling of emptiness.[10]

HOW PSYCHEDELICS AND EMPATHOGENS HEAL

Unlike ordinary antidepressant medicines, which exert their remarkable *physical* effects over several weeks or months by balancing aberrant brain chemistry, psychedelics and empathogens work on mental, emotional, and spiritual levels by facilitating experiences that can restructure one's values, attitudes, and relationships. When a psychedelic medicine eventually leaves the body, it leaves behind very little physical evidence of its passage, but psychological changes can be profound and enduring.

Most therapists who work with these medicines agree that psychedelics open the deep unconscious to immediate observation, allowing an individual to access memories and traumas that are either so deeply repressed to be inaccessible by ordinary means, or that occurred so early in life that conscious recall is impossible. They ply their magic by stripping away the "gloss" of ordinary experience that prevents us from looking within. Free from the distracting allures of the senses, we can observe our ego at work, then contrast that essential segment of the mind with a deeper, more authentic self. This can be quite frightening for an unprepared individual; hence the need for an experienced guide to lead him through the arduous process of inner exploration.

Another theory of how psychedelics exert their therapeutic effects holds that they open a dimension of the *sacred* to ordinary experience. They reveal that we are far more than solitary, isolated individuals seeking only to fulfill our need for ever more power or possessions, but are part of a divine whole in a universe ripe with meaning and purpose. With visionary psychedelics like LSD, this can take the form of merging with a divine light, of meeting and gaining guidance from a higher spiritual entity, which may be an ancestor or even an animal, or of gazing directly at a core aspect of self that remains unaffected by worldly experience.

At the feeling-level of the empathogens, a person may find that his freshly open heart allows him to appreciate how others are reaching out to help, enabling him to shed his armor of alienation. Or he may observe how his egocentric value system obscures the deeper pleasures of relating authentically to others, enabling him to love unselfishly for the first time. In some cases, people glimpse their inner connection with a collective destiny common to humankind. This reduces their own shortcomings to the context of human nature, allowing the kind of self-forgiveness that is so difficult for depressed people to feel. A few return from the experience motivated to surrender obsessive materialistic values for the subtler joys of a new career in service-oriented professions.

One psychedelic researcher, Stanislav Grof, M.D., stands out as probably having more experience working with people in psychedelic and other altered states of consciousness than any one else. Grof has been present for over 3,500 psychotherapy sessions augmented by LSD or other psychedelics, and has diligently studied the work of others in his field.

Grof theorizes that psychedelics function as a kind of "inner radar" that scans the unconscious for troublesome residuals of early-life trauma. These "systems of condensed experience," which can include traumas imprinted during a difficult passage through the birth canal, add a distorted emotional twist to similar situations that rekindle their affective charge later in life. For Grof, the role of psychedelic therapy is to help his patients become aware of these unconscious memory systems, then to mobilize enough raw, nonverbal emotion to cleanse their toxic effects.[11]

USING SHAMANIC MEDICINES SAFELY IN THERAPY

Using any potent medicine for healing mental disorders is risky, and psychedelics and empathogens are certainly no exception. Those willing to step outside the mainstream to apply these agents contend with legal, physical, and psychological risks. Because modern cultures and religions fail to provide meaningful guidance in this realm, we must forge new techniques that blend ancient wisdom, modern science, and common sense.

Screening Candidates for Therapy

The kinds of treatments discussed in this article are not for every depressed person. These medicines provide an individual with a powerful impetus to examine his worldly ego from a unique vantage point, with the aim of radically restructuring his core values, ultimately moving toward transcendence. Many people have not matured in life to the point that their ego is strong enough to withstand this frontal assault without precipitously fragmenting and regressing to primitive levels of function, with danger of becoming stuck there. This probably accounts for wildly psychotic behavior triggered by indiscriminate use of psychedelics in the 1960s, when they were advocated as an Aquarian panacea for legions of disaffected youth who had not yet consolidated a solid self-in-the-world. With the wisdom of hindsight, it may now seem obvious that we cannot expect to transcend what we do not possess.

For this reason, common sense dictates that psychedelic therapies are inappropriate for people who have a record of personality disintegration in the face of stress, or who mobilize paranoia or other primitive defenses to deflect the anxiety of self-examination. For a depressed person to benefit from this kind of treatment, he must have developed a consistent sense of personal identity and achieved a position in life that indicates an ability to sustain efforts toward a goal. He must be capable of deep introspection without losing grip on consensual reality and possess a capacity for trust that allows him to follow a therapist's lead and be emotionally vulnerable in their presence. This usually excludes adolescents, schizophrenics, paranoiacs, and people with so-called borderline personality disorder or other fragile ego structures.

The Impeccable Warrior

Steeped in the Judaeo-Christian tradition that generally discourages solitary inner exploration, our culture has few shamanic guides who can teach us how to traverse these treacherous realms safely. An exception might be found in the extraordinary collection of allegorical tales in which Carlos Castaneda reveals the teachings of a mysterious Yaqui Indian shaman, Don Juan Mateus. Although Castaneda liberally employed poetic license in his narratives, these stories remain a rich source of native wisdom about using "power-plants" as allies. One of Don Juan's earliest communications to his apprentice was to avoid harm in his explorations by assuming the role of *impeccable warrior*. This requires four attributes: (1) to have respect; (2) to have fear; (3) to be wide-awake; (4) to be self-confident.[12]

The first of these *caveats* requires the initiate to acknowledge that he is embarking on a sacred path which requires special attention to the details of one's inner and outer environment, *set* and *setting*. As the medicine opens the door to the unconscious underpinnings of depression, one must steer through this vast labyrinth with a clear expectation of learning about one's relationships, subliminal attitudes, automatic responses, and walls of negative conditioning.

Attending to set therefore requires making an explicit *intention* before any session. This intention provides vital focus for the arduous task of exploration ahead. If an individual becomes frightened, scattered, lost, overwhelmed, or disoriented, he can center himself by recalling his original intention, examining what his momentary experience might teach him about it. The most helpful intentions are based on *healing* any physical or emotional wounds that are causing distress, or on gaining *vision* to lead one toward new life goals. One must choose an intention carefully, for it is very likely to be realized.

When attending to *setting*, psychedelic therapy for depression can be effective in either individual or group settings. In either case, a therapist must be prepared to remain with his patient(s) until the medicine has completely worn off—usually all day in the case of powerful psychedelics like LSD. The therapist must provide for safety, personal comfort, and emotional release, which can occasionally become noisy. A somewhat isolated, naturalistic setting away from home or office is ideal. Before the session commences, a prudent therapist asks all present to agree to contain the energy of the medicine within the therapeutic setting, to follow his directions, to respect the confidential nature of this kind of work, and to resist temptations to bring in outside distractions, such as making phone calls or reading.

Carefully selected music facilitates any psychedelic session, providing a mood-enhancing background for hours of solitary reflection during the peak of the experience. Music can alternate with periods of talking when a strong feeling rises to the surface. The therapist's role is not to interpret his patient's productions, but simply to "be there" for their emergence. This gives the therapist an opportunity to reflect upon his patient's experience as well as his own reactions to it before venturing interpretations.

The second attribute of an *impeccable warrior* is to acknowledge one's fear of what lies ahead. A degree of fear preceding such an uncertain journey is normal; indeed we might wonder about someone who does not feel it. A depressed person might remind himself that all treatments for that disorder—medications, shock treatment, even psychotherapy—entail a measure of risk, and that if he makes no effort to change, old habits and attitudes that lower mood are likely to persist, which is arguably more fearsome. However, unusually intense fear or a strong intuition that real danger lies ahead must also be respected as a possible sign that the timing for the journey is not right, or that other paths of exploration may be better suited for that individual.

The third feature of *impeccability* is being wide-awake. This requires watchful receptivity to any perception, emotion, anxiety, or tendency to cling to old, rigid patterns of thought. Such sensitivity can enhance perception of what Jung called the shadow, a part of the unconscious mind that stores all the disowned aspects of ourselves that we want to hide from view. Unexamined and disclaimed, the shadow drains much of our energy. As it devitalizes us, it powerfully influences our mood without our knowing it. To defend against it, we tend to project our shadow onto others, thereby absolving ourselves from the responsibility of determining the kind of person we want to be and the kind of life we want to lead. With honest use, psychedelics and empathogens do not permit such areas to remain hidden, but force them to the surface, often with feelings of great relief as one gets in touch with all aspects of his being.[13] Simply observing this dark underside of consciousness in a state of deepened awareness can diminish its power to affect our mood and self-esteem.

Self-confidence is the last aspect of an *impeccable warrior,* an attribute which imparts motivation for inner exploration and overcomes the paralyzing fear of letting go that Don Juan taught was the first enemy of a person of knowledge. Self-confidence is part of the aforementioned *set,* a recognition that one has initiated a journey into spirit, a quest for knowledge, a path of transformation. This is where a sensitive therapist can help: as inevitable fears, confusions, distractions, and urges to escape the situation arise, the therapist can gently instruct the traveler to "breathe through" the experience, reminding him that he has embarked on a voyage with a beginning, a middle, and an end, that the effects of the medicine will gradually wear off, and that each experience can teach something valuable about one's *intention.*

The Integrative Stage

At the close of the session—usually eight or more hours after the patient takes the medicine—the therapist initiates a review of the experience, focusing especially on what the traveler became aware of during the session, how this relates to his original intention, and how he intends to manifest these realizations in his ordinary life. It is common for individuals at this stage to review and heal interpersonal relationships that may be contributing to their depressed mood. The individual is likely to express strong feelings of love and gratitude toward the therapist, often experiencing an enduring bond between them, which must be acknowledged, processed, and partially surrendered as they resume their individual life roles.

The integrative stage often lasts for weeks following disciplined work with psychedelics and empathogens. As the seeker returns to the vicissitudes of ordinary life, he may find that certain events trigger new insights about previously unexamined attitudes that have previously undermined his mood and self-concept. Several follow-up sessions with the therapist will be helpful to transfer the learning, the new attitudes and feelings, into everyday reality. Repeatedly reviewing the original intention is crucial during the integrative stage, as it acts as a kind of bridge between states of consciousness. Some return of depressive feelings may be expected as old patterns of thought and behavior reassert themselves; these can be used to deepen the insights gained during the psychedelic session.

Individuals vary in the way they may benefit from these medicines. Some are satisfied with a single, powerful experience that they feel will last for a lifetime. Others benefit from renewing their contact with this experiential realm once or twice a year. Still others choose to explore aggressively and frequently. Regardless of the frequency, it is essential that the previous experience has been well integrated before embarking on the next.

The guidelines offered here should not in any way be construed as an encouragement to use illegal substances. Rather, they are applicable to any state of heightened awareness, regardless of how it is generated. This kind of intense transformative work is certainly not for every depressed person or therapist. Choice must be based on full knowledge of the risks and benefits involved.

Successful healing with psychedelic and empathogenic medicines especially requires uncommon courage, dedication, and *impeccability* on the part of a therapist. This latter quality empowers the therapist to consistently hold his own center as well as that of his patient or group, even under conditions of extreme emotional release. He must collect, prepare, self-test, and administer the medicines precisely and with consideration for individual patients, artfully alternating between permissiveness and control as circumstances dictate. There are no legitimate training programs and only a few teachers in our society willing to assume the risk of supervising this kind of work. Anyone who wishes to assume the shamanic vocation must place himself under the tutelage of a teacher for a considerable time, absorbing what remains a significant, esoteric oral mystery-teaching in our over-regulated age.

20. Reactions to Spiritual Awakening

A DESCENT FROM THE HEIGHTS

BY ROBERTO ASSAGIOLI, M.D.

In this brief excerpt from his landmark book Psychosynthesis, *Robert Assagioli shows how depression can be triggered when the exalted state that sometimes accompanies spiritual awakening abruptly ceases. In the mode of the legendary Icarus, whose worldly wings of wax proved no match for the sun's luminous intensity, a similar fall may await people who tenuously access higher realizations during a manic episode.*

A harmonious inner awakening is characterized by a sense of joy and mental illumination that brings with it an insight into the meaning and purpose of life; it dispels many doubts, offers the solution of many problems, and gives a sense of security. At the same time there wells up a realization that life is one, and an outpouring of love flows through the awakening individual towards his fellow beings and the whole of creation. The former personality, with its sharp angles and disagreeable traits, seems to have receded into the background and a new loving and lovable individual smiles at us and the whole world, full of eagerness to please, to serve, and to share his newly acquired spiritual riches, the abundance of which seems almost too much for him to contain.

Such an exalted state lasts for varying periods, but it is bound to cease. The personal self was only temporarily overpowered but not permanently transformed. The inflow of light and love is rhythmical as is everything in the universe. After a while it diminishes or ceases and the flood is followed by the ebb.

Necessarily this is a very painful experience and is apt in some cases to produce strong reactions and cause serious troubles. The personal ego reawakens and asserts itself with renewed force. All the rocks and rubbish, which had been covered and concealed at high tide, emerge again. The man, whose moral conscience has now become more refined and exacting, whose thirst for perfection has become more intense, judges with greater severity and condemns his personality with a new vehemence; he is apt to harbor the false belief of having fallen lower than he was before. Sometimes it even happens that lower propensities and drives, hitherto lying dormant in the unconscious, are vitalized by the inrush of higher energy, or stirred into a fury of opposition by the consecration of the awakening man—a fact which constitutes a challenge and a menace to their uncontrolled expression.

At times the reaction becomes intensified to the extent of causing the individual even to deny the value and reality of his recent experience. Doubts and criticism enter his mind and he is tempted to regard the whole thing as an illusion, a fantasy, or an emotional intoxication. He becomes bitter and sarcastic, ridicules himself and others, and even turns his back on his higher ideals and aspirations. Yet, try as he may, he *cannot* return to his old state; he has seen the vision, and its beauty and power to attract remain with him in spite of his efforts to suppress it. He cannot accept everyday life as before, or be satisfied with it. A "divine homesickness" haunts him and leaves him no peace. Sometimes the reaction presents a more pathological aspect and produces a state of depression and even despair, with suicidal impulses. This state bears a close resemblance to psychotic depression or "melancholia," which is characterized by an acute sense of unworthiness, a systematic self-depreciation, and self-accusation; the impression of going through hell, which may become so vivid as to produce the delusion that one is irretrievably damned; a keen and painful sense of intellectual incompetence; a loss of will power and self-control, indecision, and an incapacity and distaste for action. But in the case of those who have had an inner awakening or a measure of spiritual realization the troubles should not be considered as a mere pathological condition; they have specific psychological causes. One of these has been indicated by both Plato and St. John of the Cross with the same analogy.

Plato, in the famous allegory contained in the Seventh Book of his *Republic,* compares unenlightened men to prisoners in a dark cave or den, and says:

> At first, when any of them is liberated and compelled suddenly to stand up and turn his neck around and walk toward the light, he will suffer sharp pains; the glare will distress him, and he will be unable to see the realities of which, in his former state, he had seen the shadows.

St. John of the Cross uses words curiously similar in speaking of the condition called "the dark night of the soul":

> The self is in the dark because it is blinded by a light greater than it can bear. The more clear the light, the more does it blind the eyes of the owl, and the

stronger the sun's rays, the more it blinds the visual organs, overcoming them by reason of their weakness, depriving them of the power of seeing. . . . As eyes weakened and clouded suffer pain when the clear light beats upon them, so the soul, by reason of its impurity, suffers exceedingly when the Divine Light really shines upon it. And when the rays of this pure Light shine upon the soul in order to expel impurities, the soul perceives itself to be so unclean and miserable that it seems as if God has set Himself against it and itself were set against God. (Quoted by Underhill, 26, p. 453.)

Before proceeding further it seems appropriate to point out that crises, less total and drastic, but in many ways similar to those taking place before and after the "awakening," occur in two main types of creative individuals—artists and scientists.

Artists have often complained of periods of aridity, frustration, inability to work. At such times they feel depressed and restless and may be affected by many psychological symptoms. They are apt to make vain attempts at escape or evasion of that painful condition by means such as alcohol or drugs. But when they have reached the depth of despondency or desperation, there may come a sudden flow of inspiration inaugurating a period of renewed and intense productive activity.

Often the work of art appears as a virtually finished product elaborated without conscious awareness at some unconscious level or region of the artist's inner being. As Murray has stated in his brilliant essay *Vicissitudes of Creativity*, speaking of the requirements of creation, "there must be sufficient *permeability* (flexibility) of boundaries, boundaries between categories as well as boundaries between different spheres of interest and—most important for certain classes of creation—sufficient permeability between conscious and unconscious pro-cesses. . . . Too much permeability is insanity, too little is ultraconventional rationality."

The proper treatment in this type of crisis consists in conveying to the sufferer an understanding of its true nature and in explaining the only effective way of overcoming it. It should be made clear to him that the exalted state he has experienced could not, by its very nature, last forever and that reaction was inevitable. It is as though he had made a superb flight to the sunlit mountain top, realized its glory and the beauty of the panorama spread below, but had been brought back reluctantly to his starting point with the rueful recognition that the steep path leading to the heights must be climbed step by step. The recognition that this descent or "fall" is a natural happening affords emotional and mental relief and encourages the subject to undertake the arduous task confronting him on the path to Self-realization.

21. *Depression As a Loss of Heart*

OPENING TO HEALING THROUGH INNER WORK

BY JOHN WELWOOD

Using time-honored principles of Buddhism, John Welwood teaches us how to cope with the pain of change and loss by embracing the part of us that is most tender and open to the world. The author concludes with a case history that lucidly illustrates how ego-based cravings can bring about depression, while surrendering to the heart's wisdom dissolves impediments to healing.

Depression is one of the most common psychological problems in modern society. It appears in chronic low-grade forms that can drain a person's energy and in more acute forms that can be completely debilitating. Our materialistic culture breeds depression by promoting distorted and unattainable goals for human life. And our commonly held psychological theories make it hard for people to make direct contact with depression as a living experience, by framing it as an objective "mental disorder" to be quickly eliminated. The current treatments of choice—drugs, cognitive restructuring, or behavioral retraining—are primarily technical, and often keep depression at arm's length. However, in order to help people with depression, we must see how they create and maintain this state of mind in their moment-to-moment experience. This will help us understand depression not merely as an affliction, but as an opportunity to relate to one's life situation more honestly and directly.

In simple human terms, depression can be seen as a "loss of heart." This view is consonant with the approach of Buddhist psychology, which grows out of intensive study of human experience through the practice of mindfulness meditation. The essence of the Buddhist path is a process of awakening the heart or cultivating *bodhicitta*. (In Sanskrit, the term *bodhicitta* literally means "awakened heart/mind"; the term *citta* refers equally to "heart" and "mind.") We could define heart as that "part" of us that is most tender and open to the world.[1]

A central discovery of mindfulness meditation is that sanity and vibrant well-being are intrinsic to human nature, because the basic nature of mind, or heart, is to be open, curious, sensitive, and connected to reality. In other words, our true nature is inherently attuned to things as they are, apart from our conceptual versions of them. For this reason, our basic nature is sane and wholesome. This connectedness to reality is unconditional, or, in Buddhist terms, "unborn and unceasing"—which means that nothing causes it. If we construct elaborate systems of defenses to buffer us from reality, this is only testimony to the raw, tender quality of the open mind and heart underlying them. The basic goodness of the human heart, which is born tender, responsive, and eager to reach out and touch life, is unconditional. It is not something we have to achieve or prove. It simply *is*.

BITTERNESS TOWARD WHAT IS

Although there are many varieties of depression, we could describe this pathology in general phenomenological terms as a feeling of being "weighed down" by reality. The feeling of being cast down leads to a desire to close the eyes and turn away from having to face reality. Depression may also contain anger and resentment toward the way things are. Yet instead of taking a defiant or fluid expression, this anger is muted and frozen into bitterness. Reality takes on a bitter taste. Depressed people hold this bitterness inside, chew it over, and make themselves sick with it. They lose touch with the basic wholesomeness of being responsive to life and become convinced that they and the world are basically bad. In this sense, depression indicates a loss of heart, that is, a loss of contact with our innate openness.

Loss of heart arises from a basic sense of grief and defeat. Specific losses may be involved: loss of a loved one, a career, cherished illusions, material possessions, or self-esteem. Or there may be a more global sense of defeat carried over from childhood. In either case, the depressed person feels a sense of powerlessness and loss of control, and is unable to trust reality.

The primary sorrow underlying depression is a reaction to the loss of stable reference points that have provided security and support in the past. Yet the intensive practice of mindfulness meditation reveals that this loss of stable reference points is actually happening all the time. Buddhist psychology describes this situation in terms of the "three marks of existence." These three unavoidable facts of life constitute the basic existential context in which all human life unfolds. The first mark of existence, *impermanence,* means that things are always changing, without exception. Meditators experience this by observing the ceaseless arising and passing away of their mental and emotional states.

The second mark of existence, called *egolessness,* follows from this pervasive impermanence. Because everything is constantly changing, no continuous, solid self can be found or experienced. In discovering how they are continually trying to maintain fixed ideas of themselves, meditators see that the self is a rather arbitrary construction rather than a substantial entity or essence. This discovery can give rise to either profound relaxation or intense fear.

The third mark of existence is that the nature of life always entails *pain* or suffering. There is the pain of birth, old age, sickness, and death; the pain of trying to hold onto things that change; the pain of not getting what you want; the pain of getting what you don't want; the pain of being conditioned by circumstances; and so on. Pain is inevitable insofar as being human involves being completely exposed to the larger forces of life and death that are beyond our control.

These three marks of existence do not present any insurmountable problem if we can maintain our basic openness toward reality in the face of them. Psychopathology arises, however, out of freezing into a position of rejecting what is. From a Buddhist point of view, different pathologies express different postures that people assume in reacting against the three marks. For example, rage against one's pain might lead to a paranoid state of mind: "Who did this to me? Why is everybody trying to hurt me? I'm better than all this." Trying to gain the upper hand over the three marks so as to never feel vulnerable might lead to a sociopathic condition. Catatonia involves a decision not to relate to these circumstances of life at all. And depression results from punishing oneself for the way things are.

Depression sets in when we conclude that there is something basically wrong with us because we experience pain, we feel vulnerable or sad, we cannot hold on to our achievements, or we discover the hollowness of our self-created identity. In feeling this hollowness of identity, we are very close to experiencing the larger openness of our being. However, those who fall into depression are unable to appreciate the fullness of the openness they stumble upon in this experience. Instead they react against this open, hollow feeling and interpret it as bad.

This negative interpretation is an ordinary pathology that all of us experience in one form or another. The openness of human consciousness springs from a ground of uncertainty—not knowing who we are and what we are doing here. Unfortunately, we come to judge this uncertainty as a problem or deficiency to be overcome. In so doing, we turn against our basic being, our intrinsic openness to reality, and invent negative stories about ourselves. We give in to our "inner critic"—that voice that continually reminds us that we are not quite good enough. We come to regard the three marks of existence as evidence for the prosecution in an ongoing inner trial, where our inner critic presides as both prosecutor and judge. And imagining that the critic's punitive views are equivalent to reality, we come to believe that our self and world are basically bad.

THE SOCIAL CONTEXT OF DEPRESSION

Our materialistic culture helps foster depression. Not only do we lack a living wisdom tradition to guide modern society, but we find it more and more difficult to achieve even the ordinary worldly satisfactions of adult life: finding rewarding work, maintaining a long-term intimate relationship, or imparting a meaningful heritage to our children. Our sense of personal dignity and worth is quite fragile in a society where stable families, close-knit communities, commonly held values, and connection with the earth are increasingly rare. In a society such as ours, where the motivating ideal is to "make it" through social status and monetary success, depression is inevitable when people fail to find the imagined pot of gold at rainbow's end.

Furthermore, many in the psychiatric profession seem determined to view depression as an isolated symptom that can be excised from the psyche with the help of modern technology. The fact that drugs have become the treatment of choice indicates that we as a society do not want to directly face the existential meaning of this pathology. If we believe that depression is primarily physiological and treatable by drugs, we will not confront the ways in which we create it, both as individuals and as a culture. The view that depression is an alien force that descends on the psyche actually interferes with genuine possibilities for healing.

One young man who came to me for treatment of a clinical depression illustrates this alienated view common in our culture. At age twenty-seven, he suddenly discovered that he no longer enjoyed the things he used to: surfing, going out with the guys, chasing women, and so on. He was undergoing a major identity crisis, but because he believed in the ideology of materialism so thoroughly, he was ill-prepared for the life passage facing him. Rather than considering that his depression might hold an important message for him—for example, that he could no longer live the carefree life of a perpetual adolescent—he only wanted to get rid of the depression so that he could go back to his old life-style. He regarded his depression as an arbitrary quirk of fate that had singled him out for mysterious reasons. Although he was getting his first real glimpse of the three marks of existence, the only framework he had for interpreting them made them seem like the ultimate horror. No wonder he felt so depressed!

STORIES AND FEELINGS

Depression is maintained through stories that we create about ourselves and the world being fundamentally bad or wrong. In working with depressed people, it is important to help them distinguish between actual feelings and the stories they tell themselves about these feelings. By "story" I mean a mental fabrication, a judgment, an interpretation of a feeling. We usually do not recognize that these stories are inventions; we think that they represent reality. If we can sharpen our awareness, then we can catch ourselves in the act of constructing these stories and so begin to see through them. One of the most effective ways to learn to do this is through the practice of mindfulness meditation.

When practicing meditation, we alternate between simply being present while following our breath, and getting caught up in our busy thought patterns. Mindfulness practice involves first acknowledging our thoughts, then letting them go and returning to a sense of simple presence. In the process, we begin to witness how we are continually making up stories about who we are, what we are doing, and what will happen to us next.

With continued practice, meditators can learn to develop a healthy skepticism toward this storytelling aspect of mind. In Buddhist terms, they develop *prajñā*, a discriminating awareness that allows them to distinguish between what is real and what is a fabricated story about reality, between simple attention to immediate experience and interpretations of that experience. A psychotherapist who has a well-developed meditation practice can help clients discern when they are caught up in stories about their experience and when they are actually in touch with their experience in a more immediate way. In this way, clients more readily discover a sense of well-being that does not depend on stories about their experience.

Beneath the stories that maintain the frozen state of depression are more simple, fluid, and alive feelings, such as sorrow, anger, or fear. These feelings are quite different from the stories the inner critic constructs from them—such as "I'm no good," or "I'll never get it together," or "I'm just a weak person"—which are judgments or conceptual interpretations that freeze feelings of vulnerability into a more hardened state. Frozen fear leads to the constriction, dullness, and inactivity commonly associated with depression. Yet where there is fear of life, there is also sensitivity and openness to life. Fluid fear allows a person to connect with the tenderness of the heart. Frozen anger is turned inward against oneself and becomes a self-punishing weapon wielded by the critic. Yet anger also indicates a blocked desire to live more fully. Fluid anger is dynamic energy that can be drawn on to effect change. When we construct bitter stories about ourselves and the world out of these vivid feelings, they coagulate and turn into the monotones of depression.

Aside from fear and anger, the central feeling underlying depression is sorrow or sadness. Sadness is a particularly interesting feeling. The word *sad* is related etymologically to "satisfied" or "sated," meaning "full." So sadness indicates a fullness of heart, a fullness of feeling in response to being touched by the fleeting, hollow quality of human existence. This sense of empty fullness is one of our most essential, direct experiences of what it is to be human. As an awareness of the vast and hollow quality of the open heart, sadness connects us with the rawness of not knowing who we are and not being able to control or hold on to our quickly passing life. It invites us to let go of the reference points we normally use to prop ourselves up and make ourselves feel secure. If we reject our sadness or judge it negatively, then its poignant quality, which is vibrantly alive, congeals into the heaviness of depression. In overlooking the opportunity that sadness provides for touching and awakening the heart, we quite literally lose heart.

It is important to help people suffering from depression to be more mindful of their actual feelings so that they can see through the negative stories told by their critic and touch their genuine, open heart. The more carefully they examine their experience, the more likely they are to discover that it is actually impossible to *experience* their nature as basically bad. The idea of their basic badness is only a story told by their inner critic; it is always a fabrication, never an immediate felt experience. Therefore, by helping people reconnect with their moment-to-moment experiencing, a psychotherapist can help them glimpse their basic goodness and sanity—which is their unconditional openness and sensitivity to life itself. Unlike their fictional basic badness, their basic goodness *can* be concretely felt.[2]

A CASE EXAMPLE

One of the clients who has most challenged my own trust in basic goodness is a successful lawyer in his mid-fifties whom I have been seeing for more than two years. When he first came to see me, Ted had hardened into one of the most unyielding states of depression that I have worked with. Growing up during the great depression as the son of immigrant parents who taught him to hate and fear the white Anglo-Saxon world, he had learned to get ahead at all cost, and had driven himself for years to achieve material and professional success. He had reached the top of his profession, yet was completely miserable and desperate. His body gave the impression of an armored tank, and his health was suffering from the amount of tension he carried around. He spoke at a raised pitch, as though he were preaching a series of sermons about himself and the world.

Ted had a sharp lawyer's mind that quite literally attacked whatever he turned his attention to. His mind continually constructed arguments to buttress his views of reality. His themes were always the same: his weariness with life, his fear of death and letting go, the meaninglessness of everything, the demands people were always making on him, and the distrust he felt toward everyone because his rule of life was "attack or be attacked."

His life had been a series of unsuccessful attempts to escape the three marks of existence. The more he struggled to gain the upper hand over them, the more aggressive he became, and the more he fell victim to the very circumstances he was trying to avoid. He had tried to escape his fear of egolessness and death by climbing the professional ladder, but in doing so, he was literally killing himself. He desperately wanted to be *somebody*. Yet in continually trying to win recognition, he had become so overbearing that people rejected him—which left him feeling even more like a nobody. In trying to overcome his pain, Ted had numbed himself into a profound state of depression. The three marks of existence persistently haunted him in the form of a continual sense of emptiness, loneliness, and death-in-life.

Initially I felt assaulted by Ted's manner and presence. In order to be able to stay present in the room and listen to him at all, I found that I had to engage in swordplay with his sharp mind during our first few months together. Through these encounters, which involved much more intense confrontation than I usually engage in with clients, I was eventually able to penetrate his stories and contact him in a more human way. As Ted began recognizing the difference between his actual feelings and the stories he fabricated about them, he could see how these stories only dug him deeper into his rut. He began to slow down and stop broadcasting the same stories again and again. Eventually he was able to be more still and pay attention to what he was feeling in the moment.

The next step in my work with Ted involved helping him to recognize and step back from the inner voice that kept telling him what "he should, must, ought" to do. We came to call this voice by various names: "the critic," "the driver," "the tyrant," "the judge." As we proceeded, Ted discovered that his main aim in life was to win approval and recognition from others, as well as from his own inner critic. He had chosen to pursue the more tangible comforts of recognition and approval as a substitute for having to feel his own need for love. Feeling that need only put him back in touch with the despair, fear, and helplessness he had felt as a neglected child. Ted had come to hate his vulnerability so much that he had abandoned his own tender heart. As he realized this, he began to touch his anger, sadness, and fear directly, instead of just blaming the world for his condition.

Eventually Ted reached an important turning point that has enabled him to start choosing life over death-in-life. Underneath all his compulsive striving and attempts to win recognition, he felt the tremendous sorrow of having lost touch with his own heart. It took a long time for him to really let this pain touch him. In the process, Ted has started to acknowledge his desire just to "be," without having to be an important *somebody*. He has started to soften and to feel his humanness.

INVITATION TO THE DANCE

All our reference points are continually slipping away. We can never create an unassailable identity that will guarantee happiness and security. Shall we be depressed by this fact of existence or shall we dance with it? The grand cosmic dance of Siva in the Hindu tradition or Vajrayogini in the Tibetan Buddhist tradition takes place on the groundless ground of everything arising and slipping away. These ancient images of the cosmic dance symbolize the way in which egolessness and impermanence can be a source of energy, rather than depression. Depression is the loss of heart that results from turning against the flux of things as they are. And yet at the root of depression—in the rawness, vulnerability, and poignancy underlying it—our basic sanity is always operating. That is why depression, like all psychopathology, is not merely a disease to be quickly eliminated. Instead, it can be an opportunity to awaken one's heart and deepen one's connection to life.

22. *Opening the Heart in Hell*

HEALING·THROUGH GRIEF WORK

BY STEVEN LEVINE

Psychologists have long known that suppressing the normal grief that follows a tragic loss can lead to chronic depression. Thanatologist Steven Levine's extensive work with the terminally ill and their families is exemplified in this moving account of his therapy sessions with a woman in deep mourning.

Marcia first called at six in the morning. "My daughter was viciously murdered about six weeks ago and I am just having a very hard time. I am calling because someone told me of the work you did with the Gregorys when their daughter was abducted and murdered. I don't know if there is anything you can do to help, but I have nowhere else to turn."

S: How are you feeling?

M: I don't know how we will ever possibly survive this, but somehow it helps to talk to someone who has some understanding of what has happened.

S: In a sense, understanding is not what is needed right now. That might come later. What is needed right now is to have the mercy on yourself that somehow allows the pain to be acknowledged. When the Gregorys lost their daughter, their heart was torn open as yours must be. And there is a place in the mind where it just grabs at its security, but there is just no security to be found because, in a way, there is just no way we can be protected from any of the changes that happen in the world. All we can do is allow ourselves to be open to the moment, to allow what we feel to arise, to honor the pain in our heart.

M: (After a long silence.) What we have found, and this is very strange, is that she has come into us so much. We were so close to her that she has become a part of the four of us who are left here. More than just the four of us, because there has been an outpouring of so many people who knew her—so many of her friends—and she seems to be such a part of us that that seems to make it possible to survive for a while, and then suddenly the loss—it's just such a cavern. . . ."

S: Well, you know, when the Gregorys' daughter was abducted and murdered, there was another fourteen-year-old girl that was also killed, her best friend, Sarah. Both disappeared and were later found tortured and strangled. As you can imagine, this has been an incredibly difficult year for both families. But the two families responded very differently to the event. The Gregorys allowed themselves to be torn open to their daughter's murder and of course suffered greatly, but somehow, because they allowed the pain to enter their heart, their heart seemed yet more in touch with their other children and with the spirit of their daughter. She became, as you have said, more and more a part of the family. The other family, the Spinells, had lived their life in a stiff kind of orthodoxy that they expected would protect them—a bargaining with God—and when Sarah was murdered, they lost their faith. Their hearts closed to each other and the world and they have become more and more destroyed by this experience. They raged against the universe. Their relationship is in tatters.

Meanwhile, the Gregorys have never been so close. They shared the pain. They met her death in love. They allowed their rage. It burned through them. It may never be completely gone, but still there is a sense of unity with life that has been the legacy of their daughter's death. The Spinells' younger children feel abandoned, frightened. The younger children in both families felt strongly the doubt that the world was a safe place to be. In each case the older daughter had been murdered and the younger children felt that they were completely unprotected. The Gregorys' children have come more and more into the heart of the family, of their parents, of their friends. The Spinells' children have become depressed and very unsure of themselves. Marcia, undoubtedly this is the most difficult experience of a lifetime, and in many ways it has just begun.

M: I know. I get sight of that. I know that we are going to have a time that is going to be very difficult.

S: You may also have a time where for some reason beyond anything you can put a finger on, your heart is more open and you feel more love than you have ever felt. That is what happened with the Gregorys. The other couple closed and became outraged with God.

M: We went through that when it first happened and we have been going through that for years with what is happening in the world. But what happened with our daughter somehow opened us up. She was working after school at the local newspaper, just a few blocks from where we live. She was a young girl who seemed to have everything. Just sixteen years old. She was so very beautiful, she was like the sun. She had sort of a classic Renaissance face. She had very long blond hair and she walked so proudly and beautifully.

S: You know, her face is gone and her walk is gone, but her beauty will remain forever.

M: I know. Believe it or not, I know. She was like sunshine and we have been having a lot of that lately. And she was walking home when two men got her, raped her and killed her—they beat her and finally stabbed her. When she wasn't home at the time she usually arrived, I started worrying. After a short time I walked to the newspaper, but she was nowhere to be seen and they said she had left some time before. And then I knew. Because she wouldn't ever go anywhere else without letting us know. That just wasn't the kind of relationship we had.

So we went through the whole horror of trying to get the authorities to go out and look for her, and they did. We were out looking all over for her. I was out looking for her and I couldn't find her. She was only three blocks from home where they found her. They came with a priest. They didn't know we were Quakers.

We have had letters from people all over the country that we have never met. Their support has somehow helped us live from day to day. Some of the letters were from parents who had lost a child through violence. Those letters seemed to be helpful.

S: Well, you know, nothing I can say is going to be very helpful right now. In a sense, this is a time when you touch your powerlessness and your fear of the world. As a Quaker you have the long-established practice of 'listening to the small voice within.' But that voice is going to be difficult to get in touch with sometimes, because the mind naturally is going to be agitated and in such a spin.

M: Yes. We go on and off. Right now I can function.

S: Can you allow yourself to not function?

M: Yes. I do what I have to do.

S: What would be useful right now is to allow yourself to feel all that you are feeling.

M: I don't seem to have much choice.

S: Well, there are many kinds of feelings. The full range of emotions are going to arise. Just have the mercy on yourself to leave them room to happen.

M: Well, this just happened about a month ago, and now the men have been arrested who killed her and we have to appear at their trial. I sense this is going to be very difficult for both of us. But anything that is hiding under there will most likely be brought out by this awful trial. I feel anger toward them, of course. I feel like the whole world has been hurt. I feel like it is some mindless, senseless evil that she fell in the path of. What I feel is this horror for my child. She used to be frightened sometimes, and I would go in when she would have nightmares and say, "Give it to me." She would tell me and then go to sleep, and I would take the nightmares—and I am trying to take this nightmare . . .

S: But you can't take this nightmare for her. It is your nightmare now. Her nightmare was just a moment long and has long since dissolved behind her. Yours continues as you repeat it again and again in your mind. For you she is accosted and raped a thousand times. For her it happened only once. For you, each time she is beaten and raped, at the end of that rape she is once again beaten and once again raped, over and over again. But for her each moment was followed by the next. Death only happened once, for a moment, and then the next moment arose. Her experience is different from your imagination of her experience, than your fears, than your feeling of impotent rage because you could not protect her from this "senseless evil" that she was touched by.

Feel the love, the anger, the fear, but know that what you feel exists only for a moment and then becomes the next moment. In a situation like this there is a tendency for the mind to replay the incident a million times. But you know, if you thought right now about breaking a leg as you walked across the lawn, there you would be, walking along the lawn, tripping over the sprinkler, falling down, breaking your leg, and then you would start thinking about walking across the lawn again, falling again, breaking your leg again, walking across the lawn— again and again it repeats in the mind. But in actuality when that happens, you walk across the lawn and the lawn is past. You trip over the sprinkler and the sprinkler is past and there is a moment when the bone breaks and that one is done, and then the next moment comes. But in your reflection about what happened to your daughter, the next moment never comes. You always go back to the beginning again. She did not suffer what you are imagining. She went through it only one time.

M: I know. I go through it every morning.

S: You go through it a million times. Your fear of what happened to her, in a sense, is worse than what happened to her. As you know, when you hurt yourself, you are right in the midst of that pain. Everyone else around you is trying to help and there is confusion in their mind and fright and all kinds of feelings that may not be in your mind at the time. At that time you are just with what is happening, just with the broken leg, just with the pain of the moment trying to figure out what the next step is. What she experienced is perhaps a moment of incredible fright, but then, as we have been told by many in similar experiences who lived to relate the tale, because the imminence of the danger is so great, something else seems to occur. A kind of disconnecting. Not a dissociation where you are pulling back and have gone mentally catatonic, but a displacing of the mind from the body.

We shared with Marcia the stories we have been told not only by those who had been violently attacked but also by those who had experienced the violence we imagine occurs to the mind and body during the process of drowning. One might think drowning would be one of the most terrifying deaths that could happen, but having spoken with several people who had nearly drowned and were on respirators and in treatment for some time thereafter before recovering, this apparently was not the case. Each said there was a moment when the water was above their head and when there was no chance for escape, when there was a burning in their lungs and the first recognition of what was happening—that they were going to die—when all of a sudden what came over them was an extraordinary peace, that though they saw their body thrashing in the water gasping for air, their experience was not the experience one would have imagined looking at that body wildly struggling in the water. Their experience was a peacefulness that "this too was somehow perfectly OK."

   S: Yes, your daughter may have been very frightened. But that was not the only quality in her mind during that experience. When the body recognizes that it is so thoroughly threatened, something else seems to happen, so your daughter's experience can only be imagined. For her the experience was only a few moments long, and then it was over and the next moment occurred: the dissolving out of her body, the going on which apparently is in peace, without fear and without pain.

   M: Yes. It is the mind replaying it that is the greatest difficulty right now. Like today. I saw her hand in my mind. It was very difficult, it was very hard for me to see her hand, because she was an artist and her skills had taken some enormous steps forward just in the last few months. I could see her hand with a knife cutting the paper, and with the sureness of the pen she was using, and this whole thing has just been very hard for me this morning because of that hand.

   S: Because of who she was in the world.

   M: Yes. And I held that hand so many times. We walked together all over. We had been so close—all of us.

   S: How old are your other children?

   M: One is just a few years younger than his sister was, the other is in second grade.

   S: One of the things you might want to be aware of is that a child, even one who is in his early teens, still has the feeling that his parents can protect him from anything. Now your children see their sister killed, and somewhere deep inside they may be saying that there is no real security in this world.

M: Yes. The older boy says it isn't safe for him to walk the streets.

S: And that is one you may find you will be working with off and on for some time. The death of his sister has probably had a very strong affect on his view of the world right now. But with all the unity and love that your family feels, his sense of security will re-establish itself in time.

I have seen many younger siblings become the 'oldest child' with a kind of strength and courage and pride, taking the position of the eldest in a new kind of responsibility toward life.

All of it will change just as your feelings are going to change. Indeed, you couldn't make these feelings stay even if you wanted to. Because they are all part of a process, the process of grief. You are experiencing what comes next just as your daughter did.

M: For a long time I couldn't go upstairs into her room. I would pass by her door and it would make me feel so sad. I guess I am still worried about her well being. At first after she had died, the house was filled with people and there were so many distractions, but then when everyone left, every time I would walk past her door, I would feel my heart just burst. It was almost as though I was waiting for her to come out that door all shiny and bright, ready for a new day.

But then one day her boyfriend, who had been almost catatonic for the first couple of weeks after her murder, came over and asked if he could go up into her room and just sit there quietly by himself for a while. Of course, we said that was fine. After about an hour he came downstairs and asked us all to come up into her room. And when I went upstairs and went into her room, there was an incredible peace there. It wasn't so much that I was avoiding her room before but just that I didn't know what to do. But when I went up there, it was just incredible. I sat there for a long time and since then I have sat there several times with her friends and we have talked and laughed about her. Now and again, I am so filled with joy, with the beauty of the life she lived, for the love of the people she knew.

S: And that joy will be there on and off. As you experience the grief less in your mind, as you experience her less as her separateness, as her form, as a being who had come into life as your daughter and instead just begin to experience her as being itself, the grief will sink from the mind's incessant agitation into the heart and you will just be with her in oneness, in your essential connectedness. And then the form which seemed so important but is now denied you may be seen through as an illusion which in some ways always kept you separate. Separate from the most profound, silent, inner penetration of each other. In an odd way now you can go beyond the forms that always kept you separate, of mother and daughter, of elder and child, of someone who knew and someone who had something to learn. Then the essence of being is shared in love and the grief will burn its way to completion. She is gone now into her next perfect evolutionary step, just as the unbearable pain you feel propels you toward your next stage of life and being.

M: I so wanted her to be old and me to have grandchildren and for us to laugh and talk.

S: Well, that is not going to be given, but what may be given to the degree that you can stay open to it, as it seems you are, is to let your heart be torn open. She had quite a basis for love and self-acceptance in her life. Two hundred thousand people die every day on this planet. Of that two hundred thousand, how many do you think approach death with their hearts as clear and open as hers was, with a life so full?

M: In the last six months she opened up in an astonishing way. Her friends had great confidence in her and often confided. She was, as some of her friends said, 'an old soul.' She had really been coming into her own in these last months. The last six months of her life had been just incredible, so full, so complete.

S: It sounds like she was finishing a lot of business with herself, with the world. She was very fortunate to have those last months.

M: When I talk about her being there, I mean she is in me, her brothers, her father. . . .

S: And you have the same lessons to learn that she did, that we all do. She may have learned those lessons in an instant six weeks ago, I just don't know. It may have been given to her to learn all that she had come to learn in just those few moments of life she was granted, much less those sixteen loving years.

We spoke for some time more about how the family, including grandparents and cousins, were relating to this sudden loss. Her loss had brought the family together as never before. The grief was being shared by all in a deep caring for themselves and each other.

Over the next year, we spoke to Marcia, her husband, and oldest son on various occasions and watched as the pain sank deeper and as they slowly again surfaced into life with a new commitment to compassion and mutual support. The healing was slow and profound. Her younger brother began playing the piano as she once had. As he started slowly to take the position as the oldest child, he began baby-sitting for his younger brother in a way he had never wished to in the past. And his playing piano too as he feared he never could because "she was always so good at everything and now I am too."

It is not that Marcia's family's grief will ever be completely gone but rather that it has caused them to open to life in a way they may never have imagined in the past. In a sense, they have allowed themselves to die into life, to appreciate the precious moment in which this sharing is to be experienced, letting go of the fears and worries that may have in the past kept life somewhat stiffer.

There are a few dozen families with whom we have shared over the past few years the healing that accompanies the grief of a murdered child. In most cases we have seen a slow reorientation, a deepening to life, while for a few, talking to us has just become too painful and they seldom write or call.

Often as I am talking on the phone to the parent of a murdered child, our children will come into the room filled with the urgency of adolescence, "We can't wait, we're off to town, what time are we supposed to be home?" And though the mind may be momentarily frustrated by the distraction while I am on the phone, the heart opens to the preciousness of each sharing, of each moment we are allowed together. The priorities become clearer and clearer: to honor each being as they unfold without holding them back or pushing them aside. Each day we learn a bit more and let go of the pain that keeps us separate, the isolation of father and son, of mother and daughter, and continue to merge in the one being we all share.

23. The Medicine Buddha

COMBINING ANTIDEPRESSANT MEDICATIONS WITH
SPIRITUAL PRACTICE

BY MARK EPSTEIN, M.D.

*Is taking Prozac or other mood-altering medications inimical to spiritual growth?
Transpersonal psychiatrist and Buddhist scholar Mark Epstein demonstrates how
the ancient teaching of "the middle way" allows us to artfully combine both.*

Despite ten years of dharma practice and five years of psychotherapy, Leslie was
still miserable. To those who knew her casually, she did not seem depressed, but
with her close friends and lovers she was impossibly demanding. Subject to
brooding rages when she felt the least bit slighted, Leslie had alienated most of
the people in her life who had wanted to be close to her. Unable to control her
frustration when sensing a rejection, she would withdraw in anger, eat herself
sick, and take to her bed. When her therapist recommended that she take the
antidepressant Prozac she was insulted, feeling that such an action would violate
her Buddhist precepts.

There is a story in the ancient Buddhist texts that relates how the King of
Kosala once told the Buddha that unlike disciples of other religious systems who
looked haggard, coarse, pale, and emaciated, his disciples appeared to be "joyful
and elated, jubilant and exultant, enjoying the spiritual life, with faculties
pleased, free from anxiety, serene, peaceful, and living with a gazelle's mind." The
idea that the Buddha's teachings ought to be enough to bring about such a
delightful mental state continues to be widespread in contemporary Buddhist
circles. For many, Buddhist meditation has all of the trappings of an alternative
psychotherapy, including the expectation that intensive practice should be
enough to turn around any objectionable emotional experience. Yet the unspoken truth is that many experienced dharma students, like Leslie, have found
that disabling feelings of depression, agitation, or anxiety persist despite a long

commitment to Buddhist practice. This anguish is often compounded by a sense of guilt about such persistence and a sense of failure at not "making it" as a student of the dharma when afflicted in this way. This situation is analogous to that in which a devotee of natural healing is stricken with cancer, despite eating natural foods, exercising, meditating, and taking vitamins and herbs. As Treya Wilber pointed out in an article written before her early death from breast cancer, the idea that we should take responsibility for all of our illnesses has its limits.

"Why did you choose to give yourself cancer?" she reported many of her "New Age" friends asking her, provoking feelings of guilt and recrimination that echo much of what dharma students with depression often feel. More sensitive friends approached her with the slightly less obnoxious question, "How are you choosing to use this cancer?" which, in her own words, allowed her to "feel empowered and supported and challenged in a positive way." With physical illness it is perhaps a bit easier to make this shift; with mental illness one's identification is often so great that it is extremely difficult to see mental pain as "not I," as symptomatic of treatable illness rather than evocative of the human condition.

Of course, the First Noble Truth asserts the universality of *dukkha*, suffering, or, in a better translation, pervasive unsatisfactoriness. Is the hopelessness of depression, the pain of anxiety, or the discomfort of dysphoria (mild depression) simply a manifestation of *dukkha*, or do we do ourselves and the dharma a disservice to expect any kind of mental pain to dissolve once it becomes an object of meditative awareness? The great power of Buddhism lies in its assertion that all of the stuff of the neurotic mind can become fodder for enlightenment, that liberation of the mind is possible without resolution of all of the neuroses. Many Westerners feel an immediate relief in this view. They find they are accepted by their dharma teachers as they are, and this attitude of unconditional acceptance and love is one that evokes deep appreciation and gratitude. This is a priceless contribution of Buddhist psychology—it offers the potential of transforming what often becomes a stalemate in psychotherapy, when the neurotic core is exposed but nothing can be done to eradicate it.

Eden's situation typifies this. A writer whose crisis manifested in her twenty-ninth year, Eden suffered from an oppressive feeling of emptiness or hollowness for much of her adult life. Already a veteran of ten years of intensive psychotherapy, she understood that her feelings of numbness and yearning stemmed from emotional neglect in her youth. Her father, a cold and aloof physician, had avoided the children and retreated to a rarefied intellectual world of scientific research, while her mother was fiercely loving and protective but indiscriminate in her attention, praising Eden for anything and everything and leading her to distrust her mother's affection altogether. Eden was angry and demanding in her interpersonal relationships, impatient with any perceived flaw, with any inability of her partner to satisfy all of her needs. She had recognized the source of her problem through psychotherapy but had found no relief; she continued to idealize and then devalue her lovers and could not sustain an intimate relationship.

Eden's inner emptiness was a good example of what psychoanalyst Michael Balint has called the regret of the basic fault. "The regret or mourning I have in mind is about the unalterable fact of a defect or fault in oneself which, in fact, had cast its shadow over one's whole life, and the unfortunate effects of which can never fully be made good. Though the fault may heal, its scar will remain forever; that is, some of its effects will always be demonstrable." No antidepressants were effective in Eden's case. In order for her to find some relief, she had to confront directly her inner feeling of emptiness with the understanding that she was yearning for something that would no longer prove satisfying. Having missed a critical kind of attention relevant only to a child, she found that if someone tried to give her that as an adult, it felt oppressive and suffocating. Only through the tranquil stabilization of meditation could she stand the anxiety of this inner feeling of emptiness without reacting violently against it.

This illustrates the Buddhist approach. A person must find the courage and mental balance to confront the neurotic core or "basic fault" through the discipline of meditative awareness. In the Buddhist view, all of the elements of personality have the potential to become vehicles for enlightenment, all the waves of the mind are but an expression of the ocean of big mind. Mental illness is not an especially developed concept in Buddhist thought, except in an existential sense, where it is exquisitely developed. Buddhist texts speak of the two sicknesses: an internal sickness consisting of a belief in a permanent and eternal self and an external sickness consisting of a grasping for a real object. The focus, in Buddhist psychology, is always on the existential plight of the subjective ego.

It is this existential longing for meaning or completedness and the inner feelings of emptiness, hollowness, isolation, fear, anxiety, or incompleteness that Buddhist psychology approaches most directly. Depression, as a critical entity, is rarely addressed. The fifty-two mental factors of the Abhidhamma (the psychological texts of traditional Buddhism), for example, list a compendium of afflictive emotions such as greed, hatred, conceit, envy, doubt, worry, restlessness, and avarice, but do not even include sadness except as a kind of unpleasant feeling that can tinge other mental states. Depression is not mentioned.

Mind is described in the traditional Abhidhamma as a sense organ, or "faculty," like the eye, ear, nose, tongue, or body, that perceives concepts or other mental data, surveys the fields of the other sense organs, and is subject to "obscurations," veils of afflictive emotions that obscure the mind's true nature. The faculty of mind and the consciousness produced by it are seen as the primary source of the feeling of "I am" that is then presumed to be real. There is little discussion in Buddhist literature, however, of the mind's propensity toward disruptions that cannot be remedied through spiritual practice alone. As Buddhism evolved, its emphasis became even more focused on discovering the "true nature" of mind, rather than bothering with discussions of mental illness. This "true nature" is mind revealed as naturally empty, clear, and unimpeded. The thrust of meditation practice became the experience of mind in this natural state.

A glimpse of this reality can be quite transformative from a psychotherapeutic point of view, but quite elusive for those who do not have the capacity to let their mind rest in its natural state because of the depths of their anxieties, depressions, or mental imbalances.

Timothy was a successful photographer whose life suddenly unraveled one year. His therapist of four years died unexpectedly of a heart attack; his wife was diagnosed with breast cancer and needed both surgery and chemotherapy; and his dealer suddenly went bankrupt, closed her gallery, and folded without paying him the thousands of dollars that he was owed. His studio felt contaminated by anxious hours on the telephone with his wife and her doctors; he could no longer take refuge there and what was the point, anyway, without a dealer to sell his work? He was immersed in meaninglessness, death, and grief and he began to worry obsessively about his own health. With no active spiritual practice, Timothy lacked a context in which to place the suffering that had suddenly overwhelmed him, no means of being in his pain while still actively living and little ability to be there for his wife's trauma.

Reluctantly, he went with his wife to a workshop on coping with serious illness by Jon Kabat-Zinn, which generated an interest in Buddhist practice. Slowly, he rediscovered his vitality and took possession of his studio once again while relating to his wife in a way that his unexamined grief had prevented him from doing previously. More than anything else, his dharma practice seemed to give him a method of experiencing mental agony without succumbing to the incredible pain that it produced. His was a situation in which medication would have missed the point. His crisis was an existential or spiritual one as much as a case of unexplored grief; and he was able to find a bit of the relief that Kalu Rinpoche refers to.

The wish that meditation could, by itself, prove to be some kind of panacea for all mental suffering is widespread and certainly understandable. The psychiatrist Roger Walsh remembers an early retreat at which he had the opportunity to watch Ram Dass be with a young man who had become psychotic in the midst of his practice. "Oh, good," he remembers thinking. "Now I'll get to see Ram Dass deal with a psychotic person in a spiritual way." After watching Ram Dass chanting with the young man and trying to center him meditatively, Walsh observed that it was necessary to restrain him because of his increasing agitation and violence. At this point, the young man bit Ram Dass in the stomach, prompting an immediate call for Thorazine, a potent anti-psychotic drug. The desire to avoid medication when doing spiritual practice, to confront the mind in its naked state, is certainly a noble one, but it is not always realistic.

There continues to be a widespread suspicion of pharmacological treatments for mental anguish in dharma circles, a prejudice against using drugs to correct mental imbalance. Just as the cancer patient is urged to take responsibility for something that may be beyond her control, the depressed dharma student is all too often given the message that no pain is too great to be confronted on the zafu, that depression is the equivalent of mental weakness or lassitude, that the problem is in the quality of one's practice rather than in one's body. I remember those prejudices from my early psychiatric training. I was quite suspicious of all the psychotropic drugs, equating Lithium with the antipsychotics like Thorazine which mask or suppress psychotic symptoms but do not correct the underlying schizophrenic condition. One of the only concrete things worth learning in all of those years of training was that there actually are several psychiatric conditions which can be cured or prevented through the use of medications and that denial of such treatment is folly. This is not to say that it is always so clear when a problem is chemical, when it is psychological, or when it is spiritual. There are no blood tests for depression, for example. And yet, the presence of certain constellations of symptoms invariably point to a treatable condition that is unlikely to resolve through spiritual practice alone.

Peggy came to dharma practice in her early twenties while seriously de-pressed. Adrift in the counterculture, estranged from her divorced, alcoholic, and abusive mother, tenuously bound to her self-involved and indulgent father, she was contemplating suicide when she came upon her first dharma teacher in San Francisco. She felt "found" by that teacher, surrendered the idea of suicide, and threw herself into dharma practice for the next seventeen years. She became gradually disillusioned by a succession of teachers, however, getting to know enough of them personally to lose any ability to idealize them in the way she had originally. When her mother became ill with cancer, a five-year relationship broke up, and her best friend had a baby as Peggy approached her fortieth birthday, she became increasingly withdrawn and agitated. She felt tired and anxious, weak and lethargic but unable to sleep, filled with hateful thoughts and obsessive ruminations, and unable to concentrate on her work or her dharma practice. She took to her bed, lost interest in her friends, and began to imagine that she was already dead. Her friends took her to a spiritual community, to a number of healers, and to several respected Buddhist teachers who finally referred her for psychiatric help. As it turned out, there was a history of depression on her mother's side of the family. Peggy was convinced she was doomed to repeat her mother's deterioration; she felt she had failed as a Buddhist and yet was resistant to seeing her depression as a condition that warranted treatment with medication. She got better after about four months of taking antidepressants, which she took for a year and has not needed since. While depressed, she was simply unable to muster the concentration necessary to meditate effectively; the "ultimate view" that Kalu Rinpoche describes was unavailable to her consciousness.

The psychiatric tradition with the most experience in differentiating existential from biological mental illness is probably the Tibetan one, which developed in a culture and society completely immersed in the theory and practice of Buddhism. The Tibetan medical authorities recognize a host of "mental illnesses," it turns out, for which they recommend pharmaceutical, not meditative, interventions, including many that correspond to Western diagnoses of depression, melancholia, panic, manic-depression, and psychosis. Not only do they not always counsel meditation as a first line of treatment, they also recognize that meditation can often make such conditions worse. Indeed, it is well known that meditation, itself, can provoke a psychiatric condition, an obsessive anxiety state, which is a direct result of trying to force the mind in a rigid and unyielding way to stay on the object of awareness. According to the late Terry Clifford in her book *Tibetan Buddhist Medicine and Psychiatry,* the Tibetan tradition holds that these medical teachings were expounded by the manifestation of Buddha in the form of Vaidurya in the mystical medicine paradise called Tanatuk, literally, "Pleasing When Looked Upon." Here Vaidurya is said to have commented that "all people who want to meditate and reach nirvana and want health, long life, and happiness should learn the science of medicine." Treatments for mental illnesses are not antithetical to dharma practice; rather, the Tibetan teachings seem to say, they can be venerated as manifestations of the Medicine Buddha himself.

Yet many of today's dharma students who suffer from such mental illnesses have trouble identifying effective treatments as manifestations of the Medicine Buddha. They seem to prefer to regard their symptoms as manifestations of the Buddha-mind. A recent patient of mine, for example, was a brilliant conceptual mathematician named Gideon who taught on the graduate level and was a proud, willful, creative man who had gravitated toward Buddhist practice while in graduate school. He had suffered one "nervous breakdown" during that time: for a six-month period he had become restless and agitated with bursts of creative energy, a racing mind in which thoughts tumbled one on top of the next, a labile mood in which laughter and tears were never far from each other, and a profound difficulty in sleeping. He finally "crashed," spent a week in the hospital, and emerged with no further difficulty for the next five years. He had several depressive episodes in his thirties, during which time he became much less productive in his work, felt sad and withdrawn, and retreated in a kind of uneasy solitude. He was vehemently anti-medication, however, and weathered those depressions by closing himself into his apartment and lying in his darkened room. Again, the episodes passed, and Gideon was able to continue his work. In his forties, he had a succession of episodes, much like the nervous breakdown of his graduate years, in which he also became paranoid, hearing special messages sent to him through the television and radio warning him of a conspiracy. Psychiatric hospitalization was required after he was moved to take cover in Central Park.

Gideon's condition was manic-depression, an episodic mood disturbance that usually first manifests in young adulthood and can cause either recurrent depressions, ecstatic highs, or some combination thereof. It is characteristic of this illness that the episodes come and go, with the person returning to an unaffected state between episodes. Many people with this illness find that the episodes are fully preventable or at least markedly diminished by the daily intake of Lithium salt. Gideon was markedly resistant to the idea that he had this illness, however, and he was equally resistant to the idea of taking Lithium, quoting the dharma to the effect of "letting the mind rest in its natural state" to support his refusal to take medication. The manic episodes came rapidly in Gideon's forties, hitting him every year or so and effectively ruining his academic career. For a while, his family attempted to put medication in his food without his knowledge, an endeavor which only supported his paranoia, but to this day he has refused to take medication voluntarily. He remains a brilliant and proud man with the ability to work productively between episodes, but the illness has been destabilizing him relentlessly.

Through these examples I mean to make the point that neither meditation nor medication is uniformly beneficial in every case of mental suffering. Meditation practice can be enormously helpful or can contribute to the force of denial. There is a continuing ignorance in dharma circles of the benefits to be had from psychiatric treatments, just as there is a corresponding ignorance in traditional psychiatric circles of the benefits to be had from meditation practice.

In addition, there is an uncomfortable parallel in the history of psychoanalysis to the current prejudice against pharmacological treatments in dharma circles. Freud's initial group of followers and adherents were the intellectual radicals of their day. Their excitement and faith in this new and profound method of treatment led them to embrace it as a panacea in much the same way that our contemporary avant-garde has embraced Buddhist practice. The daughter of Louis Comfort Tiffany, Dorothy Burlingham, a seminal New York figure of the early 1900s, for example, left her manic-depressive husband after his relentless and unending series of breakdowns and took her four young children to Vienna in 1925 to seek analysis with Freud. Eventually moving into the apartment below Freud's, Dorothy Burlingham began a lifelong relationship with the Freud family that evolved into her living with Anna Freud for the rest of her life (she died in 1979). Anna Freud became her children's analyst, but at least one of them, her son Bob, seems to have inherited the manic-depressive illness from his father. In a tragic story outlined by Ms. Burlingham's grandson Michael John Burlingham in his book *The Last Tiffany,* Bob suffered from unmistakable manic and depressive episodes and died an early death at the age of fifty-four. So great was Anna Freud's belief in psychoanalysis, however, that even when Lithium was discovered as an effective prophylactic treatment, she would not consider its use. He was only permitted treatment that lay within the parameters of Freudian ideology, an approach notoriously ineffective for his condition.

There are undoubtedly dharma practitioners who are depriving themselves in the same way, out of a similar faith in the universality of their ideology. Such people would do well to remember the Buddha's teachings of the Middle Path, especially his counsel against the search for happiness through self-mortification in different forms of asceticism, which he called "painful, unworthy, and unprofitable." To suffer from psychiatric illness willfully, when treatment is mercifully available, is but a contemporary ascetic practice. The Buddha himself tried such ascetic practices, but gave them up. His counsel is worth keeping.

Note: All names, identifying characteristics, and other details of the case material in this article have been changed.

24. Suicide and Transcendence

CROSSING THE GREAT DIVIDE

BY CARYN LEVINGTON, PSY.D., AND FRANK
GRUBA-McCALLISTER, PH.D.

Rather than characterizing a suicide attempt as a "sick" act committed by a "sick" person, this original article portrays suicide as unfolding in an altered state of consciousness brought on by intense psychological trauma. What is needed is an additional altered state in which the self recognizes itself as lovable, worthy of life, and intrinsically good. A case history lucidly illustrates the technique.

At first glance, drawing a parallel between transcendence and suicide appears an improbable endeavor. As a willful act of self-destruction, suicide seems blatantly antithetical to self-renewal. Thus, we tend to view a genuinely suicidal individual as seeking negation rather than affirmation; choosing premature death sharply stands in contrast to our conception of transcendence as living out our individual potentials for living with wholeness and integrity.

Commonly, transcendence is associated with positive, life-affirming experiences. Humanistic psychologist Abraham Maslow showed how such "peak experiences," a form of transcendence, occur to most individuals at least once in their lifetimes, often with great transformative impact. Maslow characterized these experiences as intense feelings of unity with the universe, accompanied by awe, wonder, and reduced fear and anxiety.[1] Transcendence—the experience of "going beyond" oneself to attain a higher, or more complete, understanding of oneself—is, by no means, limited to the experience of surviving a suicidal act. However, surviving a suicide attempt bears a unique transcendent potential because it confronts us with the ultimate paradox of life and death. It enables the survivor to travel across the great divide of existence and ultimate loss.

Existential philosophers have eloquently explored the relationship between great anguish and transcendence. Existentialists view anxiety as built into the very fabric of our being and linked to humanity's unique awareness of the inevitability of death.[2] German existentialist Martin Heidegger wrote that a resolute awareness of death as an ever-present possibility can lead to a more authentic posture in which we freely seek to fulfill as many of our possibilities as we can. Thus, the process of becoming, by its very nature, is inherently arduous.

Our quest to explore opportunities for spiritual growth in personal crises led us to the rapidly expanding discipline of transpersonal psychology. The works of transpersonal theorists Stanislav and Christina Grof and Ken Wilber emphasize how extraordinarily painful tribulations may be necessary stages in self-transcendence.

THE CHALLENGE

Although many who attempt suicide sincerely wish to end their lives, far more people survive suicide attempts than succeed in killing themselves, despite the well-known frailty of the human body and the variety of lethal methods readily available. This discrepancy can be taken to suggest that the suicidal person harbors unconscious ambivalence about her death—not surprising given there can be no decision more serious or final. It also hints that a permanent, physical death, is not necessarily desired, but that an attenuated death, a *metaphoric* one, may be sought.

Nevertheless, suicide is the eighth leading cause of death in the United States. Approximately thirty-five thousand people commit suicide annually, but experts believe a more accurate figure to be one hundred thousand, as many suicides are erroneously characterized as accidents.[3] Current estimates indicate that five million individuals in the United States have attempted suicide, and that as many as 40 percent of those who succeed had made prior attempts.[4] Thus, there are tremendous numbers of people who have tried suicide at least once, and remain at great risk for future fatal attempts.

These statistics underline the need to foster healing, life-affirmation, and transcendence in survivors of suicide attempts. In our work, we have found a simple, effective approach that both survivors and suicidal persons intuitively appear to recognize as an essential healing force in their struggle with self-annihilating anguish. The heart of this approach is conveying unconditional respect for the experience of the individual. Thus, the therapist must establish a relationship with clients in which they experience an open, loving, and non-judgmental attitude. This enables them to openly explore their pain, and the decision to end their lives.

This emphasis on "openness" echoes Heideggerian philosophy, which defines truth as an attitude that allows life's meaning to be fully disclosed to us. When we address human experience with this receptive attitude, we allow an important truth about what it means to be human to articulate itself. Our search for transcendence is inextricably tied to our search for meaning. Survivors report that discussing the will to die, and its origins, is essential to embarking upon the transition to transcendence.[5]

Communicating about pain and our desire for self-annihilation brings the specter of death back to life, teaching us to live more fully. Additionally, many suicide survivors acknowledge intense loneliness and isolation as primary precursors of suicide attempts. Not only does cutting oneself off from the suicide experience create a further internal rift but experiencing fear or condemnation from others only serves to reinforce deep and pervasive experiences of loneliness and isolation. An open attitude taken toward an individual's ability to decide to end life offers the important message that suicide is a shared human experience.

However, survivors and suicidal individuals often hesitate to communicate their experiences, fearing involuntary commitment, misunderstanding, or guilt and shame around being suicidal or failing an attempt. This trepidation is reported by survivors to be enhanced when the listener is a mental health professional. Some survivors state that if suicidality were not bluntly handled as a "red flag" by the mental health profession, engendering drastic measures, such as involuntary commitment, they would have actively sought help rather than attempting suicide in the first place.

This wariness does not arise from fantasy, for Western civilization historically regards suicide with a heartless insensitivity that contaminates the way we assess and treat self-destructive persons. This callous attitude can emerge from therapists' unresolved defenses, blinding them to their own natural anxieties about death, loss, and the kind of relentless suffering that leads a person to take her own life. Cultural attitudes that deny the inevitability of anguish and death in our lives only further alienate suicide survivors from their inner world.

Thus, how a person can transform pain into transcendence imparts meaning for us all. Anguish and its survival are universals in life's journey, and present in each of our lives in different and unique forms. And though this journey is suffused with familiar experiences of loss, despair, joy, creation, and transformation, ultimately, like our very births and deaths, it remains veiled in mystery. As Jungian James Hillman wrote, suicide is one way in which some choose to respond to this mystery, and from the perspective of the psyche, it may not be as emphatic a gesture of annihilation as it might appear:

The soul goes through many death experiences, yet physical life goes on; and as physical life comes to a close, the soul often produces images and experiences that show continuity. The process of consciousness seems to be endless. *For the psyche, neither is immortality a fact, nor is death an end.* We can neither prove nor disprove survival. The psyche leaves the question open.[6]

THE GREAT DIVIDE OF LIFE AND DEATH

Existential philosophers have conceptualized experiences of profound pain, annihilation, and self-renewal, as being "boundary experiences" because these take us to the extremes of human existence. Such experiences act as "wake-up calls," rousing us from our typical posture of slumbering through our lives, oblivious to our life's central themes of existence. Though the act of suicide is extreme, like all boundary experiences, it reminds us that we regularly experience death in life and life in death, and that ultimately, life and death are not divided but remain inseparable.

Thus, surviving suicide, similar to other life-and-death ordeals such as coping with severe illness, surviving a spouse's death, or enduring through a natural disaster, can lead to the kind of transcendence that follows intense and unexpected situations. While suicide differs from such ordeals in that it is an act of individual choice, the anguish leading to the brink of suicide is seldom chosen intentionally—at least from the suicidal person's conscious awareness of her predicament.

If we are to understand suicide, we must supplant our culture's unnatural distinction between life and death with the idea that life and death form a dialectic in which each is necessary for the other to have meaning. When we misunderstand this essential balance, suicide may seem a reasonable way to deal with an internal rift, the experience of oneself as physically alive, yet spiritually dead, or dying. By enacting death, we seek transcendence, spiritual rebirth. This tragic misunderstanding is what the Grofs call equating suicide with "egocide"— the intuition that our faltering worldly values and attachments must die. Egocide is a symbolic death that dissolves our constricted psychic baggage and readies us for an expanded, more spiritually awakened self.

Subjectively, transcendence arrives in many different forms. The survivor of a suicidal act may not have a "big bang" experience of transcendence with profound feelings of liberation, personal and spiritual visions, and deep gratitude for life. Rather, experiences of transcendence may resemble that of Tim, a seventeen-year-old African-American adolescent client of one of the authors. Tim described surviving a self-inflicted gunshot as:

> . . . the first time I ever knew that I was really alive, that if I want to grow up, I can. I live in a real bad place in the city—gangs, bad guys, drugs, guns. Death is

everywhere, but I guess so is life. I'm glad I missed offing myself. I wanted to, but . . . I'm glad I didn't. It's like now I know, hey, I'm alive!

Suicide is an extreme attempt to resolve the ambiguous dialectic of life and death on the streets of Chicago, or a symbolic internal death following great loss. But because it is an act with the capacity to so mightily reach into the human soul, suicide, when survived, has potential to kindle renewed appreciation for the human condition in its balanced state—a state in which life is once again felt to be worth its inherent struggles and suffering.

INVITING THE ASCENT

In order to encourage transcendence for the survivor of suicide, we must avoid characterizing suicide as a "sick" act committed by a "sick" person. Much of the literature on suicide paints such a negative picture, linking it, in medical-model rhetoric, to depression, character disorder, weak will, self-centeredness, self-defeat, arrested development, and so forth. While suicide does not necessarily express mental health, it seems simplistic to exclusively consider it an indicator of mental illness.

Yet suicide is undeniably an act of self-defeat. One's experience of being alive must become profoundly altered in order for self-destruction to appear as a viable alternative to continuing life. But pain alters our conscious experiences of ourselves. Our perceptions and abilities drastically change following such physical traumas as breaking a limb, sustaining a high fever, or difficult childbirth. Similarly, suicide is no more nor less than a reaction to intense psychological trauma, an ascent into pain whose remedy is not as familiar to us, nor as clear-cut as is the salve for a burn or the cast for a broken limb. Thus, pathologizing this experience—or, for that matter, *any* human experience—is rarely healing. Furthermore, because survivors of suicide often feel estranged and isolated from others, pathologizing serves only to confirm this painful perception.

The survivor of suicide needs an experience of an *additional* altered state of consciousness in which the self is felt to be worthy of life, lovable, and intrinsically good. Altered states of consciousness in therapy are not limited to LSD experimentation or primal screams. Rather, they are ways to counteract the altered state the client is already in—the altered state of pain. Throughout the gamut of "talk therapy" runs the potential for offering clients new and unexpected experiences of themselves. Reframing pain in ways that normalize and confirm the humanity of our clients while also suggesting that pain itself has a healing function is but one way in which to induce an altered state. To ground this assertion, we present a brief vignette taken from the first session with Tim, the adolescent mentioned earlier:

Tim: I don't wanna to be here.

Caryn: Here with me or here in the world?

Tim: Anywhere. I don't wanna be anywhere.

Caryn: Where do you want to be?

Tim: I . . . I dunno. Nowhere. Not alive but not dead either. I got to get outta here—out of nowhere. I can't take it anymore. There's stuff in my head I can't deal with.

Caryn: Ok. You're in a lot of pain, but we can do something about it. There's stuff in your head that hurts, but it can also help you to feel better, and it may be hard to know that now, but we're going to try to find out what your pain is trying to tell you so you can feel better.

Tim: I hope.

Caryn: Will you try something with me? (Tim nods assent.) Ok. I want you to close your eyes and take a deep breath. That's good. Keep breathing deeply, letting your mind and body do the good work of helping you to relax, more and more, and just let whatever needs to come into your head come there. Nothing will come that you aren't ready to handle. I'm going to ask you to keep relaxing and try to picture yourself being nowhere. Take as much time as you need to visit this place inside, imagine it, and see yourself there. (2-minute pause)

Tim: I'm scared.

Caryn: Is it a scary place?

Tim: Yeah. It's like . . . a just burned-out house and you don't know if there's still fire anywhere. You could get burned to death, but you can't get out of the house. It's ruined and . . . (begins crying) it really hurts. It really hurts. I'm stuck in this crazy house.

Caryn: It hurts because you're alive and trapped in a sort of dead place where you're not safe being alive.

Tim: I'm alive all right. Alive and crazy.

Caryn: Feeling this hurt is part of being alive and sane.

Tim: Is offing yourself sane? You call it normal?

Caryn: A normal thing people do when they feel so out of options and sometimes so out of control that they don't know what else to do. But there are other ways to handle pain besides dying.

Tim: I don't wanna die.

We worked with this further, until Tim felt he could freely enter and exit the "house" on his own. Tim brought drawings of the house into therapy for three more sessions, finally commenting that he "wanted to move into a new place in my head." In the fourth week of therapy his depression began markedly to improve. Two months after his attempt, he continued to work in therapy and made application for junior college. Techniques such as guided imagery, when combined with meditation and relaxation, can help survivors achieve a sense of detachment from the crisis they face and reconceptualize it in a way that facilitates mastery.

A TRAVEL GUIDE

In order to promote transcendence in suicidal individuals or survivors, we must meet them at the point their consciousness was altered by suffering. We must respect this alteration and address it not in the voice of negation, but of invitation.

There are many ways of extending the invitation to transcendence. We can explore with survivors the meanings that their suffering has for them without forcing our own beliefs on them. We can help survivors distinguish between beliefs that promote transcendence and those that lead to self-defeating cycles that create even more suffering. Finally, conducting life reviews with survivors invites them to talk about past situations in which they grew in response to adversity. This offers hope and confidence that they can again be successful in their current situation.

To be human is to be a wayfarer between the great valleys of living and dying, of love and loss; in short, to be human is to live within an ever-unfolding process that we call existence. Because process involves change, and change involves loss, life unavoidably involves pain. Sometimes this pain causes us to lose faith in life and in ourselves. In the midst of such despair, we may seek to rid ourselves of pain, no matter what the cost. Unfortunately, the price may be all too dear. Because pain is inherent to what it means to be human, our efforts to escape from it may end up as futile attempts to escape from ourselves.

Suicide can represent the most extreme form of such self-escape. However, the same situations leading one to consider suicide also contain within them the potential for transcendence. For it is only when we openly stare into the stark emptiness of death that we are able to turn our attention once more to the abundant promise of life.

25. The Paradox of Finding One's Way by Losing It

THE DARK NIGHT OF THE SOUL AND THE EMERGENCE OF FAITH

BY MICHAEL WASHBURN

"Existential" depression is characterized by a pervasive sense of disillusionment, meaninglessness, and alienation that can lead to loss of self. In this penetrating and intellectually challenging essay, transpersonal philosopher Michael Washburn holds that such a "sickness unto death" can stimulate a deeper kind of faith that draws from a person's concealed inner resources. Readers will find it rewarding to spend a bit of extra effort to grasp the author's profound and exceptionally lucid ideas.

There comes a point in some people's lives when worldly goals lose their significance and life loses its perceived value. When this happens, it seems as though life in any meaningful sense has come to an end. In fact, however, this apparent endpoint can be a turning point toward a new beginning. It is a paradox that we sometimes need to lose our way in order truly to find it, or, as Jesus says in the Gospels, that to save one's life is to lose it and to lose one's life for his sake is to save it.

In existential terms, the paradox is that despair is sometimes a precondition of faith. The process of losing one's way and the spiritual possibilities that can ripen within it have been recognized in the world's spiritual traditions. The overall process, for example, has been described as the dark night of the senses, the spiritual desert or wilderness, the state of self-accusing (Islam), the great doubt (Zen), the ordeal of dying to the world, and the death of the self.[1]

The process in question has many expressions. Among its expressions, the following are perhaps the most important and will be considered in this essay: depression, alienation, deanimation, despair, and the emergence of faith.

DEPRESSION

Depression can be caused not only by unfortunate circumstances but also by neurochemical and psychodynamic imbalances that arise irrespective of life circumstances. Most clinical cases of depression probably involve combinations of these factors. The type of depression discussed here differs in that its primary cause is not to be found in any negative events or situations or in any neuro-chemical or psychiatric conditions but rather in a loss of faith in an existential project: the pursuit of happiness.

Depression as we ordinarily experience it is a passing mood triggered by specific setbacks in life. We are depressed, for example, because we did not get into the college of our choice or because we are experiencing problems in a relationship or at work. Depression of this sort is painful, but we rebound from it. New opportunities arise, the problems vexing us are resolved, and we move back into the mainstream of life. Depression as we ordinarily experience it is indeed a form of acute unhappiness; setbacks in life can be stinging blows. We usually survive these blows, however, and resume the pursuit of happiness. Our energy is restored, and we experience a renewal of the drive for worldly fulfill-ment.

Many people who have been fortunate enough to enjoy some of the rewards of life never lose faith in the pursuit of happiness. And even many people who meet with major setbacks in life do not lose faith. Nevertheless, such a loss of faith is something to which we are inherently susceptible. For the pursuit of happiness is based on a false assumption, namely, that happiness is to be found "out there" in the world. This assumption is false because the world cannot provide what ultimately must be found within ourselves. Accordingly, although the goods of the world are indeed gratifying, we are nonetheless prone to being disillusioned in the pursuit of happiness. If and when such disillusionment sets in, the character of depression changes.

Disillusionment manifests itself initially in the form of vague feelings of dissatisfaction and futility. These feelings can lead to such questions as "Is there no more to life than this?" and "What is the use of trying?" The emergence of feelings of dissatisfaction and futility can understandably lead to depression. But the point here is that this depression is of a special type. For unlike the depressive episodes that follow setbacks in life, this depression can occur without a trigger-ing cause. It can even set in after what normally would be a gratifying worldly experience or accomplishment. Also, this depression is tenacious; it is difficult to rebound from. People who suffer from depression of this sort frequently seek treatment, and properly so. For this type of depression, although "existential" rather than neurochemical or psychiatric in the strict sense, can be seriously debilitating.

ALIENATION

Disillusionment can lead to alienation, to a sense of being cut off from the world. For in losing faith in the pursuit of happiness, one tends to withdraw from worldly involvement. This withdrawal is two-sided; it expresses itself both inwardly in one's feelings and outwardly in one's perception of the world. Inwardly, it consists of a gradual loss of interest, drive, and capacity for engagement. And outwardly, it consists in an alteration in the appearance of the world, which seems gradually to lose its "realness" and meaning. One becomes apathetic, confused, and cut off; simultaneously, the world becomes barren, purposeless, and out of reach.

Alienation is not a voluntary process. Alienation follows upon disillusionment as an effect follows upon a cause, not as a decision follows upon an insight. It is therefore a process that one is powerless to reverse. Alienation is not renunciation. The alienated person does not give up the world; rather, the world simply slips away, becoming remote and unreal.

If any one idea captures the essence of how the alienated person perceives the world, it is flatness. The world goes flat because withdrawal from the world is at the same time a withdrawal of the projected meanings (cognitive intentions) and values (cathexes) by which we interpret and enliven the world. Accordingly, when alienation sets in, the world begins to lose all modes and gradations of lived depth. It loses its peaks and valleys, challenges and disappointments, profundities and banalities, heroes and fools. It becomes a world in which everything is "equal" in the sense of being equally shallow, neutral, and gray. Actions become "equal" because they are all reduced to mere motions. And persons become "equal" because they are all reduced to mere personas. The world of the alienated person becomes flat throughout, for in withdrawing from the world the alienated person ceases intersecting in depth with the world.

A perfect example of what it is like for the world to go flat is available from the domain of the cinema. Everyone is familiar with what happens when one is suddenly drawn out of the action of a film. Let us consider an example. Let us suppose that a man and a woman are viewing a mystery-suspense film. The woman is totally absorbed. The world of the film is, for the present, her world. She identifies with or responds to the characters and is caught up in the action. The man on the other hand, having already seen the film, is not absorbed, and let us suppose that, in a moment of impatience, he reveals the conclusion to the woman—which conclusion, let us also suppose, the woman finds disappointing. Given this situation, it is likely that the woman would suffer disillusionment and would lose interest in the film. That is, she would become alienated from the *world* of the film. Simultaneously, the film itself, as everyone has experienced, would go flat. Without the depth factor provided by outreaching thought and feeling, the film would cease being a self-contained world, a reality unto itself, and would become instead only a film, a fiction. The characters would be reduced to mere actors saying lines, and what was a compelling drama would be reduced to a mere plot or story line. The world of the film would no longer be engaged, and so it would cease being an engaging reality. It would become only a setting, a sequence of scenes.

The experience of the alienated person is virtually identical with that of the moviegoer. For the alienated person, like the moviegoer, ceases being absorbed in a world of possible experience and watches as that world goes flat, becoming remote and unreal. For both, what were meaningful deeds become only idle motions or empty roles; what were real people become only surface characters. The experience of the alienated person parallels that of the moviegoer in all these ways. The alienated person's experience, however, differs from the moviegoer's in one crucial respect, for the world that the alienated person loses is not a fictional world but rather the world of material and social reality. Accordingly, whereas the moviegoer is temporarily estranged from an optional world of fantasy, the alienated person, it seems, is permanently estranged from life itself.

In clinical terms, the flattening of the world that results from the alienation process is a special case of *derealization* in which a person's everyday experience loses its sense of immediacy and familiar reality. Like the depression discussed earlier, however—and like the rest of the conditions to be discussed in this essay—the derealization associated with alienation has existential roots rather than neurochemical or strictly psychiatric causes.

DEANIMATION

The derealization of the world is at the same time a deanimation of ego identity, for ego identity—or, henceforth, simply *identity*—is inextricably a part of the world: it is selfhood *in the world*.[2] Identity is selfhood as defined and justified in terms of worldly categories. Hence, when alienation renders the world remote and unreal, it does the same to identity.

The deanimation of identity leads those suffering from alienation to perceive themselves in the same way they perceive others. Just as alienated people perceive everyone and everything else in the world as flat and dead, so they perceive themselves as flat and dead. People suffering from alienation sense that they are no longer real people in a real world but are rather only assemblages of traits, habits, routines, and roles played out on a lifeless stage. In suffering deanimation, alienated people begin to perceive their identity as only a mask, a persona, a disguise.

The loss of identity is experienced as a death of self. Usually, our sense of being derives from our identity in the world, and therefore the loss of identity carries with it the feeling of loss of being, of death. Alienated people therefore feel as though they are undergoing an irresistible process of dispossession leading in the direction of death. They are "dying to the world." As Kierkegaard, using biblical language, says, they are suffering from a "sickness" that is "unto death."

This process of dying, however, can be interrupted by the eruption of materials from the dark underside of the personality, that is, from that part of the personality that C. G. Jung called the shadow. The shadow remains unconscious so long as identity is unchallenged. So long as a person *lives* her or his identity, the shadow remains securely repressed. When, however, following the onset of alienation, identity undergoes deanimation, the shadow, simultaneously, undergoes derepression—and it rises into consciousness and triggers a host of unwelcome insights.

Alienated people, accordingly, are afflicted with much gnashing of teeth and many stings of conscience. They confront the hidden, dark side of the personality. Having already been disillusioned about the world, they are now disillusioned about themselves. They are jolted into a rude awakening. No longer able to *be* their identity, they are forced to acknowledge (what seems like) the exclusive reality of the shadow.

This derepression of the shadow eventually comes to an end, however. For the shadow is also a part of the world; it is an alter-identity in the world. Consequently, the derealization of the world that is part of the alienation process entails an eventual deanimation not only of identity but of the shadow as well. The shadow, however, must be derepressed and owned before its deanimation can begin. The typical sequence, then, is (1) derealization of world and concomitant deanimation of identity, (2) derepression and owning of the shadow, and (3) deanimation of the shadow. As the shadow begins to undergo deanimation, the process of "dying to the world" resumes and leads toward a limit point of complete deanimation. This limit point is the point of despair.

DESPAIR

The alienation process eventually deprives a person of all vestiges of hope and leads to despair. Despair signals that the world is irretrievably lost and that identity (and the shadow, too) is completely defunct, beyond all possibility of reanimation.

Despair should be distinguished from depression, for although both of these conditions involve a sense of hopelessness, the hopelessness of despair is deeper and more final than the hopelessness of depression. If we remember, the hopelessness experienced by the depressed person—that is, by the person suffering from the existential depression discussed earlier—is a sense of dissatisfaction and futility that, deriving from initial disillusionment, precedes the alienation process. The hopelessness experienced by the despairing person, in contrast, is a sense of utter dissociation and death that emerges after the alienation process has run full course. The person suffering depression has lost faith in the world and therefore is no longer *of* the world. The depressed person, however, is at least still *in* the world. The despairing person, in contrast, is no longer even *in* the world. Completely alienated from the world, the despairing person has not only given up on the pursuit of happiness but has also lost access to the world and all sense of being in the world. Whereas the depressed person can still struggle, even if vainly, to return to his or her "old self," the despairing person is incapable even of mounting such a struggle. For the despairing person is completely dead to the world.

In arriving at the limit point of despair, one ceases to have any kind of meaningful relationship with the world. Dissociated from the arena of action and divested of identity, the despairing person feels as though she or he is a complete nonentity without any justifying purpose, a mere spectator without either *être* or *raison d'être*. This condition—which mimics schizoid personality disorder—is, it seems, a condition of the most dire possible hopelessness.

THE EMERGENCE OF FAITH

Appearances notwithstanding, despair is not an utterly negative condition. It is a condition astir with positive possibilities. For the process of dying to the world that leads to despair stimulates a yearning for life that, unbeknownst to the despairing person, draws on hidden spiritual resources. This yearning is not a hope; it is part of the despairing person's despair. It is experienced as an *unquenchable* thirst, as a yearning for something *impossible,* as a yearning, therefore, that only exacerbates the hopelessness of despair. The only hopes that the despairing person understands are those that are now lost: the hope of achieving happiness in the world, the hope of salvaging at least a vestige of worldly being. With these hopes extinguished, the despairing person cannot understand the yearning that he or she experiences; it is an incomprehensible and therefore completely agonizing yearning.

This yearning for a seemingly impossible "I know not what" signals the beginning of a new kind of faith, a faith that draws deeply on a person's inner resources. This new faith is not the faith of affirming creeds and worshipping a god representation. That kind of faith dies, in the alienation process, along with worldly identity. This kind of faith is a faith that emerges when one is totally lost and can do nothing in one's own behalf other than yearn for what seems impossible. It is a dark faith that at first is not recognized as a spiritual faith at all. But this is precisely what it is.

Few people go through a dark night as severe as the one I have described. Many people suffer from bouts of depression and periods of alienation. But most bounce back and become their "old self" again. Few people follow the path discussed in this essay all the way to the limit point of despair. Those who do, however, arrive at the threshold of a new kind of faith. For their "sickness" is "unto death." For them, the old self does not bounce back; it dies and therefore makes way for the birth of a new self. This new self is a self born of faith, a spiritual self that knows that fulfillment arises from within and therefore need not be pursued as an outer, worldly goal. Accordingly, although this new self is very much a worldly self in the sense of being a self actively engaged and completely at home in the world, it is a self whose basic purpose is no longer the pursuit of worldly goods. It is a self whose basic purpose is, rather, to grow in spirit and to reach out in spirit to others.

The emergence of faith does not necessarily mean that the dark night of the soul is over. St. John of the Cross, in *The Dark Night*, explains that the period of aridity and withdrawal—the night of the senses, which we have discussed in this essay—is sometimes followed by a period of even more difficult trial: the night of spirit. For the night of the senses, as a "sickness unto death" subdues without really transforming the "old self." Accordingly, the dark night of the senses must sometimes be followed by a more radical purgation if a person is to be truly cleansed of all dispositions resistant to the spontaneous expression of spirit. Whether or not the emergence of faith is followed by the night of spirit, however, the point here is that sometimes it is only in the depths of despair that genuine spiritual life is found. It is a paradox that we sometimes have to lose our way in order to find our true self. We sometimes have to die to the world and to our worldly self before we can discover that our deepest and truest self was within us all the time.

26. *Transforming Depression Through Egocide*

SYMBOLIC DEATH AND NEW LIFE

BY DAVID H. ROSEN, M.D.

In this excerpt from his book Transforming Depression, *psychiatrist and Jungian analyst David Rosen draws upon his work with suicide survivors to show that it was not physical death they sought but* symbolic *death, a release from the incessant demands of the ego and its worldly attachments. The author shows how this arduous and sometimes perilous process can ultimately lead to rebirth of a larger and more aware Self.*

Although I had suffered painful losses before, they were not as unbearable as the circumstances surrounding the end of my first marriage, which unfolded not long after I entered medical school. The enormous demands imposed upon my time and energy by the end of the first year in medical school strained our relationship to the limit. My wife, an actress, wanted to go away alone during the summer break, to perform summer-stock repertoire at a theater on Hilton Head Island in South Carolina. Unfortunately (or fortunately), I insisted on accompanying her.

One night, as I sat waiting for her in a bar, she walked in with her leading man. Ignoring me, she went on to demonstrate that her romantic involvement with this man did not stop when the acting did. As I watched the two of them, afraid of what might happen if I vented the rage I was feeling, I ran out of the bar, jumped into my car and sped wildly through the narrow and winding island roads. I envisioned crashing into an embankment, or going off a bridge, thinking death would be far better than the pain I was living through.

Then something very unusual happened. I spun the car into a field, stopped it, got out, and began running through the moonlit, junglelike terrain. As I ran, I could see myself from above, disappearing and reappearing beneath the trees.

The quality of the vision, and with it my state of mind, became clearer and clearer—until finally, I heard a voice say, "Leave!" Later I came to realize that this inner voice issued from what has been termed the "Real Self."[1] The uncanny sensation from this experience remains my only out-of-body experience, which I now understand as one that is beyond ego.[2] Through this extravagant act of physical expression, I had unwittingly found my soul and spiritual center, and my Self had found me. My self-preservation instinct took command of my fate.

I left Hilton Head immediately, knowing and accepting that my marriage was finished. But the fact that I had been rescued did not mean my conscious mind was spared feelings of despair, helplessness, and worthlessness. I drove to New York City and consulted a psychiatrist, who was also a family friend. I blurted out, "I'm a failure." "It's hopeless. Why live?"

His reply was simple and wise, and it has shaped my response to many setbacks ever since. "You are not a failure," he said. "You failed at a marriage."

WHAT I LEARNED FROM MY EXPERIENCE

The strangeness surrounding this traumatic episode left an indelible impression on my life and on my practice as physician, psychiatrist, and analyst. I came to realize that my spontaneous out-of-body-ego experience was an example of what I now call *egocide*, the letting-go of a hurt and hurting dominant ego-image or identity. The suffix *-cide* means kill. However, egocide is a symbolic killing of the ego that is experienced as ego death: a sacrifice of the ego to the Self, a higher principle. Egocide is the core strategy for transforming depression. In my case, it was the ego-image I had of myself as a husband that was sacrificed. When I released that image, I found I could surrender to a higher power within myself— the Self.[3]

From this powerful incident, I learned to appreciate that egocide represents an antidote to suicide, a way out of depression by affirming life instead of rejecting it. But egocide does not necessarily work like a switch, changing a sad person instantly to a happy one. A person who has experienced egocide still has to go through a grieving process for the ego-image that has been left behind, as I did after driving away from South Carolina. Nevertheless, the ability to let go and surrender does represent a transcendence over the limitations imposed by the previous dominant ego-image, and it does clear the way for an eventual transformation of one's ego and self-identity. (I am using ego to represent an awareness of one's conscious identity, and Self to represent the person's unique personal being and expressions of self-esteem and self-realization.)

By the time I finished medical school, I had two significant leads from personal experience as to how one commits egocide. Creatively redirecting my despair on Hilton Head Island by racing through treacherous territory, I had, quite literally, risen above my suicidal ego-image as a rejected husband. Also, during my undergraduate and medical school years, painting had helped me to capture and vanquish depressive states. I was nineteen when I first learned this lesson as an undergraduate at the University of California at Berkeley. It did not come to me, however, in the classroom. Immersed in a period of deep depression, waiting for it to pass, I was inexplicably moved to paint my first emotional landscape—a spontaneous, free-style rendering of what I felt to be my state of mind at the time. Much to my wonder, this single activity completely dispelled my melancholic mood.

Only years later, when I read A. Lommel's *Shamanism: The Beginnings of Art,* did I fully appreciate why I had been able to paint myself out of my depression. From the beginning of human history to the present day, shamans have functioned as healers in tribal societies, assuming a multifaceted role that is analogous to the combined roles of a medical doctor, a psychotherapist or analyst, and a religious leader in our modern world. A shaman becomes a shaman by facing a personal, life-threatening illness (usually severe depression) and overcoming it, using creative activities such as drawing, crafting art objects, chanting poetry, or journeying (an intense, almost trancelike form of visualization) to do so. After self-ordination and tribal acceptance, the shaman uses his or her creative talents to assist others in dealing with their physical and emotional problems. Thus, the value of what I had done by instinct to transform my own depressed mood was confirmed by history. Today I see it confirmed again and again in the lives of patients in psychotherapy and analysis.

Ahead of me, as a medical school graduate, lay the pursuit on a professional level of further knowledge about depression and suicide.[4] Appropriately, one of the earliest and most important destinations in that pursuit turned out to be the Golden Gate Bridge.

MORE CLUES: WHAT SURVIVORS OF SUICIDE SAY

Aside from being a singularly handsome structure in its own right, the Golden Gate Bridge has exceptional symbolic beauty as a passageway between city and country, harbor and ocean, sea and sky. It is little wonder, therefore, that the Golden Gate Bridge is the place of choice for people planning their own leaps from life to death. Since the bridge opened in 1937, it is estimated that over two thousand individuals have jumped to their deaths, making it a suicide shrine.[5] Jumping is almost invariably fatal: The distance from rail to water is about 255 feet; a jumper hits the water at about 75 miles per hour. Nevertheless, one percent of the people who jump do survive.

As a resident in psychiatry at the University of California Medical Center in San Francisco, I was interested in finding out what it was like to confront and survive such a grandly staged and apparently certain suicide attempt. This interest was sparked by reading a front-page newspaper account of a survivor of a leap off the Golden Gate Bridge. I decided to formulate a research study and interview this person and other such survivors. When I discovered that there were only eight known survivors still living, I expanded my field of possible interviewees to include survivors of jumps from the San Francisco–Oakland Bay Bridge, which is also an imposing platform for committing suicide and offers the same low odds of survival. Initially, I was able to set up interviews with six of the eight Golden Gate Bridge survivors and one of the two San Francisco–Oakland Bay Bridge survivors. Later, I interviewed three more survivors of jumps off the Golden Gate Bridge.

In addition to gaining insights from these survivors that might be useful in detecting and preventing possible suicides, I was hoping to gather information that would help in treating people who go through the types of partial or symbolic deaths I have already mentioned, such as loss, failure, rejection, depression, or any psychological subjugation to a negative ego-image. Specifically, I wanted to refine my egocide theory and make it more therapeutically useful. For these purposes, I especially wanted answers to these two questions: (1) How have the survivors subsequently handled such an upsetting traumatic event—an experience so close to death? (2) What have been the long-term effects of such events on their lives?

The message I received from the interviewees was clearer and more significant than I had expected. The ten survivors gave varying reasons for jumping, but there was a common core feeling of aloneness, alienation, depression, rejection, worthlessness, and hopelessness. Although the ten had widely divergent views of religion before attempting suicide, they all admitted to feelings of spiritual transcendence after they had leaped.

The words of two survivors are particularly meaningful:

At first everything was black, then gray-brown, then light. It opened my mind—like waking up. It was very restful. When I came up above the water, I realized I was alive. I felt reborn. I was treading water and singing—I was happy and it was a joyous occasion. It affirmed my belief that there is a higher spiritual world. I experienced a transcendence—in that moment I was refilled with new hope and purpose of being alive.[6]

Another survivor expressed his spiritual transcendence and transformation in more ecumenical terms:

> It's beyond most people's comprehension. I appreciate the miracle of life—like watching a bird fly—everything is more meaningful when you come close to losing it. I experienced a feeling of unity with all things and a oneness with all people. After my psychic rebirth I also feel for everyone's pain. Surviving confirmed my belief and purpose in my life. Everything was clear and bright— I became aware of my relationship with my creator.

By surviving self-chosen-death leaps, all ten of my interviewees wound up committing *symbolic suicide*—what I have termed *egocide*—instead of actual suicide.[7] In retrospect, they each realized that they had planned their jump in a confused and demoralized state, during which they had inappropriately defined their whole being in terms of a specific failing or negative ego or self-image. Even more noteworthy, they each recommended that suicide barriers be constructed on both bridges. In every case, I interpret this plea as a projection of an inner barrier against suicide: Contrary to most survivors of very serious suicide attempts, who are at much greater risk for subsequent suicide, none of the ten survivors whom I interviewed had gone on to suicide.

In developing my egocide and transformation theory, some of my most important teachers have been these survivors. These ten individuals, who set out to commit suicide but survived, found out that they had somehow cleared the way for psychic regeneration. In surviving, they had symbolically killed their previous negative ego-identities. Each of these individuals transcended the split between inner death and life forces, between the negative ego and the Self. Through the act of surviving their depressive and suicidal states, they had transformed themselves. Their experiences became the basis of a new paradigm for me and for my patients.

A COMMONSENSE MODEL OF EGOCIDE AND TRANSFORMATION

Expressed as simply as possible, my theory of egocide and transformation presents a Bad News/Good News scenario of psychological development. The Bad News is that we all occasionally become depressed: We fail, lose, or fall. For some individuals, depression can reach a point where they feel completely worthless. In this dark abyss, the person experiences a loss of soul and spirit: Hope's flame is sputtering out. Suicide seems like the only solution. However, the

Good News is that only a part of the ego has to die (or be killed). This Symbolic Death (or egocide) can usher in a positive psychic transformation, or New Life.

To reiterate, the model of egocide and transformation involves four aspects: Bad News, Good News, Symbolic Death, and New Life. The Bad News is a state of demoralization, a negative turn leading to despair, or depression caused by a precipitating failure, such as loss of a job. This is on an ego (I, me) level. The Bad News, which involves loss, is based on rejection and is experienced as a wounding of the ego. If we can endure and persist, the untoward is followed by Good News. The Good News is that after the fall, we are able to pick ourselves up. We may need a helping hand, support, encouragement, and therapy, but we *can* get back up. There is ascent after descent; there is joy after despair; there is success after failure. Based on this Good News, the ego again feels that it is in control. The person then has an enhanced self-image.

People spend most of their lives on an ego level. However, when there is a major fall, a life crisis of some kind, there is a confrontation with death. At this time, we tend to become severely depressed, if not suicidal, and experience a feeling of losing our soul. Stuck in hopelessness, we become preoccupied with ending our life. Alcoholics Anonymous maintains that a person must hit *rock bottom*, hardly able to function, before major change occurs. In such an instance of extreme dejection, the ego can turn on itself in its last desperate act of control. The only recourse the ego feels it has left to master the situation of ultimate failure is to commit suicide. It is a conscious ego act.[8]

Therefore, in that fateful moment, if the person can transcend the inner struggle between death and life and gain insight and understanding, he or she can choose egocide and transformation, preserving the self and relationships with significant others. Anyone can talk and analyze a tragic situation to *death*, and go through a loss of that negative dominant ego-image, which has led to this confrontation with the cessation of life.

To reach the point of suicide, the negative ego colludes with what Carl Jung called the Shadow—one's darkest repressed side.[9] The way to survive involves both egocide (killing the negative ego) and shadowcide (killing the negative Shadow). In sum, this is killing the *false self*. This Symbolic Death leads to a further and greater fall, which actually feels like death. It is like entering an eternal void. This is a frightening transitional phase characterized by a death-rebirth struggle. When the ego is fragmented, the person feels lost. But when the individual contacts the center of the psyche, the Self (Supreme Being), it leads to a reorganization and reconstitution of the ego, which is now secondary to a higher principle. This is the emergence of the *true self* (genuine being).

The final phase involves New Life, based on the person surviving (suffering through) a death-rebirth experience. The individual feels reborn and morale is restored.*

Now I want to present a novel approach to treating depressed persons and those who want to kill themselves. It involves egocide, transcendence, and transformation. The method I advocate for treating depressed and suicidal patients differs from the other approaches I have described, although it works in harmony with any one or more of them. I call this approach *egocide and transformation.*

Let's look at some well-known examples of people who made this kind of healing journey through dark nights of their souls. Each example illustrates that an individual must first endure depression in order to transcend it and transform his or her life. After this healing, each of these individuals made vital contributions to bettering the lives of others.

Abraham Lincoln suffered from recurrent bouts of severe depression, no doubt resulting from the death of his mother at an early age and the harsh treatment at the hands of his father. When he was twenty-nine years old, he became morbidly depressed after the death of his beloved fiancée, Ann Rutledge. He wandered the Illinois river banks confused and grief-stricken. His friends thought he might be suicidal, so they removed his knives and razors and kept watch over his activities. At the age of thirty-two, Lincoln began experiencing deep depressive spells, as he describes in a letter to his law partner, John Stuart:

> If what I feel were equally distributed to the whole human family, there would not be one cheerful face on earth. Whether I shall ever be better, I cannot tell; I awfully forbode I shall not. To remain as I am is impossible. I must die or be better.[10]

Karl Menninger, in his book *The Vital Balance,* offers another telling account of Lincoln's depression:

> On his wedding day all preparations were in order and the guests assembled, but Lincoln didn't appear. He was found in his room in deep dejection, obsessed with ideas of unworthiness, hopelessness, and guilt. Prior to his illness, Lincoln was an honest but undistinguished lawyer whose failures were more conspicuous than his successes. This was when he was considered well—before his mental illness made its appearance. What he became and achieved after his illness is part of our great national heritage.[11]

---

* See Table one.

TABLE ONE

Commonsense Model of Egocide and Transformation

BAD NEWS	In a period of failing, falling, or losing, the depressed individual experiences such grief or despair that the person wants to die, i.e., commit suicide.
GOOD NEWS	The depressed person does not have to die totally; only part of the individual's psyche has to die or be symbolically killed off.
SYMBOLIC DEATH	Letting go of or killing off the destructive part of the psyche, the dominant ego-image or negative identity, through egocide.
NEW LIFE	Egocide makes possible a psychic transformation and a new ego-Self axis evolves, allowing for one's full potential to develop and one's personal myth to be affirmed.

In 1821, the English philosopher John Stuart Mill, then only twenty years old, became morbidly depressed. Apparently, he couldn't escape thinking that he would never be happy, even if he were to obtain everything he desired. Eventually, however, he was able to push himself beyond this state, by some means that were apparently not clear even to himself. In his *Autobiography*, Mill states:

> The experiences of this period . . . led me to adopt a theory of life, very unlike that on which I had before acted, and having much in common with what at that time I certainly had never heard of, the anti-self-consciousness theory of Carlyle. I never, indeed, wavered in the conviction that happiness is the test of all rules of conduct, and the end of life. But I now thought that this end was only to be attained by not making it a direct end. Those only are happy (I thought) who have their minds fixed on some object other than their own happiness; on the happiness of others, on the improvement of mankind, even on some art or pursuit, followed not as a means, but as itself an ideal end. Aiming thus at something else, they find happiness by the way.[12]

Another meaningful example of a person overcoming depression is William James, the founder of both American psychology and American philosophy. At the age of twenty-five, James dropped out of medical school because he was severely depressed and was entertaining suicidal thoughts. Cameron, his biographer, writes:

> He awoke every morning with a horrible dread. For months he was unable to go into the dark alone ... he wondered how other people could live so unconscious of the pit of insecurity beneath the surface of life. . . .
>
> The world owes a great deal to those personal misfortunes. James was thrown heavily upon his own resources; his incapacities and frustrations at such a time gave him an intense and intimate appreciation of the deepest philosophical and religious problems; his illness clearly developed and deepened the bed in which the stream of his philosophic life was to flow.[13]

Menninger suggests that by transcending their illnesses, these three individuals became what he terms *weller than well*. They were able to enter into the darkness and commit egocide rather than suicide; afterward, they were able to transform their identities. Each of them was involved in a journey toward wholeness that was related to a cycle of living and symbolically dying, and living again, which is the antithesis to the ego's ultimate claim to control, i.e., suicide.

Whatever impels a person to seek death, there is virtually always a better alternative than killing oneself. Sometimes the temptation to commit suicide can be strong and even comforting. Nietzsche, for example, said: "The thought of suicide is a great consolation: By means of it, one gets successfully through many a bad night." However, thoughts of suicide, under certain conditions, may be dangerous to entertain. I propose a different maxim: Contemplate egocide, a humbling but healing act of creative transformation; by means of it, one goes through a Symbolic Death, and on to New Life.

EGOCIDE AND SHADOWCIDE: SYMBOLIC KILLING OF EGO AND SHADOW

Why symbolically kill the disaffirming introjected parental ego and negative ego-image? In dreams and in the Jungian practice of active imagination (creative artistic expression of unconscious conflicts), the reason for such an act is usually clear. Marion Woodman gives an example of such a reasonable killing in a dream told to her by a young woman suffering from a crippling father complex.[14] "My brothers and I killed our father," she said, recounting her dream. "He was haunting us, terrorizing us. We pounded him with stones in the alleyway. We put his body in the car trunk and buried him in a field." Woodman, claiming that her patient's dream illustrates her transition into mature womanhood, states, "She must *symbolically kill* her father."

Jung also refers to the patient's need to "kill the symbolic representative of the unconscious . . . the Terrible Mother who devours and destroys."[15]

Egocide for the bridge-jump survivors represented an extreme case of symbolic suicide—a dramatic, real-life extension of a psychic dilemma analogous to the symbolic killing of the father in the dream of Woodman's patient. In the case of each attempted suicide the Self survived, while the problematic ego-image and identity, along with the negative pole of the shadow—which was adversely influencing the ego-image and identity—were destroyed.

One of my patients, Stephen, a middle-aged professional, came to see me after the only other males in his immediate family had destroyed themselves. His father had died from alcoholism and his brother had committed suicide. Stephen was also on a path toward sacrificing himself but, after a little more than two years of analytical therapy using my model, he committed egocide instead. The telling moment came in a dream in which he climbed up to a platform atop one of the towers of a suspension bridge. Then he jumped off. When he leaped, he left his former destructive ego-image and evil shadow identity behind. Upon awakening, he miraculously found himself alive, uninjured, and reborn, and his new identity was no longer dependent solely upon the ego. In the surrender of ego, the Self had been experienced and his new ego was secondary to this higher power.

Analytical therapy nearly always involves shadowcide. Initially the Shadow is projected and then dealt with in problematic interpersonal relationships, including negative transference reactions. As the projections are withdrawn, Shadow dreams of evil same-sexed figures are more common. For example, when I was dealing with my own negative Shadow, I had dream confrontations with vicious male figures; at one point I killed a cruel male mafia leader, which is an example of shadowcide. At that time, my identity or dominant ego-image was associated with a self-harmful father complex. Shortly thereafter, I psychically murdered my father. This symbolic killing of my negative ego, Shadow, and father complex cleared the way for transformation. Years later, I had a dream in which my deceased father came back from the realm of the dead and moved toward me, uncharacteristically smiling, then he embraced me. He had substance to him, but I knew that he was from the other side. This is an image of acceptance of my personal Shadow and father complex (as well as my father) based on a psychic transformation.

The adolescent wants and needs to psychically kill off and let go of his or her dominant ego-image and identity, which is tied up with parental introjects. Neumann, too, calls for the murder of parental figures on a symbolic level, as not only okay but necessary.[16] This experience would be egocide; ideally the adolescent would transform the parental image into his or her own ego-image and unique identity, and his or her own personal myth would begin to unfold (the individuation process).

Goethe extolled the adolescent experience and claimed that he repeatedly chose to go through self-generated adolescentlike crises (death-rebirth experiences) throughout his life. In other words, he was recommending periodic experiences of egocide and transformation or Symbolic Death and New Life. The killing energy is harnessed and undergoes metamorphosis; when the suicidal complex is transformed, the individual is changed. But every death experience, literal or symbolic, requires mourning.

Even though egocide is based on letting only a part of the ego die, it feels like total ego death, and one feels dead. Therefore, the person so afflicted needs to go through a mourning process for the lost ego-image and identity.

I want to emphasize the importance of the mourning process in egocide, because a death experience has transpired even though it is symbolic in nature. As Kast notes:

> The dreadful despair must be accepted as such and must be regarded as appropriate to this particular life situation. In addition, the chaotic emotions, especially the anger, must be endured. This is made easier by an understanding that this emotional chaos represents the dismantling of the old patterns of relationship and the old habits and therefore also the creation of a new potential.

Over time, through the mourning process, the killed ego part becomes an accepted inner figure, a friendly ghost. The energy of the accepted Symbolic Death of the previous dominant ego identity is transformed into New Life. One's new ego-image based on a deeper ego-Self connection leads to better relationships with others. In my egocide model, the painful death experience (Symbolic Death) is undeniably an evil of sorts, a kind of destruction (Bad News); but it is followed by creative reconstruction (Good News) and renewal (New Life). Beethoven's words are apt here: "I am patient, for I remember that every evil is attended with some good."

THE HEALING JOURNEY

In mapping a territory it is wise to learn from those who have gone before. Just as I was taught by the bridge-leap survivors, analytical work with my patients has led to trail blazing through a wilderness of depression.

In the first stage of healing, you feel extremely depressed and suicidal. Whether or not you are alone in your personal life (often you are), you feel isolated and alienated. Usually you have suffered some Bad News, some loss that has triggered a feeling of helplessness, which frequently progresses to a feeling of hopelessness. Internally, your candle of hope is flickering. You feel like a failure and assume a negative ego-image and identity: The Shadow takes over the ego, so that you feel worthless. Your persona is marred and you are unable to perform effectively. The false self is predominant, and you experience inauthenticity, emptiness, and meaninglessness. There is unbearable suffering, a living hell as many people describe it, and you feel disorganized, disabled, and incapable of working. Your ego is dying. This is the actual experience of egocide or Symbolic Death.

After I published my first article on the bridge-jump survivors, Stanislav Grof contacted me. He was intrigued by my empirical study, because he had made some of the same observations when he studied the use of LSD in psychotherapy with suicidal patients. He carried out this study with a series of suicidal patients for whom every other kind of therapeutic intervention had failed. Grof discovered that all of these patients went through what he called an ego death experience and none went on to commit suicide.

Grof outlines three Death-Rebirth Stages utilizing a model of clinical delivery. He describes the first stage of a patient's illness as *antagonism with mother* with ego death, accompanied by a feeling of total annihilation and disintegration. The patient then enters the second stage of illness and therapy, where his or her experience is archetypal, within the collective unconscious. During this second stage, which Grof calls *synergism with mother*, the patient grapples with the mother archetype, that which gives and takes back all life. Thus, the death-rebirth struggle is both positive and nurturing as well as negative and devouring. The third stage, *separation from mother*, involves the death-rebirth experience itself—an emergence from darkness into light that parallels the physical birth experience.

EMOTIONAL BLUEPRINT OF THE HEALING JOURNEY

At each stage of a depressive illness, there is a correspondingly different stage in the therapeutic analytical process. During the first stage, you nearly always exhibit resistance and express a lot of negativity and rage. This behavior is an understandable test to see if your therapist can genuinely accept you and empathize with you. Be wary of a negative response (hateful rejection) by your therapist.[17] You can always leave your therapist and find one who is accepting and caring. Building trust with your therapist allows you to go through a constructive "regression in the service of the ego."[18] This regression is to be in the service of positive ego. Your therapist ought to point out and support every ego strength you have, emphasizing all your assets, capabilities, and talents, thus giving you a safe place to identify, confront, understand, and abandon ego deficits and liabilities.

Once your initial resistance has been overcome, conflicts related to the personal unconscious can be faced and resolved. In Stage I the primary task is to understand and work through complexes (conflicts) you have with your parents. Again, this is a time to acknowledge your strengths and capabilities and thereby reinforce your positive ego-image. Then, through the analytical process, negative introjects (negative mother and father complexes), i.e., disaffirming parts of the ego, are identified and killed off (or allowed to die)—in other words, talked or analyzed to death. This is the essence of what I term *egocide*. During the final part of the first stage, you actually feel as if you are dying. The dying negative ego-image and false self are pulling your healthy ego and identity into the sea of the unconscious to join them in Symbolic Death. To say the least, this is a very painful and difficult time in therapy.

During Stage II of your illness and therapy, you usually feel dead and are extremely dependent: a confirmation that your previous ego-identity is dead. You become anxious, confused, despondent, and withdrawn; there is synergism with your therapist, who becomes a mother surrogate. It is as if you are back in the womb and totally reliant on your mother. The strength of the positive transference and therapeutic alliance is critical at this stage. There is a "regression in the service of the Self."[19] You experience Good News and begin to see light at the end of the tunnel. Your reintegrated, reconstituted, and stronger ego, which includes more of the Shadow and the contrasexual aspect of the psyche (anima or animus), helps you to contact your center, the Self, which encompasses all of consciousness and unconsciousness. During this stage the ego-Self axis develops, and it is at this point that you begin working with the collective unconscious complexes and archetypes. At the end of the second stage, you begin to feel hopeful and less depressed, which ushers in the next stage.

The third and final stage of your illness and therapy is characterized by separation from your therapist and a death-rebirth experience. You work on ending therapy, and the frequency of sessions decreases. You create expressions of integrated wholeness which represent a union of opposites (examples include: yin [female] and yang [male], and good and evil). The way to transcend opposites is to integrate them. The Self, a union of opposites, often manifests itself in creative acts such as mandalas, which are found in all human cultures past and present. Rebirth or New Life is the culmination of the last stage which signals self-realization. It is in this closing phase that the *self-Self axis* develops,[20] and you feel that life has meaning and purpose. Action and resolution become apparent in your outer life, often in the form of creative productions and life changes (e.g., spontaneous healing images, changes in significant relationships and careers).

Controlling the process of egocide and transformation in the midst of a real-life crisis can be extremely difficult. Psychotherapy offers a container within which that process can be more effectively handled and, therefore, geared more toward *individuation,* Jung's term for the healing journey toward wholeness.[21] Carl Rogers postulates a similar concept and process in what he terms *self-realization,* which he describes "as a life-long process of realizing an individual's potentialities to become a fully functioning person . . . to be that self which one truly is."[22] Abraham Maslow's parallel view is that the ultimate value is the human spiritual need for *self-actualization,* in other words, you must be true to your own divine nature.[23] The psychotherapeutic relationship between you and your therapist creates a *temenos,* a sacred space, where such a transformation can take place in privacy and relative security.

The survivors of jumps off the Golden Gate Bridge were able to transcend their depressive and suicidal states and commit egocide and shadowcide (rather than suicide) and undergo a transformation of their conscious identities. They embodied Ecclesiastes' "A time to kill and a time to heal." What they symbolically killed was the negative ego and Shadow, not the self (their unique personal being). They did not commit suicide from which there is *no* return, but rather their healing was based on Symbolic Death, reconnecting with the soul, and reorienting by the Self. They were involved in a journey toward wholeness that was and is related to living and dying naturally—the antithesis to suicide. Egocide, the Symbolic Death of the false self, leads to New Life and the rebirth of the true self.

THE DANGERS AND POWERS OF EGOCIDE

Egocide is not to be embraced lightly as a mode of therapy or life. It is a soul-wrenching process and must be pursued with immense respect for the dangers involved. The most serious of these dangers is suicide, which should always be regarded as an ever-present possibility. The agony of the first stage of therapy is so painful that in a moment of desperation, when severely depressed, you may want to act on a wish to escape into permanent sleep. To forestall this from happening, your psychic pain level needs to be monitored as carefully as possible. If you are unable to tolerate the pain of worsening melancholia, then admission to a hospital ought to be considered.[24] The protective confines of a womblike shelter can be just what the inner healer ordered!

Psychosis is another possible problematic outcome of egocide.[25] The term egocide literally means killing the ego; but in practice it actually refers to the symbolic death of a dominant ego-image and disaffirming identity. If, instead, your entire ego disintegrates, then you will be psychotic (i.e., without an ego). This eventuality is comparable to what happens to a small minority of people who take LSD: Their egos dissolve and they remain egoless psychotics. The threat or possibility of such an outcome during the egocidal process might require the use of anti-psychotic medication and, possibly, hospitalization.

The final egocide-related danger is regression to a former persona.[26] This regression does not lead to New Life, but rather to a former state of being, or old life, like a recently divorced person returning to his or her parents' home and staying there permanently. The divorced person regresses from a spouse persona to a dependent-child persona. Such a regression is a negative development with the person getting stuck in a former and superficial as well as inappropriate role and identity; that is, a false self.

Having warned about the dangers of egocide, let me end this chapter by praising its positive powers. Egocide is a vital step in transforming a depressed and suicidal individual into a life-affirming person.

> Only through critical times of suffering and despair can transformation occur; for when push comes to shove the individual's limitations are accepted, forcing the ego to renounce its centrality and thereby allowing the Self to emerge. Now a dialectic relationship between the Self and ego can engage so healing and wholeness may occur.

Agreeing with Goethe, I want to stress that egocide is a recurring process. Peter Mudd comments on "the ego's achieved capacity to die repeatedly an ongoing series of conscious voluntary psychological deaths in the service of individuation."[27] This statement seems to affirm that egocide is an ongoing and repetitious phenomenon.

Finally, I cite Oliver Wendell Holmes and say that the power of egocide and transformation can rescue lives, which may help to atone "For those who never sing/But die with all their music in them."

27. *Gifts of Depression*

HEALING THE WOUNDED SOUL

BY THOMAS MOORE

Poetically reaffirming the primeval role of Saturn—the ancient archetype of life's somber side—Thomas Moore shows us how pathologizing our melancholy moments alienates us from powerful sources of inner healing. In this perceptive excerpt from his bestseller Care of the Soul, *the author shows how depression can become an initiation, a rite of passage to higher levels of self-realization.*

The soul presents itself in a variety of colors, including all the shades of gray, blue, and black. To care for the soul, we must observe the full range of all its colorings, and resist the temptation to approve only of white, red, and orange— the brilliant colors. The "bright" idea of colorizing old black and white movies is consistent with our culture's general rejection of the dark and the gray. In a society that is defended against the tragic sense of life, depression will appear as an enemy, an unredeemable malady; yet in such a society, devoted to light, depression, in compensation, will be unusually strong.

Care of the soul requires our appreciation of these ways it presents itself. Faced with depression, we might ask ourselves, "What is it doing here? Does it have some necessary role to play?" Especially in dealing with depression, a mood close to our feelings of mortality, we must guard against the denial of death that is so easy to slip into. Even further, we may have to develop a taste for the depressed mood, a positive respect for its place in the soul's cycles.

Some feelings and thoughts seem to emerge only in a dark mood. Suppress the mood, and you will suppress those ideas and reflections. Depression may be as important a channel for valuable "negative" feelings, as expressions of affection are for the emotions of love. Feelings of love give birth naturally to gestures of attachment. In the same way, the void and grayness of depression evoke an awareness and articulation of thoughts otherwise hidden behind the screen of lighter moods. Sometimes a person will come to a therapy session in a dark mood. "I shouldn't have come today," he will say. "I'll feel better next week, and we can get on with it." But I'm happy that he came, because together we will hear thoughts and feel his soul in a way not possible in his cheerful moods. Melancholy gives the soul an opportunity to express a side of its nature that is as valid as any other, but is hidden out of our distaste for its darkness and bitterness.

SATURN'S CHILD

Today we seem to prefer the word *depression* over *sadness* and *melancholy.* Perhaps its Latin form sounds more clinical and serious. But there was a time, five or six hundred years ago, when melancholy was identified with the Roman god Saturn. To be depressed was to be "in Saturn," and a person chronically disposed to melancholy was known as a "child of Saturn." Since depression was identified with the god and the planet named for him, it was associated with other qualities of Saturn. For example, he was known as the "old man," who presided over the golden age. Whenever we talk about the "golden years" or the "good old days," we are calling up this god, who is the patron of the past. The depressed person sometimes thinks that the good times are all past, that there is nothing left for the present or the future. These melancholic thoughts are deeply rooted in Saturn's preference for days gone by, for memory and the sense that time is passing. These thoughts and feelings, sad as they are, favor the soul's desire to be both in time and in eternity, and so in a strange way they can be pleasing.

Sometimes we associate depression with literal aging, but it is more precisely a matter of the soul's aging. Saturn not only brings an affection for the "good old days," he also raises the more substantive idea that life is moving on: we're getting old, experienced, and maybe even wise. A person even in his middle or late thirties will be in conversation and offhandedly recall something that happened twenty years ago. He will stop, shocked. "I've never said that before! Twenty years ago. I'm getting old." This is Saturn's gift of age and experience. Having been identified with youth, the soul now takes on important qualities of age that are positive and helpful. If age is denied, soul becomes lost in an inappropriate clinging to youth.

Depression grants the gift of experience not as a literal fact but as an attitude toward yourself. You get a sense of having lived through something, of being older and wiser. You know that life is suffering, and that knowledge makes a difference. You can't enjoy the bouncy, carefree innocence of youth any longer, a realization that entails both sadness because of the loss, and pleasure in a new feeling of self-acceptance and self-knowledge. This awareness of age has a halo of melancholy around it, but it also enjoys a measure of nobility.

Naturally, there is resistance to this incursion of Saturn that we call depression. It's difficult to let go of youth, because that release requires an acknowledgement of death. I suspect that those of us who opt for eternal youth are setting ourselves up for heavy bouts of depression. We're inviting Saturn to make a house call when we try to delay our service to him. Then Saturn's depression will give its color, depth, and substance to the soul that for one reason or another has dallied long with youth. Saturn weathers and ages a person naturally, the way temperature, winds, and time weather a barn. In Saturn, reflection deepens, thoughts embrace a larger sense of time, and the events of a long lifetime get distilled into a sense of one's essential nature.

In traditional texts, Saturn is characterized as cold and distant, but he has other attributes as well. Medical books called him the god of wisdom and philosophical reflection. In a letter to Giovanni Calvalcanti, a successful statesman and poet, Ficino refers to Saturn as a "unique and divine gift." In the late fifteenth century, Ficino wrote a book warning scholars and studious people in particular to take care not to invite too much Saturn into their souls; because of their sedentary occupations, scholars can easily become severely depressed, he said, and have to find ways to counter their dark moods. But another book could be written about the dangers of living without study and speculation, and without reflecting on our lives. Saturn's moods may be dangerous because of their darkness, but his contributions to the economy of the soul are indispensable. If you allow his depression to visit, you will feel the change in your body, in your muscles, and on your face—some relief from the burden of youthful enthusiasm and the "unbearable lightness of being."

Maybe we could appreciate the role of depression in the economy of the soul more if we could only take away the negative connotations of the word. What if "depression" were simply a state of being, neither good nor bad, something the soul does in its own good time and for its own good reasons? What if it were simply one of the planets that circle the sun? One advantage of using the traditional image of Saturn, in place of the clinical term *depression,* is that then we might see melancholy more as a valid way of being rather than as a problem that needs to be eradicated.

Aging brings out the flavors of a personality. The individual emerges over time, the way fruit matures and ripens. In the Renaissance view, depression, aging, and individuality all go together: the sadness of growing old is part of becoming an individual. Melancholy thoughts carve out an interior space where wisdom can take up residence.

Saturn was also traditionally identified with the metal lead, giving the soul weight and density, allowing the light, airy elements to coalesce. In this sense, depression is a process that fosters a valuable coagulation of thoughts and emotions. As we age, our ideas, formerly light, rambling, and unrelated to each other, become more densely gathered into values and a philosophy, giving our lives substance and firmness.

Because of its painful emptiness, it is often tempting to look for a way out of depression. But entering into its mood and thoughts can be deeply satisfying. Depression is sometimes described as a condition in which there are no ideas—nothing to hang on to. But maybe we have to broaden our vision and see that feelings of emptiness, the loss of familiar understandings and structures in life, and the vanishing of enthusiasm, even though they seem negative, are elements that can be appropriated and used to give life fresh imagination.

When, as counselors and friends, we are the observers of depression and are challenged to find a way to deal with it in others, we could abandon the monotheistic notion that life always has to be cheerful, and be instructed by melancholy. We could learn from its qualities and follow its lead, becoming more patient in its presence, lowering our excited expectations, taking a watchful attitude as this soul deals with its fate in utter seriousness and heaviness. In our friendship, we could offer it a place of acceptance and containment. Sometimes, of course, depression, like any emotion, can go beyond ordinary limits, becoming a completely debilitating illness. But in extreme cases, too, even in the midst of strong treatments, we can still look for Saturn at the core of depression and find ways to befriend it.

One great anxiety associated with depression is that it will never end, that life will never again be joyful and active. This is one of the feelings that is part of the pattern—the sense of being trapped, forever to be held in the remote haunts of Saturn. In my practice, when I hear this fear I think of it as Saturn's style, as one of the ways he works the soul—by making it feel constrained, with nowhere to go. Traditionally, there is a binding theme in saturnine moods. This anxiety seems to decrease when we stop fighting the saturnine elements that are in the depression, and turn instead toward learning from depression and taking on some of its dark qualities as aspects of personality.

INSINUATIONS OF DEATH

Saturn is also the reaper, god of the harvest, patron of end-time and its festival, the Saturnalia; accordingly, imagery of death may permeate periods of depression. People of all ages sometimes say from their depression that life is over, that their hopes for the future have proved unfounded. They are disillusioned because the values and understandings by which they have lived for years suddenly make no sense. Cherished truths sink into Saturn's black earth like chaff at harvest time.

Care of the soul requires acceptance of all this dying. The temptation is to champion our familiar ideas about life right up to the last second, but it may be necessary in the end to give them up, to enter into the movement of death. If the symptom is felt as the sense that life is over, and that there's no use in going on, then an affirmative approach to this feeling might be a conscious, artful giving-in to the emotions and thoughts of ending that depression has stirred up.

The emptiness and dissolution of meaning that are often present in depression show how attached we can become to our ways of understanding and explaining our lives. Often our personal philosophies and our values seem to be all too neatly wrapped, leaving little room for mystery. Depression comes along then and opens up a hole. Ancient astrologers imagined Saturn as the most remote planet, far out in cold and empty space. Depression makes holes in our theories and assumptions, but even this painful process can be honored as a necessary and valuable source of healing.

In the ancient texts Saturn was sometimes labeled "poisonous." In recommending some positive effects in saturnine moods, I don't want to overlook the terrible pain that they can bring. Nor is it only minor forms of melancholy that offer unique gifts to the soul; long, deep bouts of acute depression can also clear out and restructure the tenets by which life has been lived. The "children of Saturn" traditionally included carpenters, shown in drawings putting together the foundations and skeletons of new houses. In our melancholy, inner construction may be taking place, clearing out the old and putting up the new. Dreams, in fact, often depict construction sites and buildings just going up, suggesting again that the soul is *made:* it is the product of work and inventive effort. Freud pointed out that during bouts of melancholy the outer life may look empty, but at the same time inner work may be taking place at full speed.

COMING TO TERMS WITH DEPRESSION

In Jungian language, Saturn may be considered an *animus* figure. The *animus* is a deep part of the psyche that roots ideas and abstraction in the soul. Many people are strong in *anima*—full of imagination, close to life, empathic, and connected to people around them. But these very people may have difficulty moving far enough away from emotional involvement to see what is going on, and to relate their life experiences to their ideas and values. Their experience is "wet," to use another ancient metaphor for the soul, because they are so emotionally involved in life, and so they might benefit from an excursion to the far-off regions of cold, dry Saturn.

This dryness can separate awareness from the moist emotions that are characteristic of close involvement with life. We see this development in old people as they reflect on their past with some distance and detachment. Saturn's point of view, in fact, can sometimes be rather hardhearted and even cruel. In Samuel Beckett's melancholy play *Krapp's Last Tape,* we find a humorous, biting depiction of saturnine reflection. Using a tape recorder, Krapp plays back tapes he has made throughout his life, and listens with considerable gloom to his voices from the past. After one of the tapes, he sits down to make another: "Just listening to that stupid bastard I took myself for thirty years ago, hard to believe I was ever as bad as that. Thank God that's all done with anyway."

These few lines reveal a distance between past and present, as well as a cooler perspective and a deconstruction of values. In most of Beckett's plays we hear characters express their depression and hopelessness, their inability to find any shreds of former meaning; yet they also offer an image of the noble foolishness that is part of a life so riddled with emptiness. In the absolute sadness of these characters, we can grasp a mystery about the human condition. It is not a literal aberration, although it may feel that way, to suddenly find meaning and value disappear, and to be overwhelmed with the need for withdrawal and with vague emotions of hopelessness. Such feelings have a place and work a kind of magic on the soul.

Krapp, whose name suggests depression's devaluation of human life, shows that cold remorse and self-judgment do not have to be seen as clinical syndromes, but as a necessary foolishness in human life that actually accomplishes something for the soul. Professional psychology might try to correct Krapp's self-criticism as a form of neurotic masochism, but Beckett shows that even in its ugliness and foolishness it makes a certain kind of sense.

Krapp playing his tapes and muttering his curses is also an image of ourselves turning our memories over in our minds again and again, in a process of distillation. Over time something essential emerges from this saturnine reduction—the gold in the sludge. Saturn was sometimes called *sol niger,* the black sun. In his darkness there is to be found a precious brilliance, our essential nature, distilled by depression as perhaps the greatest gift of melancholy.

If we persist in our modern way of treating depression as an illness to be cured only mechanically and chemically, we may lose the gifts of soul that only depression can provide. In particular, tradition taught that Saturn fixes, darkens, weights, and hardens whatever is in contact with it. If we do away with Saturn's moods, we may find it exhausting trying to keep life bright and warm at all costs. We may be even more overcome then by the increased melancholy called forth by the repression of Saturn, and lose the sharpness and substance of identity that Saturn gives the soul. In other words, symptoms of a loss of Saturn might include a vague sense of identity, the failure to take one's own life seriously, and a general malaise or ennui that is a pale reflection of Saturn's deep, dark moods.

Saturn locates identity deeply in the soul, rather than on the surface of personality. Identity is felt as one's soul finding its weight and measure. We know who we are because we have uncovered the stuff of which we are made. It has been sifted out by depressive thought, "reduced," in the chemical sense, to essence. Months or years focused on death have left a white ghostly residue that is the "I," dry and essential.

Care of the soul asks for a cultivation of the larger world depression represents. When we speak clinically of depression, we think of an emotional or behavioral condition, but when we imagine depression as a visitation by Saturn, then many qualities of his world come into view: the need for isolation, the coagulation of fantasy, the distilling of memory, and accommodation with death, to name only a few.

For the soul, depression is an initiation, a rite of passage. If we think that depression, so empty and dull, is void of imagination, we may overlook its initiatory aspects. We may be imagining imagination itself from a point of view foreign to Saturn; emptiness can be rife with feeling-tone, images of catharsis, and emotions of regret and loss. As a shade of mood, gray can be as interesting and as variegated as it is in black-and-white photography.

If we pathologize depression, treating it as a syndrome in need of cure, then the emotions of Saturn have no place to go except into abnormal behavior and acting out. An alternative would be to invite Saturn in, when he comes knocking, and give him an appropriate place to stay. Some Renaissance gardens had a bower dedicated to Saturn—a dark, shaded, remote place where a person could retire and enter the persona of depression without fear of being disturbed. We could model our attitude and our ways of dealing with depression on this garden. Sometimes people need to withdraw and show their coldness. As friends and counselors, we could provide the emotional space for such feelings, without trying to change them or interpret them. And as a society, we could acknowledge Saturn in our buildings. A house or commercial building could have a room or an actual garden where a person could go to withdraw in order to meditate, think, or just be alone and sit. Modern architecture, when it tries to be cognizant of soul, seems to favor the circle or square where one joins community. But depression has a centrifugal force; it moves away from the center. We often refer to our buildings and institutions as "centers," but Saturn would probably prefer an outpost. Hospitals and schools often have "common rooms," but they could just as easily have "uncommon rooms," places for withdrawal and solitude.

Leaving a television running when no one is watching, or having a radio playing all day long may defend against Saturn's silence. We want to do away with the empty space surrounding that remote planet, but as we fill in those voids, we may be forcing him to assume the role of symptom, to be housed in our clinics and hospitals as a pest, rather than as a healer and teacher—his traditional roles.

Why is it that we fail to appreciate this facet of the soul? One reason is that most of what we know about Saturn comes to us symptomatically. Emptiness appears too late and too literally to have soul in it. In our cities, boarded-up homes and failing businesses signal economic and social "depression." In these "depressed" areas of our cities, decay is cut off from will and conscious participation, appearing only as an external manifestation of a problem or an illness.

We also see depression, economically and emotionally, as literal failure and threat, as a surprise breaking in upon our healthier plans and expectations. What if we were to expect Saturn and his dark, empty spaces to have a place in life? What if we propitiated Saturn by incorporating his values into our way of life? (Propitiate means both to acknowledge and to offer respect as a means of protection.)

We could also honor Saturn by showing more honesty in the face of serious illness. Hospice workers will tell you how much a family can gain when the depressive facts of a terminal illness are discussed openly. We might also take our own illnesses, our visits to the doctor and to the hospital, as reminders of our mortality. We are not caring for the soul in these situations when we protect ourselves from their impact. It isn't necessary to be *only* saturnine in these situations, but a few honest words for the melancholy feelings involved might keep Saturn propitiated.

Because depression is one of the faces of the soul, acknowledging it and bringing it into our relationships fosters intimacy. If we deny or cover up anything that is at home in the soul, then we cannot be fully present to others. Hiding the dark places results in a loss of soul; speaking for them and from them offers a way toward genuine community and intimacy.

Care of the soul doesn't mean wallowing in the symptom, but it does mean trying to learn from depression what qualities the soul needs. Even further, it attempts to weave those depressive qualities into the fabric of life so that the aesthetics of Saturn—coldness, isolation, darkness, emptiness—makes a contribution to the texture of everyday life. In learning from depression, a person might dress in Saturn's black to mimic his mood. He might go on a trip alone as a response to a saturnine feeling. He might build a grotto in his yard as a place of saturnine retreat. Or, more internally, he might let his depressive thoughts and feelings just be. All of these actions would be a positive response to a visitation of Saturn's depressive emotion. They would be concrete ways to care for the soul in its darker beauty. In so doing, we might find a way into the mystery of this emptiness of the heart. We might also discover that depression has its own angel, a guiding spirit whose job it is to carry the soul away to its remote places where it finds unique insight and enjoys a special vision.

Notes

PROLOGUE

1. Greenberg P., et al. (November 1993). The economic burden of depression in 1990, *Journal of Clinical Psychiatry*, 54:11.

1. THE MANY FACES OF DEPRESSION

1. M. Siskind and F. A. Whitlock (1979). Depression and cancer: A follow-up study, *Psychological Medicine*, 9, 747–752.
2. *Diagnostic and Statistic Manual of Psychiatric Disorders* (1994). Fourth edition. Washington, D.C.: American Psychiatric Association Press.
3. Research by Michael T. McGuire is cited in P. Kramer (1993). *Listening to Prozac*. New York: Viking Books, 168–69.
4. Donald F. Kline (1977). Psychopharmacological treatment and delineation of borderline disorder, in P. Hartocollis, ed., *Borderline Personality Disorder: The Concept, the Syndrome, the Patient*. (New York: International Universities Press), 365–83.
5. Fieve's work contains a wealth of factual information about bipolar disorder. He was instrumental in introducing lithium treatment into the United States. See Fieve, R., *Moodswing*, Bantam Books, 1975.
6. J. Nelson (1994). *Healing the Split; Integrating Spirit Into Our Understanding of the Mentally Ill* (rev. ed.). Albany, NY: SUNY.

4. MEETING THE SHADOW AT MID-LIFE

1. C. Jung (1944). Psychology and alchemy, in H. Read (ed.), *The collected works*. Trans. R.F.C. Hull. Vol. 12, p. 336. Princeton, N.J.: Princeton University Press.
2. J. Hillman (1979). *The Dream and the Underworld*. New York: Harper & Row.
3. C. Jung (1958). Flying saucers: a modern myth of things seen in the skies, in H. Read (ed.), *The collected works*. Trans. R.F.C. Hull. Vol. 10, pp. 355–356. Princeton, N.J.: Princeton University Press.
4. Joseph Campbell (1949). *The Hero with a Thousand Faces*. Princeton: Princeton University Press.
5. Diane Wolkstein and Samuel Noah Kramer (1983). *Inanna: Queen of Heaven and Earth: Her Stories and Hymns from Sumer*. New York: Harper & Row.
6. Sylvia Brinton Perera (1981). *Descent to the Goddess*. Toronto: Inner City Books.

7. Kathleen Raine (1983). The inner journey of the poet, in M. Tuby, *In the Wake of Jung.* London: Coventure Ltd.

8. Ginette Paris (January 1994). Unpublished lecture presented at Pacifica Graduate Institute, Carpinteria, CA.

7. "THE DARK NIGHT OF THE SOUL"

1. Evelyn Underhill, *Mysticism.* New York: New American Library, 1974, p. 386.

2. Ibid., 381.

3. Ibid., 400.

4. Ibid.

5. St. John of the Cross, *Dark Night of the Soul.* (1959). Trans. E. Allison Peers. Garden City, NY: Doubleday and Co., pp. 109–10. Jeremiah vividly bewails his suffering in the Dark Night of the Abyss, complaining:

"I am the man that see my poverty in the rod of His indignation; He hath threatened me and brought me into darkness and not into light. So far hath He turned against me and hath converted His hand upon me all the day! My skin and my flesh hath He made old; He hath broken my bones; He hath made a fence around me and compassed me with gall and trial; He hath set me in dark places, as those that are dead for ever. He hath made a fence around me and against me, that I may not go out; He hath made my captivity heavy. Yea, and when I have cried and have entreated, He hath shut out my prayer. He hath enclosed my paths and ways out with square stones; He hath thwarted my steps. He hath set ambushes for me; He hath become to me a lion in a secret place. He hath turned aside my steps and broken me in pieces, He hath made me desolate; He hath bent His bow and set me as a mark for His arrow. He hath shot into my veins the daughters of His quiver. I have become a derision to all the people, and laughter and scorn for them all the day. He hath filled me with bitterness and hath made me drunken with worm-wood. He hath broken my teeth by number; He hath fed me with ashes. My soul is cast out from peace; I have forgotten good things. And I said: mine end is frustrated and cut short, together with my desire and my hope from the Lord. Remember my poverty and my excess, the wormwood and the gall. I shall be mindful with remembrance and my soul shall be undone with me in pains."

6. Ibid., 107.

7. Ibid., 100.

8. John Ferguson (1982). *Encyclopedia of Mysticism and Mystery Religions.* New York: Crossroads Publishing Co., p. 19.

9. Theodore Roethke (1975). *The Collected Poems of Theodore Roethke.* New York: Doubleday & Co., p. 129.

10. Underhill, op. cit., 319.
11. *Parabola*, Summer 1987, p. 71.

9. SEEKING THE SPIRIT IN PROZAC

1. P. Kramer (1993). *Listening to Prozac; A Psychiatrist Explores Antidepressant Drugs and the Remaking of the Self.* New York: Viking.
2. D. Klein (1971). Approaches in measuring the efficacy of drug treatment of personality disorders: An analysis and program, in *Principles and Problems in Establishing the Efficacy of Psychotropic Agents.* Washington, D.C.: U.S. Dept. of HEW, Public Health Service No. 2128. Cited in Kramer, op. cit., 74.
3. M. McGuire et al. (1984). Social and environmental influences on blood serotonic concentrations in monkeys, *Archives of General Psychiatry*, vol. 41 pp. 405–10. Cited in Kramer, op. cit., 212–13.
4. Kramer, op. cit., 214.

11. DEPRESSION IN BORDERLINE PERSONALITIES

1. Peter Knudtsen (1975). Flora: shaman of the Winter *Natural History Magazine*, 12.
2. Carl Faber (1976). *On Listening.* Perseus Press.

12. ALTERNATIVE MEDICAL TREATMENTS FOR DEPRESSION

1. Michael Rosenbaum and Murray Susser (1992). *Solving the Puzzle of Chronic Fatigue Syndrome.* Tacoma, WA: Life Sciences Press.
2. Jay Goldstein (1993). *Chronic Fatigue Syndrome: The Limbic Hypothesis.* Binghampton, NY: The Haworth Medical Press.
3. William Crook (1983). *The Yeast Connection.* Jackson, TN: Professional Books.
4. John Parks Trowbridge (1986). *The Yeast Syndrome.* New York: Bantam Books.
5. Hal Huggins (1989). *It's All in Your Head.* Tacoma, WA: Life Sciences Press.
6. Broda Barnes (1976). *Hypothyroidism, The Unsuspected Illness.* New York: Harper and Row.
7. Devi Nambudripad (1993). *Say Good-bye to Illness.* Buena Park, CA: Delta Publishing.
8. Priscilla Slagle (1987). *The Way Up From Down.* New York: Random House.

17. CHAOS THEORY AND DEPRESSION

1. J. Wieland-Burston (1989). *Chaos and Order in the World of the Psyche.* New York: Routledge.
2. I. Prigogine and I. Stengers (1984). *Order out of Chaos: Man's New Dialogue with Nature.* New York: Bantam Books, Inc.
3. Ibid., p. xv.
4. W. Styron (1992). *Darkness Visible: A Memoir of Madness.* New York: Vintage Books, 47.
5. I.D. Yalom (1980). *Existential Psychotherapy.* New York: Basic Books, 159.

18. TRANSPERSONAL PSYCHOLOGY AND DEPRESSION

1. A. Huxley (1972). The perennial philosophy, in J. White (ed.), *The Highest State of Consciousness.* New York: Anchor Books, 58.
2. J. Nelson (1994). *Healing the Split, Integrating Spirit Into Our Understanding of the Mentally Ill* (rev. ed.). Albany, NY: SUNY. See also J. Nelson (Summer 1994). Madness or transcendence? Looking to the ancient east for a modern transpersonal diagnostic system, *ReVision*, Vol. 17, No. 1, 14–23.
3. K. Wilber (1983). *Eye to Eye.* New York: Anchor Books, 293.
4. R. Sheldrake (1988). *The Presence of the Past.* New York: Vintage Books.
5. R.D. Laing (1982). *The Voice of Experience.* New York: Pantheon Books.
6. M. Harner (1980). *The Way of the Shaman.* New York: Bantam Books, xiv.
7. Goldstein and Kornfield (1987). *Seeking the Heart of Wisdom.* Boston: Shambhala.
8. H. Kohut (1977). *The Restoration of the Self.* Madison, CT: International Universities Press.
9. C. Castaneda (1966). *The Teachings of Don Juan: A Yaqui Way of Knowledge.* New York: Simon & Schuster.

19. THE PATH OF THE DRAGON

1. A. Weil (1973). *The Natural Mind.* Boston: Houghton Mifflin. See also R.K. Siegal (1992). *Fire in the Brain.* New York: Dutton.
2. R. Strassman (Jan–Mar 1991). Human hallucinogenic drug research in the United States: A present-day case history and review of the Process, *Journal of Psychoactive Drugs*, Vol. 23 (1).
3. L. Grinspoon and J. Bakalar (1979). *Psychedelic Drugs Reconsidered.* New York: Basic Books.

4. E. Mascher (1967). Psycholytic therapy: Statistics and indications, in H. Brill, J. O. Cole, et al., *Neuro-psychopharmacology*. Amsterdam: Excerpta Medica.

5. L. Grinspoon and J. Bakalar (1986). Can drugs be used to enhance the psychotherapeutic process? *American Journal of Psychotherapy* 40 (3): 393–404. Reported in T. Riedlinger and J. Riedlinger (1994). Psychedelic and entactogenic drugs in the treatment of depression, *Journal of Psychoactive Drugs*, 25(1).

6. C. Savage et al. (1962). LSD transcendence, and the new beginning, *Journal of Nervous and Mental Disease* 135:425–39. Reported in T. Riedlinger and J. Riedlinger, op. cit.

7. P. Kramer (1993). *Listening to Prozac.* New York: Viking.

8. C. Grob, G. Bravo, and R. Walsh (1990). Second thoughts on MDMA neurotoxicity, *Archives of General Psychiatry.* 47: 288.

9. T. Riedlinger and J. Riedlinger, op. cit.

10. S. Adamson (1985). Foreword by Metzner, R. *Through the Gateway of the Heart.* San Francisco: Four Trees Publications.

11. Stanislav Grof (1975). *Realms of the Human Unconsciousness; Observations from LSD Research.* New York: Viking Press.

12. Carlos Castaneda (1968). *The Teaching of Don Juan: A Yaqui Way of Knowledge.* New York: Pocket Books.

13. Myron Stolaroff (Winter 1993). Using psychedelics safely, *Gnosis*, No. 23, 26–30.

21. DEPRESSION AS A LOSS OF HEART

1. C. Trungpa (1984). *Shambhala: The Sacred Path of the Warrior.* Boston: Shambhala.

2. J. Welwood (1983). *Awakening the Heart: East/West Approaches to Psychotherapy and the Healing Relationship.* Boston: Shambhala.

24. SUICIDE AND TRANSCENDENCE

1. A. Maslow (1971). *The Farther Reaches of Human Nature.* New York: Press.

2. M. Heidegger (1962). *Being and Time.* Translated by J. Macquarrie and E. Robinson. New York: Harper & Row.

3. L. Dolce (1992). *Suicide.* New York: Chelsea House.

4. Colt, G. Howe (1991). *The Enigma of Suicide.* New York: Summit Books.

5. C. Levington (1987). *The Sane Suicide.* Unpublished manuscript.

6. J. Hillman (1976). *Suicide and the Soul.* Dallas, Spring Publications, 66.

26. TRANSFORMING DEPRESSION THROUGH EGOCIDE, SYMBOLIC DEATH, AND NEW LIFE

1. A. Maslow (1980). A theory of metamotivation: The biological rooting of the value-life, in Walsh and Vaughan, 121–131.

2. K. Wilbur (1980). A developmental model of consciousness, in Walsh and Vaughan, 99–114.

3. I mean surrender in the Buddhist sense of surrendering one's ego which leads to transformation. See Wilbur (1980) and C.G. Jung (1968). *Aion: Researches into the Phenomenology of the Self. CW.* Vol. 9, II.

4. I had already started investigating the problem of suicide while I was still in medical school. D.H. Rosen (1970). The serious suicide attempt: Epidemiological and follow-up study of 886 patients, *American Journal of Psychiatry*, 127: 764–770. D.H. Rosen (1976). The serious suicide attempt: Five-year follow-up study of 886 patients, *Journal of the American Medical Association*, 235: 2105–2109.

5. This estimate was arrived at by calculating the supposed number of suicides from a 1:100 ratio of survivors to suicides. As of 1990, there had been 20 known survivors of leaps off the Golden Gate Bridge; the actual number of survivors or suicides is not known.

6. This quote and the other quotes from this study are taken from D.H. Rosen (1975). Suicide survivors: A follow-up study of persons who survived jumping from the Golden Gate and San Francisco Bay bridges, *Western Journal of Medicine*, 122: 289–294.

7. D.H. Rosen (1976). Suicide survivors: Psychotherapeutic implications of egocide, *Suicide and Life-Threatening Behavior*, 6: 209–215.

8. Regarding this statement, Joel Weishaus made this insightful comment: "The 'conscious ego act' is done with the ego not believing in its own demise. Thus suicide, as opposed to egocide, is not a sincere act, but the ego in its trickster mode."

9. Jung has even stated, "The shadow corresponds to a negative ego personality and includes all those qualities we find painful or regrettable." See C.G. Jung (1986b). *Psychology and Alchemy. CW.* Vol. 12.

10. R.P. Basler, ed. (1953). *The Collected Works of Abraham Lincoln.* Vol. New Brunswick, NJ: Rutgers University Press.

11. K. Menninger, M. Mayman, and P. Pruyser (1967). *The Vital Balance: The Life Process in Mental Health and Illness.* New York: The Viking Press.

12. J.S. Mill (1960). *Autobiography.* New York: Columbia University Press.

13. N. Cameron (1942). *William Jones.* Madison: University of Wisconsin Press.

14. M. Woodman (1985). *The Pregnant Virgin: A Process of Psychological Transformation.* Toronto: Inner City Books.

15. C.G. Jung (1967). *Symbols of Transformation. CW.* Vol. 5. 328.

16. E. Neumann (1969). Trans. E. Rolfe. *Depth Psychology and a New Ethic.* New York: G.P. Putnam's Sons, 104–105.

17. M.T. Maltzberger and D.H. Buie (1974). Countertransference hate in the treatment of suicidal patients, *Archives of General Psychiatry*, 30: 625–633.

18. E. Kris (1952). *Psychoanalytic Explorations in Art.* New York: International Universities Press.

19. After utilizing this phrase, I came across a reference to it in H.L. Henderson (1984). Reflections on the history and practice of Jungian analysis, in M. Stein ed., *Jungian Analysis.* Boston: Shambhala. 16.

20. I am indebted to Sally Parks (1980). *The Puer Aeternus and the Narcissistic Personality—Kindred Spirits.* Unpublished thesis. The Inter-Regional Society of Jungian Analysts for two phrases: "regression in the service of the self" (associated with one's own personal being) and "self-Self axis" (associated with a Supreme Being).

21. Jung (1971). *Psychological Types. CW.* Vol. 6. 448–450.

22. C.R. Rogers (1977). *Carl Rogers on Personal Power.* New York: Delacorte. Also used the term self-actualization to express the same concept.

23. A. Maslow (1970). *Motivation and Personality.* New York: Harper & Row.

24. Long-term, in-depth psychotherapy with a chronically depressed or suicidal person focuses on identifying the negative and self-destructive aspects of the ego and the shadow. Only by analyzing these aspects to death can an individual transcend and transform them. No matter how carefully this analytical process is conducted, however, it is never without risk. When a person is committing egocide, he or she is in a precarious and confused state, and there may be risk of suicide.

25. A psychotic patient can go through actual egocide and transformation; there are many successful accounts of this process. For only one of many examples, see J.W. Perry (1953). *The Self in the Psychotic Process.* Berkeley: University of California Press.

26. Jung characterizes this as "the regressive restoration of the persona." See C.G. Jung (1966). *Two Essays on Analytical Psychology. CW.* Vol. 7. 163–168.

27. P. Mudd (1990). The dark self: Death as a transferential factor, *Journal of Analytical Psychology*, 35: 125–141.

25. THE DARK NIGHT OF THE SOUL

1. St. John of the Cross divides the dark night of the soul into the night of the senses and the darker and more difficult night of spirit. The dark night described

here corresponds to his night of the senses. I am indebted to Edith Schnapper (*The Inward Odyssey*, 2d ed., George Allen & Unwin, 1980) for the example from Islam.

2. Deanimation is more usually referred to as depersonalization, the inner dimension of the depersonalization-derealization process.

Author Biographies

ROBERTO ASSAGIOLO, M.D., was founder of the influential Psychosynthesis Movement and author of numerous works that integrate spiritual perspectives into psychotherapy.

BRUNO BETTELHEIM, M.D., was Distinguished Professor of Education, Psychology, and Psychiatry at the University of Chicago. He was a survivor of Nazi concentration camps and later authored numerous books on child development and psychoanalysis.

DAVID D. BURNS, M.D., has been one of the prime developers of cognitive therapy. In addition to treating patients, he teaches psychotherapy and drug therapy at the University of Pennsylvania and lectures to professional groups around the world. He is the author of *Feeling Good: The New Mood Therapy*.

HYLA CASS, M.D., is an Assistant Clinical Professor of Psychiatry, UCLA School of Medicine, and is a frequent commentator on radio, television, and print media. In her Santa Monica–based psychiatric practice, she combines various psychotherapeutic techniques with nutritional medicine to address imbalances in body, mind, and spirit.

KATHY CRONKITE is the daughter of Walter Cronkite and author of *On the Edge of the Spotlight*. She serves on the boards of the Mental Health Association of Austin and the Mental Health Association of Texas, and has received the Mental Health Association Media Award. She lives in Austin, Texas, with her husband and two sons.

MARK EPSTEIN, M.D., is a psychiatrist and writer with a private practice of psychotherapy in New York City. He is the author of *Thoughts Without a Thinker: Psychotherapy From a Buddhist Perspective*.

ERIC FROMM, M.D., was an internationally known psychoanalysist and educator who published numerous books on psychology, contemporary society, and human nature. He was a pioneer in introducing existential thought into modern psychology and psychiatry.

FRANK GRUBA-MCCALLISTER, PH.D., is Associate Dean and Professor at Illinois School of Professional Psychology, Chicago. Working with clients suffering from chronic disabilities, he has studied the psychology of human suffering in depth. His present focus is on existential psychology and integrating psychology and spirituality.

PETER D. KRAMER, M.D., author of the bestselling book *Listening to Prozac,* studied history and literature at Harvard and University College in London, and received his M.D. from Harvard. He is an Associate Clinical Professor of Psychiatry at Brown University and has a private practice in Providence. He writes a monthly column for *Psychiatric Times,* and is the author of *Moments of Engagement: Intimate Psychotherapy in a Technological Age.*

LINDA SCHIERSE LEONARD, PH.D., is a Jungian analyst based in San Francisco and an existential philosopher who gives workshops and lectures. She is author of *Witness to the Fire: Creativity and the Veil of Addiction.*

STEVEN LEVINE has been leading workshops in thanatology since 1980, and with his wife, Ondrea, is co-director of the Hanuman Foundation Dying Project. His books include *Who Dies?, Meetings at the Edge,* and *Healing into Life and Death.*

CARYN LEVINGTON, PSY.D., is Associate Professor at Harper College, Palatine, Illinois. Her professional interests include humanistic psychotherapy, preventative medicine, existential psychology, and spiritual practice. Her personal interests include alternative rock composition and performance, philosophical contemplation, and stargazing.

BEVERLY LOCKWOOD-CONLAN, L.C.S.W., is a graduate of the University of Southern California and has practice psychotherapy in Glendale, California, for more than two decades.

ALEXANDER LOWEN, M.D., is the creator of Bioenergetics, and author of numerous books linking emotions to the body. He practices psychiatry in New York.

JOANNA MACY is a scholar of Buddhism and general systems theory, and author of *World as Lover, World as Self,* and *Mutual Causality in Buddhism and General*

Systems Theory. A mother of three grown children, she lives in Berkeley, California, with her husband, Francis, and teaches at the California Institute of Integral Studies and Starr King School for the Ministry.

MARTHA MANNING, PH.D., is a clinical psychologist and former Professor of Psychology at George Mason University.

THOMAS MOORE, author of the bestselling *Care of the Soul,* is a leading international lecturer and writer in the areas of archetypal psychology, mythology, and the imagination. He lived as a monk in a Catholic religious order for twelve years and has degrees in theology, musicology, and philosophy.

ANDREA NELSON, PSY.D., is a licensed clinical psychologist who has worked with depressed patients in the United States and Australia. Her doctoral dissertation applied chaos theory to the process of psychological transformation. She presently practices in a California psychiatric hospital.

JOHN E. NELSON, M.D., is a practicing psychiatrist certified by the American Board of Psychiatry and Neurology. He has worked with a wide variety of psychiatric patients since 1969, and has long been a student of Eastern philosophy and transpersonal psychology. He is presently in private practice in Ventura, California.

FRANCOISE O'KANE, PH.D., is a graduate of the Jung Institute in Zurich and holds a doctorate in ethnology and social anthropology.

SHYLOH RAVENSWOOD is a free-lance writer, worried environmentalist, aging athlete, itinerant philosopher, shaman's apprentice, and consciousness explorer who roams the California costal mountains seeking the Tao.

DAVID H. ROSEN, M.D., is a psychiatrist and Jungian analyst who holds the McMillan Professorship in analytical psychology, and is Professor of Psychiatry and Humanities in Medicine at Texas A & M University. Married and the father of three children, Dr. Rosen lives in College Station, Texas.

WILLIAM STYRON is the author of *Darkness Visible, The Confessions of Nat Turner, Sophie's Choice,* and *This Quiet Dust.* He has been awarded the Pulitzer Prize, the American Book Award, The Howells Medal, and the Edward MacDowell Medal. He lives in Roxbury, Connecticut, and Vineyard Haven, Massachusetts.

MICHAEL WASHBURN, PH.D., is a Professor of Philosophy at Indiana University, South Bend, and a leading scholar and theoretician in transpersonal psychology. He is the author of *Transpersonal Psychology in Psychoanalytic Perspective*, and *The Ego and the Dynamic Ground*. He is also editor of the State University of New York Press Series in the Philosophy of Psychology.

JOHN WELWOOD, PH.D., is a psychologist and professor at the California Institute of Integral Studies. He has written on East-West psychology, meditation, and relationships. His books include *Challenge of the Heart* and *Journey of the Heart*.

CONNIE ZWEIG, PH.D., is former executive editor of Jeremy P. Tarcher, Inc., where she founded the New Consciousness Reader Series. She is editor of two collected volumes, *Meeting the Shadow*, and *To Be a Woman*, and recently received her doctorate in clinical psychology. She lives on a ridgetop in Topanga Canyon, California.

Permissions and Copyrights

Page vii: "I Love the Dark Hours" (7 lines) from *Selected Poems of Rainer Maria Rilke*, edited and translated by Robert Bly. Copyright © 1981 by Robert Bly. Reprinted by permission of HarperCollins Publishers, Inc. Chapter 1 is an original paper by John E. Nelson. Printed by permission of the author.

Chapter 2 consists of excerpts from *Darkness Visible: A Memoir of Madness* by William Styron. Copyright © 1990 by William Styron. Reprinted by permission of Random House, Inc.

Chapter 3 consists of excerpts from *On the Edge of Darkness* by Kathy Cronkite. Copyright © 1994 by Kathy Cronkite. Used by permission of Doubleday, a division of Bantam Doubleday Dell Publishing Group, Inc.

Chapter 4 is an original paper by Connie Zweig. Printed by permission of the author.

Chapter 5 consists of excerpts from *Surviving and other Essays* by Bruno Bettelheim. Copyright © 1979 by Bruno Bettelheim. Reprinted by permission of Alfred A. Knopf Inc.

Chapter 6 consists of excerpts of 2,500 words from *Undercurrents* by Martha Manning. Copyright © 1995 by Martha Manning. Reprinted by permission of HarperCollins Publishers, Inc.

Chapter 7 consists of excerpts from *Witness to the Fire* by Linda Schierse Leonard. Copyright © 1990. Reprinted by arrangement with Shambhala Publications, Inc., 300 Massachusetts Ave., Boston MA 02115.

Chapter 8 consists of 3,500 word excerpt from *Feeling Good* by David D. Burns. Copyright © by David D. Burns. Reprinted by permission of William Morrow and Company, Inc.

Chapter 9 is an original paper by John E. Nelson. Printed by permission of the author.

Chapter 10 consists of excerpts from *Listening to Prozac* by Peter D. Kramer. Copyright © 1993 by Peter D. Kramer. Used by permission of Viking Penguin, a division of Penguin Books USA Inc.

Chapter 11 is an original paper by Beverly Lockwood-Conlan. Printed by permission of the author.

Chapter 12 is an original paper by Hyla Cass. Printed by permission of the author.

Chapter 13 Reprinted by permission of The Putnam Publishing Group from *Depression and the Body* by Alexander Lowen. Copyright © 1972 by Alexander Lowen, M.D.

Chapter 14 consists of an excerpt from *Sacred Chaos: Reflections on God's Shadow and the Dark Self* by Francoise O'Kane. Copyright © 1994 by Francoise O'Kane. Reprinted by permission of Inner City Books, Studies in Jungian Psychology by Jungian Analysts, no. 64.

Chapter 15 consists of an excerpt from *The Sane Society* by Erich Fromm. Copyright 1955 © 1983 by Erich Fromm. Reprinted by permission of Henry Holt and Co., Inc.

Chapter 16 consists of an excerpt from *World as Lover, World as Self* by Joanna Macy (1991), with permission of Parallax Press, Berkeley, California.

Chapter 17 is an original paper by Andrea Nelson. Printed by permission of the author.

Chapter 18 is an original paper by John E. Nelson. Printed by permission of the author.

Chapter 19 is an original paper by Shyloh Ravenswood. Printed by permission of the author.

Chapter 20 consists of an excerpt from *Psychosynthesis* by Robert Assagioli. Copyright © 1976 by Robert Assagioli. Reprinted by permission of Sterling Lord Literistic, Inc.

Chapter 21 is a paper by John Welwood entitled "Depression as a Loss of Heart," originally published in the *Journal of Contemplative Psychotherapy*, Vol. IV, 1987. The Naropa Institute, Boulder, Colorado.

About the Editors

John E. Nelson, M.D., is a practicing psychiatrist certified by the American Board of Psychiatry and Neurology. He has worked eclectically with a wide variety of psychiatric patients since 1969, and has long been a student of Eastern philosophy and Western transpersonal psychology. He is presently in private practice in Ventura, California.

Andrea Nelson, Psy.D., is a licensed clinical psychologist who has worked with depressed patients in the United States and Australia. In her doctoral dissertation, she applied Chaos Theory to the process of psychological transformation. She presently practices in a California psychiatric hospital.